ALAN JOYCE &QANTAS

Peter Harbison is globally recognised as an authority on the aviation industry and his views are frequently sought by the industry and the media. He has been working in and writing for the industry for more than 50 years. For over 30 years, he ran an airline consulting, events and data business.

Lead researcher **Derek Sadubin** has worked closely with Peter Harbison for over 20 years as a writer and data analyst.

ALAN JOYCE &QANTAS

THE TRIALS AND TRANSFORMATION OF AN AUSTRALIAN ICON

PETER HARBISON WITH DEREK SADUBIN

PENGUIN BOOKS

UK | USA | Canada | Ireland | Australia
India | New Zealand | South Africa | China

Penguin Books is part of the Penguin Random House group of companies,
whose addresses can be found at global.penguinrandomhouse.com.

Penguin
Random House
Australia

First published by Penguin Books, 2023

Cover design by Luke Causby © Penguin Random House Australia Pty Ltd
Cover images courtesy Bloomberg/Getty Images (Alan Joyce) and
A380spotter/Getty Images (airplane)
Typeset in Sabon by Midland Typesetters, Australia

Printed and bound in Australia by Griffin Press, an accredited
ISO AS/NZS 14001 Environmental Management Systems printer.

 A catalogue record for this
book is available from the
NATIONAL LIBRARY OF AUSTRALIA National Library of Australia

ISBN 978 1 76134 529 6

penguin.com.au

 MIX
Paper | Supporting
responsible forestry
FSC® C018684

*We at Penguin Random House Australia acknowledge that Aboriginal and Torres Strait
Islander peoples are the Traditional Custodians and the first storytellers of the lands
on which we live and work. We honour Aboriginal and Torres Strait Islander peoples'
continuous connection to Country, waters, skies and communities. We celebrate
Aboriginal and Torres Strait Islander stories, traditions and living cultures;
and we pay our respects to Elders past and present.*

'It ought to be remembered that there is nothing more
difficult to take in hand, more perilous to conduct,
or more uncertain in its success, than to take the lead
in the introduction of a new order of things.'

—Niccolò Machiavelli

For Liz and our beautiful family.

CONTENTS

PREFACE

In the Spotlight

Most Australians, if asked to name the CEOs of two Australian companies, would probably fall short by one – but the one they would know is the CEO of Qantas. Australians are obsessed with Qantas. And by 2023, after his fifteen years running the airline, Alan Joyce had become synonymous with the flying kangaroo.

This addiction to the brand implies many things, positive and negative. But there are few Aussie flyers who aren't afflicted by one or other of the side-effects. 'Twas ever thus. Qantas has rarely ever been out of the headlines. As Joyce's predecessor, Geoff Dixon, once said, 'I don't think any other company in Australia attracts such divided opinion and outcry. Everybody in Australia still believes they own Qantas.'[1]

Love it or hate it, feelings run high about the national carrier. It's an iconic brand, it's an airline, it's ours and it's an employer (or not). More recently, it's a destroyer of the environment, it's a rip-off, it's 'I'll never fly with them again', it's 'Feels like home' or . . . it's 'that Alan Joyce'.

Many travellers have never known a Qantas where Alan Joyce was not the CEO. It's been that long. He appeared on the horizon when he first headed the start-up Jetstar subsidiary in 2004, but it was only after winning the Qantas prize in November 2008 that he began to accumulate the notoriety that would ultimately surround him.

Part of that has to do with the enormous obstacles he's had to negotiate during his decade and a half at the helm, but probably more importantly it's the way he's led the organisation. To an objective outside observer, under Joyce's leadership Qantas has evolved from a fragile and overweight company to an almost bulletproof, profitable operation that is fit for purpose in today's world. To an insider, it can often seem a brutal and uncaring colossus.

In its 2008 manifestation, it could survive. But years of inadequate domestic competition from a ponderous Ansett Australia and the support of a protectionist international policy through the 1990s had allowed Qantas to be mildly profitable without being efficient.

Some years later, Qantas chairman Leigh Clifford observed that there had been little appetite within the company for serious reform at the time. Clifford himself has never shied away from making the tough call. 'Frankly I think too often Qantas has pissed at the edges in the past about costs,' he said in a media interview in March 2014.[2]

As low-cost airlines appeared on the scene and international challenges swelled, Qantas was on track for a steep decline. Only a very smart move in 2004 to create a low-cost subsidiary, Jetstar, had allowed Qantas to fend off the upstart Virgin Blue.

In retrospect, it was brutally fortunate that the deterioration within Qantas was hastened by the global financial crisis (GFC). And that's where Joyce's professional and personal qualities made the difference. He has his failings – he's human – but he also has a mix of attributes that has helped set Qantas up for the future. And that's what this book is about.

As a company, Qantas is part of an intensely complex array of activities, spending billions of dollars on big, shiny jets, engaging with a dozen or more unions, negotiating with governments and intermediaries, and engaging with tens of millions of individual travellers and other stakeholders every year.

It is also naked in its exposure to 'external' threats. Input costs like oil prices, currency movements, interest rates, airport charges, parts and equipment are all subject to fluctuations. These are the household's meat and veg and electricity bills. They're the essential items, but you have almost no control over what they cost. Then there's the unexpected events: a volcano in Iceland causes millions in costs blowouts, SARS outbreaks close markets, political conflicts mean flying circuitous routings, economic downturns kill demand – to say nothing of COVID-19.

Adding spice to that mix, the industry is today about to run into a firestorm of environmental headwinds that could threaten its very existence.

There are so many conflicting interests in servicing the assortment of internal demands that it's guaranteed that many of Qantas's customers – sometimes most – will be constantly dissatisfied and unhappy with its performance.

Qantas is part of an industry in perpetual transition, impossibly competitive and consistently failing to generate returns that other self-respecting companies consider sufficient. By corporate profitability standards, the airline industry's economic performance is risible. But it's become an integral part of the global economy, directly creating millions of jobs, through tourism and by facilitating business generally. It services priceless social needs and plays a vital role in facilitating global harmony. Airlines create dreams and destroy equity.

Airlines are also superb spreaders of disease. They transmit global outbreaks like no other form of transport – yet, as we have seen, the loss to the world is catastrophic when a pandemic prevents nations, and even states, from maintaining a flow of travellers between one another.

Being the custodian of a centenarian brand like Qantas, and all that it goes with it, is consequently a stern undertaking for any ordinary mortal.

Yet that only goes part of the way to explaining why so much of the intensity of popular Australian media feeling – most of it negative – is directed very personally at the one who sits at the top, the CEO. That is nothing new: airline CEOs are responsible for everything that goes wrong in their extensive list of duties. Yet there are few, if any, companies in the country where such intensity of feeling is directed at one person.

Is it because Alan Joyce is Irish? Because he's gay? Because he's outspoken on social issues that aren't always universally popular? Or is it because he's consistently made tough decisions to keep the airline functioning in a changing world? Or is it perhaps, as consistently argued by some union leaders, because he doesn't give a damn for his workers?

From the point of view of Qantas customers, is it because the airline flunked the test when operations began again after the COVID pandemic had done its worst? There's no doubt Qantas's reputation was badly damaged in 2022, when flights were cancelled or delayed, bags were lost and refunds were refused – and yet fares rocketed. Was that down to Joyce?

It's been argued that Joyce is brutally indifferent to the needs of his staff and customers, and is interested only in self-aggrandisement, in making himself rich and in looking after the interests of company shareholders. Just how accurate are these negative assessments – or the views of Joyce's supporters, who argue that his peers consider him one of the most successful CEOs in the industry?

The Qantas CEO reports to one of the more competent boards in Australian commerce today. Its members have a wealth of industrial relations experience, as well as financial and airline experience, and they're no shrinking violets, yet have been willing to give considerable latitude to their chief executive. In the end, of course, Joyce is accountable to the board for his decisions.

Most of the time – for almost all of Joyce's fifteen years as CEO, in fact – the board has left it entirely to him to be the public face of the airline. Interestingly, though, and perhaps in recognition of the fact that things were going off the rails, chairman Richard Goyder made a rare public intervention following the 2022 post-pandemic snarl-up, to help shore up an under-fire CEO, asserting that Joyce had 'done exceptionally well to steer the airline through a crisis that sent other airlines . . . packing'.[3]

There's no shred of doubt he has transformed the airline. Whether it has been for the better or for the worse often depends on your perspective. The immediate popular judgement will inevitably be strongly – and therefore negatively – coloured by the more recent events of 2022–23. Dixon compared managing Qantas to a football team: the coaching job is simple – unless you're the coach.

In one respect if no other, Joyce is already remarkable. The average tenure of a corporate CEO is approximately three to five years; for an airline it is usually less. For an airline CEO to hold the post for a decade and a half is almost unheard of.

This book sets out to examine Alan Joyce and his record over fifteen turbulent years at the helm of an Australian icon, reviewing the issues from the inside looking out. Things can look very different from that perspective. Typically, the man and the airline are characterised two-dimensionally, but closer inspection reveals a much more variegated image.

Few experiences focus the mind like cancer. We all have a vague awareness that we are going to die, but the prospect of death is not usually something that interrupts our daily behaviour. Receiving a diagnosis of 'the big C' brings a sudden, shocking reminder of the reality of mortality. Anyone who's been given that news will have the memory of that moment engraved on their mind for life.

At the age of forty-four, with his corporate agenda filled with professional challenges, cancer simply wasn't on Alan Joyce's horizon. So in May 2011, less than three years into one of the most demanding baptisms of fire any airline CEO could have in the wake of the global financial crisis, Joyce felt like he had been hit by a train when he was diagnosed with prostate cancer.

The Qantas board had decided to send the company's top 100 executives for routine medical check-ups. And they were indeed routine for all except the CEO. Prostate cancer is the most common cancer in Australia. For men of Joyce's age, although he was otherwise found to be in good health, it's a killer unless caught in time.

'I wasn't planning to have my prostate checked until I turned 50,' said Joyce. 'But the doctor asked me about it and I thought I may as well. I was very lucky because testing showed I had an aggressive form of prostate cancer.'[4] If Joyce had waited those extra few years, he'd have had an 80 per cent chance of a painful and speedy death.

But with the bad news there was good news too: the malignant tumour was detected early, meaning better treatment options. Joyce quickly underwent a procedure known as a da Vinci robotic-assisted prostatectomy at Sydney's St Vincent's Hospital, a two- to four-hour procedure in which a guided robotic arm removes the prostate gland with the tumour fully intact. The treatment was successful, and by mid-May Joyce was back at his desk, fully recovered and firing on all cylinders.

Joyce is nothing if not driven. He'd had an almost uninterrupted upward career trajectory – an exception being when he walked away from his position in network planning at Ansett after Air New Zealand took full control, although even that proved timely as he walked across the street to Qantas just before the other two major airlines imploded in 2001.

When he was diagnosed with cancer, his overriding concern had been professional. 'I thought, "I can't die now, leaving this legacy" [at Qantas]', he says, that priority seemingly greater than any other. Such was the desire of this working-class boy from Dublin to excel.

'My lesson out of that cancer scare,' he reflected, 'was being even more passionate about that legacy and that determination to make sure that this is a successful company going forward. I'm very passionate about the Qantas brand and the legacy of leaving this great company in a great position[5] . . . You realise that you have a limited time on this planet, and that you want to make sure that what you're contributing is good, and appropriate, and that you're going to do the right thing while you're here.'[6]

Joyce was acutely conscious of the imprint he would leave behind. Certainly there hadn't been much to crow about in the short time he'd been in charge of Australia's national carrier.

Joyce had ascended to the role on 28 November 2008. Just two months earlier, the 150-year-old Lehman Brothers investment bank had collapsed, triggering the global financial crisis. Money markets froze, and banks and insurance companies in most of the developed world suddenly found they could not borrow or lend. By February 2009, the US stock market had fallen back to the levels of ten years earlier.

Airlines are in the front line when economic conditions change, for better or for worse. And the new conditions couldn't have been much worse. There was little Joyce could do about that, but now he was in charge. Qantas, already in steep decline when he took the controls, continued to struggle, its share price bumping along the bottom. The unions were restless.

Fast-forward to 2011. Fuel prices, a major operating cost item, were now near all-time highs, with oil over US$150 a barrel; jet fuel prices were at their highest level ever. This was the time of the 'Arab Spring' uprisings, which disrupted supply, as the cartel of major oil-producing nations in OPEC had cut production to force prices up, and speculators in the futures market were pouring more fuel on the fire. All of these inputs were well beyond the control of any airline boss.

At home, a discount airfare war was raging, ramped up by competition from Joyce's arch-rival John Borghetti, who was now CEO of Virgin Australia. Joyce had defeated Borghetti for the Qantas role, and there was no love lost between the two, overlaying a deliciously human aspect on the commercial battle.

Overseas, Qantas's international operations had turned disas-
trous as the Gulf carriers chewed away valuable business traffic,
and anyway, traffic was not recovering anywhere nearly as fast
as had been hoped following the lows of the GFC. Things really
couldn't have looked much bleaker.

In Geoff Dixon's last two years as CEO, Qantas had delivered
underlying profit before tax of $965 million in the 2007 financial
year, and then $1.4 billion in 2008. Under Joyce, these had dete-
riorated to $100 million in 2009 and $377 million in 2010. The
2012 financial year became even grimmer; Joyce would eventually report a meagre profit of just $95 million at the annual
general meeting. As the share price hovered around $2, with
little to suggest any improvement, shareholders were becoming
ominously restless.

It was time for stern action to stem the flow – but Joyce had
fourteen unions to talk around. Even in the short time he had been
under the robot at St Vincent's, the Australian Licensed Aircraft
Engineers Association's (ALAEA) volatile federal secretary, Steve
Purvinas, announced an end to ongoing talks with the airline,
calling his members off the job for an hour.

Now there were three major industrial voices – the always
vociferous Transport Workers' Union (TWU) and the more
discreet but threatening Australian & International Pilots
Association (AIPA), along with the ALAEA – that were agitated,
waging high-profile industrial campaigns. And one view they all
shared: Joyce was the culprit.

The TWU's national secretary, Tony Sheldon, disparaged
Joyce's leadership: 'Qantas refuses to bargain in good faith and
[attacks] its own workforce.'[7]

It didn't seem there was much more that could go wrong,
and the chances looked high that Joyce would die a professional
failure.

But the CEO wasn't that easy to knock over. Emerging from
the initial shock of his diagnosis, and with a healthy prognosis
after treatment, meant that when he was confronted by what he

saw as a major threat to Qantas, he felt battle-hardened. Less than six months later, confronted by continued obduracy from the three major unions, whose industrial actions were scaring off passengers planning their peak Christmas travel, Joyce grounded the entire airline on 29 October 2011 – along with tens of thousands of unsuspecting passengers.

If anyone had queried his resilience, there could be no doubting it now. His legacy was developing.

The new CEO's first report to the market began on the back foot, a familiar position for most leaders of airlines:

> During the first half of the year, we encountered a confluence of events that affected our reputation, negatively. Two in-flight incidents, QF30 in July 2008 and QF72 in October 2008, attracted widespread attention. Preliminary findings from independent authorities found no suggestion that Qantas safety was a cause.
>
> Customers also experienced punctuality issues deriving from a long-running engineering, industrial dispute and subsequent lateness backlog, and this led to a shift in perception that Qantas had reduced its commitment to safety . . . During the second half of the year, the Qantas group experienced the adverse effects of the downturn in the global economy . . .[8]

But Joyce strove to conclude his maiden report on a more positive note, albeit a muted one:

> We have brought our on-time performance back to industry leading standards and achieved significantly improved customer satisfaction ratings . . . We have emerged as one of the few airlines worldwide to deliver a full year profit this year, and we have more than 160 new aircraft on order over the next 10 years.

In one form or another, these messages of setback and resilience would be repeated time and again: safety, union conflict, customer satisfaction and the CEO's quest to stay above water financially.

Ultimately, it's the stock market that leaves no place to hide, and Qantas's share price over the fifteen years of Joyce leadership tells his story vividly, with many ups and downs (see appendix). Constant shocks battered the airline seemingly from every side – including the inside. The share price roller-coaster, particularly up to 2015, provides a stark pictorial summary of the turbulence the airline went through early in his tenure. A failed bid by a private-equity consortium in 2007 to delist Qantas and take it private had included a final offer of $5.60 per share. A few months later, it climbed to $6.45, but it would be almost ten years before it reached that level again.

CEOs watch their company's share price closely. For one thing, it can have a big influence on the bonuses they receive, but it also reflects more or less how well the company is going – and how well the CEO is leading. In reality, that evaluation isn't totally accurate, as other factors also influence how investors see the business. But the share price is always out there, so the board, the CEO, analysts and investors all keep an eye on it.

It's not as black and white as the football coach who's on a losing streak, but it's not completely dissimilar. One way or another, the CEO's job is always on the line. Joyce knew that to be sacked by his board would be an indelible stain on his career and his legacy – which would be a blow not just to him, but to his parents, who had got him there and to whom he owed so much, and even to his peers in the 'Irish mafia' of airline executives around the globe. He was the Irish working-class kid who just *had* to make good.

The early part of the twenty-first century was nothing short of calamitous for airlines around the world. Two major US airlines had fled into Chapter 11 bankruptcy protection: United Airlines in 2002 and Delta in 2005. This controversial procedure allowed them to default on their debts and redraw their union agreements, in the process destroying equity held by shareholders. In some cases, unfunded pension plans left many employees with little to show for their years of service. The third major US carrier, American Airlines, struggled on until November 2011, merging with US Airways before resurfacing at the end of 2013.

The US airlines had to resort to these extreme measures because they were relics of a bygone age, and were in no way competitive with the aggressive and low-cost approach that was sweeping through the industry.

Air Canada, the most similar to Qantas in terms of domestic and international profile, had also gone through a US-style bankruptcy process in 2003–04. Even so, its share price tumbled more than 90 per cent, from just under C$20 to C$0.85 between November 2006 and April 2009.

Across the North Atlantic, British Airways' share price had fallen from 760 pence in May 1997 to 150 pence when the September 11 attacks occurred. Cost slashing was unavoidable. First, former Ansett CEO Rod Eddington was brought in to address the crisis. Then, in September 2005, fresh from his success in turning Aer Lingus around, Irishman Willie Walsh took the reins. But Britain's national icon was to be a very different proposition.

In November 2009, BA reported its worst ever half-year loss as a restructuring program finally got underway, having been vigorously opposed by the unions. Despite much pain and in the face of vitriolic criticism from his British political masters, Walsh cut costs, merged and reshaped the airline.

Meanwhile, Lufthansa, Germany's pride, went on a share price roller-coaster, from €20 in December to €5.50 in March 2003, back to €16 in February 2007, then zooming down again to under €6 in February 2009. Developing airline strategy during this period was a bit like throwing darts at a dartboard while sitting on that roller-coaster.

The 2008 global financial crisis took a rapid toll on the world's economies. In the few months between the announcement of Joyce's appointment on 28 July 2008 and his taking office that November, Qantas shed a third of its market capitalisation – only for the shares to dip a further dollar to $1.57 four months later, on 6 March 2009. There was a brief respite, with signs of apparent recovery doubling the price, which peaked at $3.22 on 16 October that year.

It was to prove a false dawn, and there followed the bleakest six years imaginable. Horrifyingly, Qantas's share price dropped below $1 in 2012 – it briefly reached an intra-day trading low of 95.5 cents in December 2013 – and didn't scrabble back up to its 2009 level until March 2015.

It was during this time that Dixon, along with some mates, attacked the Qantas team 'coach' he had welcomed in 2008, making a financial play for the airline and arguing loudly that Joyce and his management should go. The CEO survived, but it was a tough time for Joyce, personally and professionally.

In 2014, Qantas recorded its biggest ever net loss, writing down the value of much of its international fleet, as management cleared the decks in preparation for a comprehensive 'transformation plan', beginning in 2014. It was brutal, but timely. The plan gained traction, the share price eventually rose and conditions stabilised.

With a new cost base and a clear long-term strategy, the outlook became much more positive. The airline was back in profit. Now for some plain sailing. Joyce could start preparing to move on.

And then along came COVID-19.

PART I

BOARDING

'I loved aviation, and I gave myself the goal . . . to be an airline CEO before I was forty. Somehow, it was something that really excited me, and I wanted that role.'

—Alan Joyce

1

Shaping the Future Leader

'My mum is very determined and I'm very much like her,' Alan Joyce says. 'Growing up as a Catholic family, I distinctly remember one Friday evening when I was thirteen, Mum had bought some fish from the local fishmonger. The fish was off, but Mum had a cold and she couldn't smell it. When we tasted it we said, "Ma, this is terrible! The fish is off!" So she went back up and asked for a refund, and the guy wouldn't give her a refund. So she stood there for three hours outside the shop.

'I went up in the middle of it and said, "Ma, we're all at home, we're starving. Are you going to come back and feed us?" and she said, "No, I'm here protesting – I'm telling everybody he sold me this shitty fish." And she just kept on going until he refunded it.'

This episode from Joyce's childhood taught him two things. First, never give up. And second, only give refunds if people complain long enough and loud enough – although he doesn't promote that idea.

When asked to sum himself up in a few adjectives, Joyce hesitates. 'I don't know. Enthusiastic,' he says at last. 'Because I think you have to be always enthusiastic about what you do. Optimistic, I hope, because I would always approach everything with a "glass half full" view of things.' Another short pause. 'I would say relentless, because I don't like giving up on something. Things would happen and people would say, "Oh, that's the end of it," and we'd say, "No, let's give it another go."'

Joyce says his sense of purpose came from his parents. 'They're phenomenal people, and they were always my inspiration, and still are today.' His father had died a few years earlier. 'They were amazing role models, because they were unbelievably hardworking and unbelievably focused on education, in order for their kids to do well.

'Your formal education really gives you a foundation for the way you deal with the rest of your career. And having a mathematics background and a science background, for me, I find very helpful. Because one of the things I definitely practise is the scientific method, coming up with a hypothesis and then getting us whatever available information is there to either validate it, prove or disprove it.'[1]

As an undergraduate, Joyce studied mathematics and physics. His postgraduate studies in management took him to Trinity College Dublin, where he strolled among the ghosts of at least two Nobel Prize winners: Samuel Beckett, for literature, and physicist Ernest Walton, who shared the 1951 physics award with John Cockcroft for their work on splitting the atom. Other Trinity alumni include writers and poets Oscar Wilde, J.P. Donleavy, Bram Stoker, Jonathan Swift, Oliver Goldsmith, Thomas Moore and Sinéad Morrissey, philosopher and statesman Edmund Burke, a host of eminent lawyers and politicians, and even singer Courtney Love, who briefly studied theology. Leo Varadkar, the first gay leader of Ireland, who came out at the time of the nation's referendum on same-sex marriage in 2015, also walked Trinity's hallowed halls.

(Although Alan Joyce's namesake James Joyce attended the rival University College Dublin, his claim to a ghostly presence lies in the fact that parts of the movie of his masterpiece, *Ulysses*, were filmed in the Trinity grounds.)

Joyce would have seemed an unlikely follower in their footsteps. The oldest of four boys – his brothers are Anthony, Maurice and Paul – Alan Joseph Joyce was born on 30 June 1966 and grew up in a government apartment in working-class Tallaght. Up to the 1960s, Tallaght was a small village in the southwestern part of the old County Dublin, linked to several nearby rural areas. When Joyce was born it had a population of around 2500. Tallaght had produced many notable boxers, footballers and musicians, but no airline executives or nuclear physicists.

One of Joyce's first jobs was a paper round, where he mixed it with Irish wolfhounds and Jack Russells to get the job done. It was an environment that instilled grit and determination from early on. Suburban development began in Tallaght in the 1970s, and a town centre developed in the late 1980s. A thirty-minute bus ride away from Trinity College, Tallaght is now very much a suburb of Dublin.

The boys' father, Maurice senior, had left school in his early teens to become a factory worker and sometime postman. He strove to give his boys the tertiary education he had missed. Joyce's grandfather had been involved in setting up the Irish Congress of Trade Unions, having grown up in a tenement building in Dublin with thirty-five others. Joyce's parents had both had tough upbringings and always struggled. But they were very focused on the power of education, 'and that was the thing that got me and my family out of poverty', according to Joyce.

As for the gritty, relentless fighter in him, Joyce credits his mother, Colette – who worked as a cleaner at a local sports complex – as the source of the determination that would become a hallmark of his tenacious leadership. 'She's only four-foot-nine,' he says. 'One of my brothers calls her the best pound-for-pound fighter in Dublin, because she really has always stood up for the family against bullies. And she was a determined individual – still is.'

Colette had to get to work by 7 am each day, so the boys would always be up at around 6 am, a daily routine that became embedded in Joyce's makeup.

Religion was a big part of family and social life. 'In the '70s in Ireland, the Catholic Church dominated,' he recalls. 'I think 80 to 90 per cent of people went to mass – we did once a week – and I went to Catholic schools. My mam wouldn't go to mass, but still a very strong Catholic, and my aunts were too.'

It was a very close-knit family. Joyce recalled a trip back to Ireland for his parents' fiftieth wedding anniversary in 2015. He hadn't visited Ireland for a while, given the trials and tribulations at Qantas at the time. Some Guinness was downed. 'It was a big party with 120 of my relatives I hadn't seen in years. We finished at 5 am and my seventy-year-old aunts outlasted me. I'm off alcohol for the month!'[2]

Joyce had a natural talent for numbers, and this was stimulated at an early stage. His father bought some little cards with the times tables printed on them and would test Alan and Anthony. 'That was probably the start of it,' he reflected in a 2023 interview with *The Australian*, '[Dad] spending the time with his kids saying, "I'm going to make your life better than mine." [But] by the time the younger two came along to our age, Mum and Dad said, "Oh God, we're so tired" and they just shoved them a packet of crayons and they started drawing.'[3]

In secondary school, at St Mark's Community School in Springfield, Tallaght, Joyce's favourite teacher, Miss Moriarty, fanned the flames of his interest in maths. 'That encouraged me to specialise in mathematics – she was a big influence in the early years,' he later recalled, 'my first mentor.'[4]

Around this time, Catholicism took a back seat. 'As we got more and more educated like the rest of the country, I became less and less religious,' Joyce says. 'In my late teens, when I started being able to vote, around that time I became an atheist and I think the same happened to all my brothers.' Even today, he chokes up when he recalls the widespread national disillusionment with the church when hidden abuse by clergy on a horrifying scale was exposed.

Paul Joyce went on to become a successful graphic designer in Ireland, while Maurice junior became an animator, spending time as a director of Disney cartoons. As Joyce quips, 'Two of us use the left-hand side of our brain, and two of us use the right-hand sides of our brain. So between the four of us, we've got two good brains!'[5]

Like Alan, Anthony studied applied science and graduated with first-class honours and a university medal; he went on to become a leading actuary. 'We have always been competitive, [but] I have to admit that Anthony was better than me at maths,' Joyce later told *The Australian*.[6]

Seeing his parents struggle to raise their four boys, Joyce at one time proposed quitting his studies to help the family, but their focus was clear: 'Get your degrees, and that'll set you up for life. They were very, very passionate about it.'[7] And so he became the first member of the family to complete a tertiary degree.

Although his parents and their parents before them had lived just a short distance from the renowned Trinity College, Joyce's father had never been through its gates until his eldest son's graduation day. 'He was so proud on that day, which made a huge difference,' Joyce says.

Joyce enjoyed the social and academic aspects of life at Trinity, and he admired the history of the institution – something he would later revere about Qantas and its historic roots. But the life of Beefy and Balthazar B, the philandering heroes of J.P. Donleavy, was not for him. 'I tried not to get caught in the [Trinity] library with a drink – that would've been a bad look! Like everybody, going through university was probably the best years. Its location right in the middle of the city centre with a lot of good pubs around meant there was a good student nightlife.' Not without pride, Joyce adds, 'It's got a great reputation, so I really enjoyed being there.'[8]

Early encouragement that recognises a natural talent can become self-fulfilling, he reasons. 'That's why I always think, in terms of management style, praise and positive reinforcement is

far better than criticism. And when you go through a change program, you should spend 80 per cent of the time on the positives,
and 20 per cent of the time on the negatives. I think that starts at
an early age.'

Joyce graduated from Trinity in 1988, the year Australia marked
its bicentenary, and after a short stint as a computer programmer
he joined Aer Lingus. He was not intoxicated by aviation fuel –
yet. It was overbooking he was attracted to.

'I came into an airline not because of the excitement of the
airline, but because of the maths!' he laughs. 'I was an operations
research analyst, building mathematical models around aviation
problems, like queuing or overbooking. I managed to apply for
the job and get in on the basis of that degree.'

Network planning requires a highly structured, logical
mindset and Joyce applied this in his disciplined approach to
decision-making. He liked to have the details and get all his ducks
in a row. He had a mathematician's mindset, and liked to understand all the pieces of the equation before moving on.

He'd briefly savoured the idea of becoming a pilot at Aer
Lingus, but his short-sightedness meant he failed the test. He
was disappointed, but quickly got over it. Even so, it wasn't long
before Joyce was savouring the scent of jet kerosene in his nos-
trils. At the age of twenty-three, he took to the skies for his first
ever flight, from Dublin to Chicago. As an airline employee,
his baptism was in business class. This was living! He never
looked back.

Once Joyce was on the inside, the glamour and dynamics of
the aviation business complemented his education. He was soon
being inspired by a handful of exceptional industry leaders of
the time. 'In the late 1980s and '90s, there were a lot of superheroes around,' he said. 'The Bob Crandalls [legendary CEO of
American Airlines] of this world, Southwest Airlines and Herb
Kelleher, and what he had done, the changes that were there.

There were a lot of superheroes and people that changed the face of travel around the globe.'[9]

He was quickly promoted to fleet planning, where he developed a mathematical model to predict the optimum number of spare Boeing 737 engines the airline needed to hold, then he spent time in market and schedule planning. He travelled extensively, supporting Aer Lingus's marketing and IT systems installed at airlines in Thailand, Albania and Ukraine, eventually returning to Dublin in 1994.

Across Europe, things were changing fast. The European Economic Community's 'single market' had come into effect in 1993, relaxing border restrictions within the European Union, and spawning new low-cost airlines such as Ryanair and easyJet. The traditional national airlines were being forced into a fundamental rethink of their strategies, which hadn't shifted much for decades, as they relied on aggregating European travellers into their national hubs and onto long-haul flights.

Until the single market, Europe was carved up into tidy bilateral markets, with specific air services agreements between each pair of countries. So Aer Lingus and British Airways controlled all services between the United Kingdom and Ireland; other airlines were carefully excluded. As a result, these flag carriers had little incentive to innovate, such as by offering discounted fares. Until 2000, things were very similar in Australia's domestic arena, with its comfortable duopoly of Qantas and Ansett.

The new European point-to-point, low-cost airlines now started to undermine the short-haul connections of legacy network airlines, including British Airways, Air France and Lufthansa. These network carriers made much of their revenue connecting these shorter sectors onto their large long-haul routes. Eating away at their intra-Europe flights was now starting to disrupt the whole model.

BA was later to experiment – unsuccessfully – with its own low-cost subsidiary, called Go!, as Ryanair and easyJet forced

European fares to unthinkable lows, and passenger numbers to unthinkable highs.

Smaller full-service airlines such as Aer Lingus were being seriously marginalised – for them it was a case of adapt or die. Radical change was needed, where only modest tinkering had been possible before. The Irish national carrier was much later to become a global model for how a full-service airline could cut costs and survive.

It had become obvious that cost awareness and restructuring were the ingredients for survival in this new world. Even more importantly, half-measures were futile when major change was clearly necessary.

At first, the airline's response had been to create its own low-cost offshoot, Aer Lingus Express. Aer Lingus had seconded Conor McCarthy to set up the subsidiary, and Joyce was assigned to help him. This experience was to have a major influence on Joyce's future roles, professionally and personally.

Another influence on Joyce's days at the airline was Garret FitzGerald, a former *taoiseach* (prime minister) of Ireland, between 1981 and 1987. More an intellectual than a politician, he was at the forefront of major reforms in the country, including reconciliation policies that ultimately led to the 1998 Good Friday Agreement.

His economic reforms also helped Ireland to become the 'Celtic Tiger', spawning, among other things, the now massive aircraft-leasing industry. One of his better-known sayings was 'It sounds great in practice, but how will it work in theory?', which he uttered while negotiating the 1985 Anglo-Irish agreement. Sometimes the Irish have a way of making you rethink the obvious.

FitzGerald, who like Joyce had a keen interest in maths and statistics, had decided at the age of twelve that he would one day work for the national airline. His hobby of memorising airline timetables had led him to apply for several airline jobs, and he secured a role as an administrative assistant at Aer Lingus in 1947. By 1950, he'd become responsible for economic planning and scheduling within the company.

'FitzGerald used to write mathematical problems in the published timetables and would solve them for relaxation,' Joyce says. Even when Joyce was at Aer Lingus, FitzGerald would still write in, saying, 'I think your utilisation of the 737s on Dublin–London could be improved.'

Joyce never memorised schedules like FitzGerald, but he collected the paper airline timetables for a while. Even today, he still has loads of them. 'They used to be phenomenal documents,' he says. 'I did get into airline timetables, but I haven't done it in ages. Now that's a very nerdy thing – I shouldn't say that, should I?'

Even though he's now a proudly naturalised Australian, Joyce's Irish origins were always enormously influential in his professional life. Industry titans such as Willie Walsh and Ryanair's Michael O'Leary blazed a trail, and their example encouraged Joyce as he strived to achieve his own ambitious goals in the industry.

Somehow, despite its tiny island, Irishmen have permeated the aviation game over the past three decades. 'The airline industry is full of bullshitters, liars and drunks. We excel at all three in Ireland,' O'Leary once said.[10] But there's arguably more to it than the Ryanair CEO's tongue-in-cheek assessment suggests.

Nonetheless, it took more than that for a working-class Irishman – and a gay one at that – to become the youngest ever CEO of Qantas, in a country a world away from his upbringing. Even in a liberal and open democracy like Australia's, the odds were surely stacked against Alan Joyce. Words such as tenacious, passionate and obsessive describe the man well, but one attribute held him in great stead when it came to the final selection: his proven leadership success.

Since 2004, Joyce had demonstrated that he could not only create a low-cost airline, but also steer it through its challenging first years, against opposition from both inside and outside the company. In doing so, he vindicated the judgement of both Qantas CEO Geoff Dixon and his board.

Joyce's key role in the establishment and success of Jetstar, and its importance in stemming the damage wreaked by the genuinely low-cost Virgin Blue model, undoubtedly played a big part in his big step upwards. Dixon and the board had seen him in action and he'd barely put a foot wrong.

On a trip back to Dublin soon after becoming Qantas CEO, Joyce told the Wings Club: 'There must be something in the water – or the Guinness – here. Because there's certainly a very special Irish connection with aviation. Even our writers look skyward. After all, Oscar Wilde thought we were all in the gutter, but the best of us are "looking at the stars". And William Butler Yeats called the passion for flying a "lonely impulse of delight". Well, the skies are hardly lonely today.'[11]

Ireland's great aviation tradition begins in the 1930s, near the small town of Limerick, on Ireland's west coast. Today, Shannon Airport ranks 680th in the world for the number of annual flights. But if you scratch the surface, it becomes clear that the fact it has a 3200-metre runway these days disguises an ancestry more vigorous than its present. Even the busiest airport in the world, Atlanta's Hartsfield-Jackson International Airport, with its five runways, has only one that is longer than Shannon's. Dublin Airport's longest falls short of Shannon's.

In 1935, a government-led survey party had set out for the west of Ireland 'to find suitable bases for the operation of seaplanes and landplanes on a transatlantic service'. The party found the ideal spot beside the water near Rineanna, in County Clare, just an hour and a half's bicycle ride from Limerick when the wind wasn't against you, although it usually was. The waterside location meant the contemporary flying boats could also come and go. The first commercial flight to land at the airport wasn't until July 1939, when a small Sabena aircraft arrived from Brussels via Croydon, but then World War II rapidly accelerated Ireland's aviation character. It scarcely looked back.

Despite Ireland's neutrality during the war, Shannon Airport quickly took on a crucial role. The airport's strategic location made it an ideal refuelling and maintenance stop for military aircraft travelling between North America and Europe. Its long runway and spacious facilities were well-suited to accommodate the large and heavy military aircraft, which needed plenty of runway. American bombers, transports and fighters frequently made stopovers on their way to or from combat zones, to refuel, restock and undergo maintenance.

The airport also served as a transit point for wounded soldiers and prisoners of war being transported to or from Europe, and its medical facilities were used to treat and care for injured military personnel, as well as proving a valuable R&R stopover.

After the war concluded, the runway at Shannon was extended to today's length and it was to be another quarter-century before technology advanced far enough for passenger-carrying aircraft to consistently make the big hop all the way across the North Atlantic Ocean, overflying Ireland. Right up until the early 1970s, Shannon continued to play an important commercial role, leveraging its duty-free shopping facility for passengers and providing convenient two-way immigration clearance as well.

Shannon was the catalyst for the Irish fixation with aviation, and for the proliferation of prominent industry leaders that far surpasses the rightful amount for a country of Ireland's size.

If there is a modern godfather of the Irish industry, it is Tony Ryan, born, appropriately enough, near Limerick, a shorter cycle ride from Shannon Airport with the tailwind. His hopes of a university education died with his father, so he too started off in Aer Lingus as a dispatch clerk, later being selected as a management trainee. In 1975, he established one of the first global aircraft-leasing companies, with financial backing from one of the country's wealthiest families, Guinness.

With creative government support and tax incentives specifically tailored to the aviation industry, including the Irish Government Aircraft Leasing Scheme (GALS) and the 'double Irish' tax arrangement, Guinness Peat Aviation (GPA) prospered. Until GPA overreached during the economic downturn of the early 1990s, Ireland had become a highly attractive location for establishing aircraft-leasing companies.

Today, some fifty aircraft-leasing companies are based in Ireland, including fourteen of the fifteen biggest, and more than half of the world's leased aircraft are owned by Irish firms (that is, over one-quarter of all the large aircraft in the world). The aviation industry contributes a billion US dollars to the national economy and supports nearly 10,000 jobs. Government-backed incentives have also stimulated extensive aviation education and training programs.

Tony Ryan went on to establish Ryanair in 1984, today the biggest airline in Europe and the biggest low-cost carrier in the world – although the airline only achieved its leadership position after Michael O'Leary became CEO in 1994.

Along the way, a deep culture of safety and regulatory policy developed in Ireland, with much sharing of ideas and knowledge. That intense aviation environment also produced one of the most highly regarded regulatory bodies, the Irish Aviation Authority.

This fecund petri dish of Aer Lingus produced a growing number of airline managers, including an outspoken young pilot named Willie Walsh, who would become CEO in 2001, before moving to run British Airways. They shared a particular brand of culture, of low-cost efficiency, and they began spreading the religion widely. One of those low-cost missionaries, serial low-cost carrier (LCC) start-up maestro Conor McCarthy, had begun his aviation career at Aer Lingus as a sixteen-year-old apprentice.

'Conor and I started doing the business case for Aer Lingus Express,' Joyce recalls, 'but then the Aer Lingus CEO at the time ended up doing a deal with the unions not to do it. So it never got up and running. We started getting aircraft and responsibility for some of the poor-performing routes, and so [the operation] was starting to happen. Conor left because he was disappointed that Express didn't launch. He went to Ryanair and worked there through their big expansion.'

Aer Lingus nearly went broke in 2002, following the September 11 attacks. CEO Willie Walsh, formerly the head of the airline's pilots' union, initiated a severe cost-cutting exercise, turning the company around and delivering a profit by 2004. It was a painful exercise, but the alternative was dire. Joyce's experience of Aer Lingus's turbulent environment would serve him well a decade later, when the same strategic tsunami struck Australia.

By now captivated by the industry, Joyce impertinently gave himself a goal: 'to be an airline CEO before I was forty'. His former boss and great friend Conor McCarthy had now moved on, and Joyce realised it was time for him to reach for new horizons too.

2

Time to Move

Homosexuality was decriminalised in Ireland in 1993. 'But I didn't feel like I could come out to many people outside of my close family, and certainly not at work,' Alan Joyce later recalled.[1] Ireland, he felt, was not the place for him.

To Joyce, Australia seemed like an egalitarian, open society, and in 1996, at the age of thirty, he migrated there on the promise of a job with Ansett Australia. He joined as a network and schedules planner under Lyell Strambi. Their roles would one day reverse, with Strambi later becoming a key executive at Qantas under Joyce.

Soon after the young Irishman arrived, Rod Eddington was brought in as chairman of Ansett by the company's half-owner, News Ltd, on a mission to streamline the airline's menagerie of fleet types, a cost-heavy operation and a culture that better suited a regulated environment.

Both handicaps had been inherited from the days when News Ltd and TNT were equal owners of Ansett. Rupert Murdoch and TNT's Sir Peter Abeles were joint managing directors, but by 1996 TNT had sold its 50 per cent share to Air New Zealand, leaving News as uncomfortable fifty-fifty partners with the airline across the Tasman.

News had wanted out before TNT sold but couldn't agree a price, which meant there was already friction between the joint owners, and now Eddington was fixing Ansett up with a view to selling News's 50 per cent to Singapore Airlines. That tie-up made a lot of sense for Ansett, and Eddington was close to Singapore's chief executive, C.K. 'Doc' Cheong.

Air New Zealand considered Singapore Airlines a competitor, and was not at all keen to share ownership with it, so in April 1999 exercised its pre-emption rights to acquire the 50 per cent of Ansett it didn't already own.

For Joyce, this tumultuous period had echoes of his time at Aer Lingus, although the task confronting Ansett was much stiffer. As he helped rationalise Ansett's lopsided operations from the ground up, Joyce was now absorbing abundant knowledge of Australia's domestic market, solidifying the foundations of his future career.

When Air New Zealand scuppered News's plan to sell to Singapore Airlines, as most Ansett staff had come to assume would happen, it threw the airline into turmoil. Ansett management was now 'New Zealandised', and many of the team – including Lyell Strambi – were shown the door. This was not one of Air New Zealand's proudest moments.

Most of the people who knew the Australian domestic market were given the sack. Joyce was appointed group head of network and fleet at Ansett, and found himself with a new boss who was a Canadian.

'In one of the first meetings, I said, "Here's what I want to do on Sydney–Brisbane and Brisbane–Adelaide," because there was a lot of capacity being added and I wanted to make some changes,' Joyce recalls. 'My new boss said to me, "Hold on a second, let's go back to basics. How many people are in Brisbane and how many flights do we have on Sydney–Brisbane? Can you give me a geography lesson?" I knew we were in trouble! You had an Irishman telling a Canadian telling a New Zealand company, "Here's how the Australian market works." I figured this isn't going to work!'

Eddington, whose appointment by News had assumed a sale to Singapore Airlines, was no longer needed by Air New Zealand and had departed to occupy the role of CEO of British Airways – which was at that time a 25 per cent owner of Qantas. But before leaving, he called Geoff Dixon, who asked him: 'Who would you nick from Ansett?'

'Oh, a few people,' Eddington said. 'Alan's one of them.'

Joyce got a call from Dixon around the same time that he was getting used to his Canadian boss.

Ansett's headquarters were at 501 Swanston Street, Melbourne, while Qantas had an office just around the corner in Franklin Street – the former head office of TAA (Trans Australia Airlines). The buildings were so close to each other that it was even possible for some staff to see into their competitors' offices. Way back in the bad old days, the companies' respective pricing teams would meet at a pub at the nearby Victoria Markets to fix prices for the day.

It's an incestuous industry. Geoff Dixon came up through the ranks at Ansett. Today's Virgin Australia CEO, Jayne Hrdlicka, was brought into Qantas by Joyce and advised for years on strategy issues, before becoming CEO of Jetstar. For years there's been a two-way flow between Qantas and Virgin.

When Dixon called, Joyce says, 'I sneaked in not wanting anybody to see me and went up to Geoff's office. He had his feet on the table. He interviewed me for forty-five minutes and made me an offer to come and run network planning in Qantas.'

Joyce walked back to Swanston Street and informed his Canadian boss that he was leaving. Within minutes, 'they got security to escort me out of the building. The security guard came up and took me down and took my ID off me.'

Joyce's timing was immaculate, as at Ansett two years of mayhem ensued.

Despite having owned a half-share in Ansett for four years, Air New Zealand had apparently failed to perform adequate due diligence. It struggled to support the loss-making, heavily indebted Australian carrier. Pouring a little fuel on the fire, News Ltd had spotted an anxious buyer and had also upped the sale price to $680 million. Rupert Murdoch was never a man to give a sucker a break.

The unwieldy and dysfunctional combination might eventually have righted itself but, with little warning, not one but two new low-cost airlines entered the Australian market during 2000: Impulse Airlines in June, followed two months later by Virgin Blue.

Impulse was a known entity – it had been publicly raising funds – so on its own it was manageable. It began with five of Boeing's 717s and a poorly formulated business plan. But with its two 737s, Virgin Blue was the real thing: co-founder Brett Godfrey had LCC experience from Europe, and the airline enjoyed a cost base not far from half that of Ansett. Godfrey had grand plans for rapid growth.

Although both new entrants were small, the jolt they gave the system was grossly disproportionate. Indeed, it was volcanic. A savage discount war broke out on the east-coast trunk routes, as Ansett and Qantas moved to fend off the challengers. This reaction partially succeeded: the underfunded Impulse quickly folded under the pressure, running out of cash and passing into Qantas's hands before being bankrupted.

Qantas adroitly persuaded the Australian Competition & Consumer Commission (ACCC) to authorise the transaction, aided by the fact there were no other buyers. No independent was going to step into that cauldron.

For the newly appointed Joyce, this created an early exposure to the talents in Qantas, and he was impressed. He attributes much of the credit for getting approval for the Impulse deal to the persistence of his then boss, Paul Edwards, in convincing the ACCC. Impulse was failing and there were no other suitors, but initially the commission, led by Allan Fels, rejected the takeover proposal.

Edwards, said Joyce, 'was relentless on it and he kept on going. I thought, "Wow, that was good," because a lot of people would've given up. In the end we got Impulse and, because it became the foundation of Jetstar, we were able to create Jetstar at scale and fast.' Making matters even better, Impulse's fourteen twin-engine 717s also came on sweetheart lease rates.

The deal involved Impulse agreeing to Qantas running the operation under the Qantas brand, with a seamless changeover. Then, in November 2001, Qantas exercised its option to buy the airline outright, moving the fleet into a beefed-up regional operation, QantasLink. Later, when Jetstar converted to new A320s in 2005–06, the 717s progressively went back into service with QantasLink.

Virgin Blue was also losing heavily under the torrent of price-cutting, and despite the deep pockets of its wealthy backer, Richard Branson and the Virgin Group, it was on the brink of selling to a willing Air New Zealand in early 2001. The New Zealand company believed that taking Virgin out would stabilise the market. But by the middle of the year, it became apparent that Ansett was in deep trouble and Virgin Blue might survive. Branson had been less than convinced the venture would work – he had only put in $10 million at start-up – but now he was convinced to stay in.

By June 2001, Ansett was losing $80 million a month and going from bad to worse. Then, in the early hours of the morning of 12 September 2001, Sydney time, Air New Zealand made the decision to push Ansett into administration.

If there was any lingering hope of a quick financial fix, this was dashed a few hours later when, at 8.45 am on 11 September in New York – Tuesday evening in Sydney – an American Airlines 767 flew into the World Trade Center, throwing the aviation world and global financial markets into chaos. The last thing any financier wanted was to invest in a defunct, debt-laden airline. The US skies were shut down for three days, with all aircraft grounded.

Prime Minister John Howard happened to be in Washington to mark the fiftieth anniversary of the ANZUS Treaty, and could see the smoke from the attack on the Pentagon building from his hotel room window. To help him home, the next day President George W. Bush engaged Air Force Two to fly him to Hawaii. For months thereafter, the PM resisted loud calls for him to 'Save Ansett' by bailing it out. He considered it would be 'politically unsustainable and economically dangerous'.

For a few months, Ansett struggled to revive in administration while buyers were sought. Dixon had a look at picking up the wreck for $1, although he was suspected by the New Zealand side to be just on an information-finding mission. On 4 March 2002, after more than sixty years' existence, Ansett finally breathed its last, putting almost 16,000 staff out of work. It was the biggest corporate collapse in Australian history. In October 2001, Air New Zealand, almost dragged into the mire itself, was saved from collapse only by its national government, which fifteen years earlier had privatised it.

Now Virgin Blue rushed to fill the gaping market void left by Ansett's demise. US air travel had slumped post-9/11, so cheap aircraft were plentiful, and Virgin was quick to take advantage of this fortune.

Qantas too was scouring the world for aircraft. The Ansett planes were out of reach while the administrator attempted to restore the airline to the air – and anyway, as it turned out, the ageing 'Ansett Ark' of aircraft types came with very complex ownership structures.

'It got really tough with the advent of the low-cost carriers and Ansett going belly-up and September 11,' one former Qantas manager says. 'That was a pretty intense period. Airline fortunes really can turn on a dime. It went very quickly from fighting hard to compete, to all of a sudden having more business than we knew what to do with.'

Almost before Qantas could react, within a year it too was under siege. With a cost base at least 20 per cent higher than Virgin's, the LCC was gobbling up market share as it brought on new aircraft, offering fares Qantas couldn't sustain, with seemingly no end in sight.

The young Alan Joyce, still only thirty-two, was gaining a remarkable education, with a view from the touchline of an industry undergoing revolution. He already had experience in the engine room of disruption in Europe, had witnessed first-hand the power of low-cost operations, had gained invaluable experience in network planning in the Australian market, and had been exposed directly to several examples of the destruction that weak management and poor decisions could wreak in a short time.

Responding to the Virgin threat, Qantas dithered for a while, first dipping a toe into low(er)-cost operations with a short-lived revival of the Australian Airlines brand in 2002, flying internationally out of a Cairns base and focusing on Asian tourism. It made most of the usual halfway steps, by then typical for legacy airlines across the world – for example, seconding staff (so they were costly) and avoiding direct competition with Virgin.

But CEO Dixon learned from the mistakes and said the Australian Airlines move was not radical enough to cope with the rapid changes to the structure of aviation. 'We did not lose money,' he said. 'But it became clear that we needed to take a more comprehensive approach.'[2]

He then took what was, for the time, a very bold step. It would leave a powerful and enduring legacy for Qantas.

Dixon moved to open up new vistas for his young but by now well-qualified network planner. Joyce was ushered into a top-secret project to establish a budget airline subsidiary for Qantas. Already impressed by the bright young man, Dixon appointed him to lead the charge.

So, in October 2003, at the age of thirty-seven, Alan Joyce became project lead and then CEO of Jetstar. 'So I just got there,' he observes. 'I wanted that [CEO] role.'

A small team was assembled to nut out the details of what was to become the most successful LCC subsidiary in the world, in turn part of a near-invincible 'dual brand' airline operation.

Among the Jetstar team was John Gissing on the operational side, who would later go on to join Joyce's executive team at Qantas.

'Alan was the network nerd and we were operations guys,' Gissing said. 'He was deeply into mathematics and I heard he read network schedules on the weekends, so I thought, "There's got to be something awfully wrong with this guy."'

Gissing first met Joyce when the board announced that Impulse was a potential launch vehicle for Jetstar. 'Maybe I was feeling old at the time and a bit weary, but Alan looked very young and with not much experience. But that first impression washed away almost immediately as I learned he was very curious – and persistent.'

Gissing recalls the time Joyce met the Jetstar team for the first time. 'I said to the guys, "It's a low-cost carrier, let's learn from round the world: ties off, open-plan office." Someone said, "He's Irish – why don't we get some green hats and we'll turn on the St Paddy's Day theme and get some clover leaves too." So Alan walks into the old Impulse building on 11th Street at Mascot, we're all lined up, the team and the operations guys, all with green hats on, and he walks in wearing a tie! And he missed the joke on the green hats because Jetstar's colour was orange. But we had a laugh anyway. From that moment, we were taking the micky and having a bit of fun. He saw that we were prepared to do that – and he was too.

'He's just got this great spring in his step and tells a great yarn and he can be a lot of fun. So this young, cheerful guy was given this big role, and that was great because it engendered immediate trust in the relationship and you could have a good chat about things.'

Joyce and Gissing were supported by Boston Consulting Group consultant Bruce Buchanan, who eventually took over from Joyce as CEO of Jetstar. The team also included David Koczkar, who went on to become CEO of Medibank Group, and Terry Bowen, the future finance director of Wesfarmers.

Through the Irish network, McCarthy flew down to Melbourne in 2003 to work closely with his former colleague. 'We also had Jerry Turner, who came in from Ryanair,' says Joyce. 'It's always good to triangulate these things, so that's what Conor and his team did.'

The strategy team worked quickly, presenting a model to the board for approval. After several runs at a name, they came up with JetX. The story goes that it was Dixon who said, 'Nah, sounds like a gas station,' then he put on his marketing hat and suggested Jetstar.

Of the many attempts by full-service airlines across the globe to set up low-cost subsidiaries as the new breed of start-ups stole their passengers, none had succeeded. By 2003, the educated wisdom was that the strategy didn't work. Many people told Dixon that Qantas wouldn't be able to make it work. Joyce and his team, meanwhile, reviewed the long list of failures and asked why they hadn't cut through.

Gissing and a few others visited JetBlue in New York, and Southwest on the ground at LAX. 'I remember a time in Dublin, literally hiding behind a flowerpot so I didn't distract them, taking notes on Ryanair's aircraft turn and how they did the headcount and ticketing count,' he says. Then they went over to easyJet to understand the very constrained terminal space at its Gatwick operation. 'It was all about learning, and not reinventing the wheel.'

The world tour turned up some helpful insights about the 'schizophrenic nature' of having an in-house low-cost carrier. In some cases, the start-up airlines became too independent. 'The cure was worse than the disease' was BA chief Rod Eddington's take on its low-cost subsidiary Go! Airlines, because it had become very competitive with its parent, which caused a lot of issues. Other airlines became too close to the legacy carrier. There was Ted by United, and Song by Delta: they had no difference in the employee arrangements, and the same overheads and supporting infrastructure. They were essentially just different brands.

These latter examples weren't true low-cost carriers, Joyce later said in a EUROCONTROL interview. The 'true' LCCs were disrupters, low-cost missionaries. Their mentality fundamentally differed from that of the full-service tradition. When they generated new business, they didn't put their prices up like a legacy airline would – they added flights. LCCs also developed new markets simply by offering very low fares.

They outsourced everything they possibly could, and focused on utilisation and seat density. By flying their fleet for twelve or more hours a day – in contrast to the eight that Qantas managed domestically – LCCs reduced fleet needs by a third. By adding thirty all-economy seats to their A320s or 737s, they increased seat numbers by 20 per cent. They used only one aircraft type, with a standard configuration, which saved costs by making everything and everyone interchangeable.

Where possible, LCCs employed non-union staff or just paid them less. And, crucially, they followed the low-cost religion. Indeed, this was the magic ingredient. As start-ups, they arrived with no legacy airline full-service baggage – literally, in many cases, as paying extra for checked bags became the norm, generating 'ancillary revenues'.

Globally, there had never been a disruptive force on this scale. Virtually every full-service airline was confronted by such start-ups, although some lobbied their governments to protect them from new competition. In Australia's open marketplace, there would be no returning to the status quo.

For established airlines, adapting to fight off the new invaders was near impossible. There was just too much of an attitude shift needed, too much bureaucracy, too many 'silos'. AirAsia founder Tony Fernandes would tell his people who spoke at industry conferences to make sure they picked up all the spare pens from the tables so they didn't go to waste. It was as much about creating a culture as about saving money.

Full-service airlines typically prioritised higher yields rather than lower costs. For them, changing course to becoming low-cost meant making a 180-degree turnabout. To use a sweet Irish saying, 'If you want to get there, you wouldn't start from here.'

According to Joyce, Geoff Dixon decided Jetstar had to be very different from its parent. 'Geoff said, "You can't be based in Sydney. Set up somewhere else. You can pick any other city so you have separation,"' he recalls.

And so Jetstar set up a Melbourne headquarters, well away from Qantas's Sydney head office. Other features followed. 'We did everything different: independent pilots, cabin crew, independent supply of ground handling, engineering, everything. And it came under Virgin's cost base by 5 per cent, which was our target,' Joyce adds.

But that wasn't all. Independent LCCs like Virgin Blue chased the high-volume traffic flows – 'cherrypicking', as the opposition disparagingly called it – although they also had the power to create a market where none existed before, simply by tapping a more discretionary segment. Success wasn't just about lower fares but more creative pricing.

In Australia, Virgin Blue focused on the short-haul routes between the east-coast capital cities. These included two of the world's five busiest city pairs (Sydney–Melbourne and Sydney–Brisbane), and it was here that Qantas and Ansett made the bulk of their profits.

This was where the dilemma arose for any full-service airline wanting to use a subsidiary to retaliate. If Qantas were to unleash a low-cost subsidiary, it too would have to operate these routes – meaning the new entity would eat away at the parent's traffic. At BA, Rod Eddington had found that network planners and revenue managers in the much larger parent airline were strongly against having another competitor, especially one from inside its own camp. As they saw it, this was cannibalisation. On the other hand, there was little point in creating an LCC subsidiary if it wasn't going to compete with the other LCCs.

Qantas needed to think hard about the issue of cannibalisation if it was to successfully repel the Virgin invasion. But that was easier said than done. In the end, it would take the Qantas group years to refine the dual-brand product to reach the optimal outcome. Even so, Jetstar began to be effective almost immediately.

'To stop the cure becoming worse than the disease, we coordinated a lot and made sure the brands were very different on the network and on pricing of revenue management,' Joyce says. 'What that meant at the start was two separate route networks. The premium Qantas brand went upmarket and thrived. Qantas Domestic became the most profitable business in our network.'

Quite simply, this early adaptation had to be successful. It was about survival. By the end of 2003, Virgin Blue's market share was growing by the day. Now Qantas was ready to fight back.

Jetstar's first flight under its new brand, between Newcastle and Melbourne, took off on 25 May 2004. It was later joined by thirteen other ex-Impulse 717s that had temporarily formed QantasLink, and by the end of the day several thousand Australians had their first experience with the orange tails. That Jetstar was able to get into the air so quickly was thanks to the Impulse launch vehicle, where Joyce's relentless boss, Paul Edwards, had so impressed him.

Gradually, Jetstar began to compete on the key routes, helping stem the inroads being made by Virgin Blue. As the start-up gained experience, the impact of the Qantas subsidiary became stunning, stopping Virgin's expansion trajectory in its tracks in a matter of months.

Meanwhile, in a March 2005 management reshuffle, Qantas Airlines executive general manager John Borghetti took over network management, including scheduling. Borghetti had decades of experience across all aspects of the operation, and this was his chance to shine. CFO Peter Gregg added fleet and long-term network development to his portfolio.

It was widely seen as a succession move by Dixon, whose contract as CEO was ending in 2007. Respected industry journalist David Knibb wrote in *FlightGlobal*: 'Historically, Qantas has groomed two executives as potential leaders and ultimately picked one. These moves are seen as a start to that process, with Gregg and Borghetti the likely candidates.'[3]

As well as leading the premium brand, Borghetti also chaired the Qantas 'Flying Committee', a high-level group created within Qantas to coordinate all route and capacity decisions for Australian Airlines, Jetstar, Qantas and QantasLink.

This posed a fresh challenge for the CEO of Jetstar: it was not going to be easy to convince Qantas's experienced and dedicated revenue management expert that the new airline should have the freedom to operate where it would be most effective, even if that caused some pain to Qantas.

The committee would meet regularly, review the market and, in effect, decide where and how Jetstar could operate, segmenting the market and learning as they went along. The impact of Jetstar's entry or pricing on any route was quickly visible. It was a uniquely valuable way of learning how the new market worked, but the mood was often adversarial.

Joyce and Borghetti were boxing over route strategy. The inherent conflict of having two airlines competing for resources and attention created the appearance, at least, of bad blood between the executives.

'What you had, which I love, was people that were passionate about the brands that they're running and we'd say, "Here's how I'd like to promote them and grow them,"' Joyce recalls. 'John would have his opinion on what Qantas should have. And I had my opinion with Bruce [Buchanan] on where Jetstar should go. When we couldn't get an agreement, Geoff would come in.'

The stage was set for rivalry and friction between two ambitious executives on converging flightpaths, the older anxious to preserve the immensely valuable Qantas brand, the younger striving to make a success of his low-cost airline. This collision of interests framed a relationship that, in the following decade, would have a massive impact on Australian aviation.

This was a time when the Australian and Asian economies were growing strongly and regulatory limitations in Asia were being relaxed. In December 2004, Jetstar Asia Airways commenced operations from its Singapore hub to Hong Kong. A year later, the Australian Jetstar operation launched international flights from Sydney, Melbourne, Brisbane and the Gold Coast to Christchurch, New Zealand. Joyce was now overseeing an international operation.

Meanwhile, the Australian Airlines experiment was being wound down. It was eventually shut down altogether in 2006, having provided Qantas with some valuable lessons and having paved the way for Jetstar.

Under Dixon's leadership, the Qantas Group's dual-brand strategy soon became a model for others to follow. Jetstar's almost immediate success in dampening Virgin Blue's expansion gave credibility to the upstart airline. As the start-up gained global industry attention, Joyce's role in Jetstar's success propelled him to a new level.

This didn't go unnoticed at his old airline. At this time, Aer Lingus CEO Willie Walsh was moving to head British Airways, and he strongly supported passing the Qantas baton to the Jetstar star.

In 2005, in the wake of Walsh's move, Joyce received an offer to become CEO of Aer Lingus. It was tempting to return to where it all started and be closer to his old friends and family, not to mention the attraction for him of leading the Irish flag carrier. Joyce returned to Ireland to speak with his father, Maurice, for career advice. The country had modernised and wore a much more liberal face than it had a decade earlier, when he had left. He would already return a hero.

Dixon, however, had other ideas, upping Joyce's pay and offering encouraging words. And, after some sage advice from his dad, the Jetstar CEO decided to stay on in Australia. His home-grown peers and heroes would remain half a world away.

3

An Australian, an Italian
and an Irishman . . .

In 2007, a year before he would leave Qantas, Geoff Dixon was a prominent part of a failed Macquarie Bank–led attempt to 'privatise' Qantas – that is, to buy and delist the airline and put it into the hands of investors, through a consortium called Airline Partners Australia (APA). Although he was CEO of the airline, Dixon was an active player in the move, which also included some large Australian, US and Canadian private-equity investors. The final offer of $5.60 a share valued the airline at over $11 billion. At the time, this would have made it the largest leveraged buyout in Australian corporate history.

As the deadline for acceptances drew nearer, the consortium was struggling to get over the line. While shareholders were being solicited to sell, the Qantas chairman (as she preferred to be called), Margaret Jackson, who would have profited grandly from the sale, made some comments about the intelligence of shareholders who declined to part with their shares. She maintained that the price being offered was too good to miss, and warned about what failure of the bid would mean. 'If anyone thinks this will happen without affecting the [share] price then they have a mental problem with how the market works,' she said in May 2007.[1]

The indelicate phrasing did not help the optics of an outcome that would have benefitted Jackson's personal interests. The deal narrowly failed to achieve the requisite number of acceptances, and Jackson, amid public censure, announced that she would step down as chair at the annual general meeting in November. She and Dixon had worked together closely, and very effectively, for most of his leadership of the airline, so Dixon himself remained as CEO despite having advocated for that failed bid. He ultimately acknowledged that the deal would have led to disaster for the airline as the GFC unfolded.

Joyce later concurred. 'A private equity bid at that time would've caused immense problems for Qantas with the debt the airline would've had,' he says. 'At the time, people thought we had a lazy balance sheet. People thought that we could gear up a lot more . . . The world was very different back then, and I think, fortunately, we are in a position where it didn't happen, and Qantas is in a very strong position compared to where it would've been.'[2]

The sale would have substantially enriched several members of Qantas management to the tune of tens of millions of dollars. Only one senior executive didn't join the party – John Borghetti.

Although it had seemed that the bid would be accepted, it fell 3.5 per cent short of a majority by the deadline, which was 7 pm Sydney time on Friday, 4 May 2007. One story has it that the last US investor needed to get over the line was playing hard to get; he was always intending to agree but miscalculated the time difference, his faxed confirmation arriving five hours too late.

The elaborate buyout deal was dead, but it had been highly divisive within the Qantas Group. Many staff were put offside, politicians from both the right and the left voiced their opposition, and the whole affair generated a bad smell among the broader public. Despite Jackson's public psychiatric assessment, the share price rose almost another dollar in 2007, after Dixon reported a record $1 billion profit in August, which only added another aromatic layer to the whole affair.

At the end of 2007, Jackson was replaced as chairman by the patrician Leigh Clifford, fresh from his role as CEO of mining giant Rio Tinto, where he'd gained a reputation for forthright dealing. In awarding him an honorary doctorate, the University of Melbourne described Clifford as being 'marked by a determination to modernise – whether in the use of technology, work practices or microeconomic reform'. It's not hard to see how these characteristics would mesh well with those of the CEO who would replace Geoff Dixon when he stepped down a year later.

While the media included Alan Joyce in their shortlists of candidates to replace Dixon in 2008, the Melbourne-based Jetstar CEO was very much the dark horse in the race. Thanks to Jetstar's high profile, he was probably better known to the public than to Qantas's own Sydney staff.

And so most inside Qantas were surprised to learn who the board had selected as their next CEO; some were even shocked. To most of those who had seen him walking the corridors of the poky Qantas headquarters at Mascot, he was just one of the network planning guys.

As one Qantas insider put it, 'I remember seeing this little nerdy guy with dark business shirt and chinos, no tie and pretty unkempt. He was wandering around with the boffins on what used to be Level Seven – strategy, network planning, scheduling. He was giving off "maths professor" kinda vibes. And I just remember at the time thinking, "Who's that guy?" He turned out to be the guy chosen to run Jetstar.'

Peter Gregg and John Borghetti were much better known. Most head office staff reported to one or the other, saw them working well together and more or less assumed there would be continuity if Gregg – most people's frontrunner – got the nod.

But aside from Joyce's track record of accomplishments, a couple of very important things worked in his favour. The new

Qantas chairman had come into the company in 2007 with fresh eyes. He'd been appointed to fill a vacancy created at least partly because his predecessor had been active in what was seen, in retrospect, as a somewhat tawdry financial play.

Making matters worse, in the few short months between Leigh Clifford's appointment and the selection of Dixon's successor, Qantas's share price had almost halved as the global financial crisis began to kick in from late 2007. It became clear what a disaster the APA buyout would have been if it had gone through. With the heavy debt burden it involved, Qantas would have been, to use the technical financial jargon, cactus.

Stripped of its major assets – its aircraft, Jetstar, the frequent-flyer program – the 88-year-old icon would have been little more than a valueless hulk, with several years of economic doldrums ahead of it as the GFC washed through the system. Five years earlier, Ansett had failed, leaving 16,000 staff unemployed. If Qantas went, there was no question it would have to be renationalised, just as Air New Zealand had been.

Dixon, Gregg and Borghetti continued to perform at their usual high standards, but their association with the APA bid must have seemed a negative in the mind of Clifford. Even though Borghetti had stood back from involvement, while Joyce signed up to it, the Jetstar CEO was more removed from the old elite. Peter Gregg, in particular, had been deeply engaged in it.

A strong point in Joyce's favour was that he had actually had five years' hands-on experience as CEO of an airline, albeit a smaller one, but that had developed in him obvious expertise across all activities. And he had performed well, commercially and publicly. Importantly, he'd shown he was competent at fronting the public when things got controversial.

And so – paradoxically, perhaps – Joyce was now seen as the safe pair of hands. As the global economy unravelled and the industry slid into loss-making, it was obvious that cost containment was going to be a major issue for some years to come.

With speculation intensifying, each of the three candidates was notified that he should prepare to be interviewed by the board. When, eventually, only Joyce was asked to present, there was some discontent: why was he getting special treatment?

Joyce's take is a bit different. This was not a classic head-hunter process, with several rounds of interviews, he argues. The candidates were internal and so were well known to the board, which had watched them perform in their roles every time they appeared before a monthly board meeting.

'I was CEO of Jetstar for five years, and before that I went to the board with business cases for new routes,' he points out. 'The board saw me in the public domain when we were presenting on Jetstar. They saw me handling the press, they saw us dealing with shareholders, they saw us doing all of those aspects that are important. So I had a lot of dialogue with the board over a space of five, six years before I even got the role – it's a long interview.

'The board is not going to suddenly interview people and say, "Oh, that was a fantastic interview. We've changed our minds – you're going to get the job." They're going to say, "What did you do over the five years? What did you do over the last decade?"

'At the end, the board said, "You're the preferred candidate. We believe that you're the person for the job, but we want you to present to us what your plan is for the business if you were to get it." It wasn't an interview. The board had to figure out what [my] intent would be for the strategy of the business. Is it continuity? Is it a complete radical change? And how different would it be going forward? When you got down to the preferred candidate, it was: "What are you going to do? And is the board going to find that that's too high-risk or too radical if we were to appoint you for the job?" That was the last test.'

One thing the board would have been looking for was an assurance that Qantas wasn't about to be turned into Jetstar. Joyce still had a lot to learn about the premium, full-service model, but he knew enough to convince the board he was the man for the job.

'I think a few people had their noses out of joint over it, but the interview process was over a long period of time,' he says.

That is quite the understatement. There were some very bent noses, Gregg's in particular, as he rightly felt he was the leading candidate. He'd guided the company's finances through a difficult period and had produced back-to-back billion-dollar profits. He'd sculpted a killer deal in late 2005 to buy and lease 115 of Boeing's new under-development technological masterpiece, the 787 Dreamliner. He had also been appointed chairman of Jetstar Asia, a key part of the Qantas Group's Asia push, replacing his boss.

Despite what Joyce says about the board's 'interview' process, the optics were not ideal. Giving Gregg and Borghetti the opportunity to present to the board would have given a better appearance of due process, removing scope for any internal criticism.

'I'd certainly say there was surprise [at Joyce's appointment],' one Qantas insider says. 'If you're taking a broad external lens – from the business community, government, tourism and travel industry – there was probably a bit of surprise about Alan because John [Borghetti], in particular, probably had a higher profile in some of those sectors than Alan. Within the Qantas Airlines part of the business, which John was running, I think there would've been a surprise when Alan popped up as the lead candidate. But I think that was more from the perspective that Alan was running Jetstar and just wasn't as visible to a lot of the people in the broader organisation.'

For John Gissing, though, Joyce's appointment came as no surprise. 'I was obviously heavily biased,' he says. 'I had been working with Alan at Jetstar and saw his amazing strengths. His strategic thinking is incredible. I hadn't known the others much at all. And maybe a bit of that was my own personal hope, knowing the culture Alan would bring to Qantas, his integrity and persistence. I had been in Qantas and saw the opportunities based on what we had applied at Jetstar. I love Qantas and always want to see it successful, so I was hopeful from that point of view.

'I'm one of the first people he called on the morning he was told formally by the board, and I confess to punching the air and saying, "Fantastic!" Then I think we had a moment of, "Oh, now we've got to get on and deliver."'

For several years Qantas had enjoyed fairly benign conditions. There had been the Asian financial crisis and SARS, but China's economy was booming and its demand for resources was pumping up the Australian economy, so travel demand was strong. In the airline industry, domestic competition was more muted now that Ansett was gone; although Virgin Blue was growing fast, its low-cost model left the extremely valuable corporate market wide open to Qantas.

Qantas Group had enjoyed solid year-on-year revenue growth and strong profits, including a new record underlying $1.4 billion before-tax profit in the twelve months to 30 June 2008.

In November 2008, in the days before he stepped down as CEO of Qantas, Geoff Dixon said he had been immensely fortunate to have had one of the great Australian jobs for eight years. But he warned that the global environment for aviation was extremely tough.

Unlike the China-driven Australian economy, the world's airlines were hurriedly downgrading their profit estimates, halving the projections of just a few months earlier. Qantas was a stark exception: it had generated around 20 per cent of total world-wide industry profits for the year. But many airlines had gone broke this year due to fuel price rises, Dixon said, 'and more are going to be under enormous pressure due to the credit crunch and the massive economic slowdown'. Qantas was not immune from this upheaval, 'but we are in a relatively strong position'.

As Dixon wrapped up, he reflected on how the decisions of his era had centred on the theme of 'competitiveness' – the drive to create a competitive aviation environment in Australia, and to make Qantas competitive in the world. That drive was underpinned by a great cultural continuity, according to Dixon, which stemmed back to the original days of Qantas. This culture was 'characterised by constant innovation in product and service, leadership in aircraft purchase, overriding commitment to operational excellence, and the highest standards of community citizenship'.[3]

These weren't just perfunctory niceties, even if some might have seen them as objectives rather than achievements. They might not exactly have laid out the company's priorities, but they certainly pointed to where they needed to be.

The outgoing CEO was a great contrast to his much younger colleague, and his predecessor. Seventy-year-old Dixon, the archetypal Aussie knockabout, was a big mate of fellow advertising and marketing larrikin John 'Singo' Singleton. The boy from Wagga Wagga was a former journalist with no tertiary qualifications, who, through astute marketing skills and a strong strategic mind, had worked his way to the top of the industry.

According to one Qantas insider, Dixon's predecessor, James Strong, 'was statesman-like and he was certainly loved by the staff. Whereas Dixon was the most divisive guy of all. He didn't suffer fools. I just think he didn't have the time of day for 80 per cent of the workforce at Qantas.

'At one of those top 200 managers' strategy sessions at the Four Seasons, Geoff got up, gave his speech and told everyone how we were going. "But it's not good enough, you need to do more," he said. And then as Peter Gregg got up to give his presentation, Geoff went to the back of the room, pulled up a chair next to the sound desk, opened the *Sydney Morning Herald*, put his feet up on the desk and just sat there reading the paper. That's how much of a shit Geoff gave about what anyone else thought or said.'

Dixon and Joyce did share working-class roots. And Joyce's smarts and persistence as the head of Jetstar certainly gave him a credibility as leader who was hard to challenge. Dixon himself said of Joyce, 'We had the wisdom to put a very talented aviation executive, Alan Joyce, in charge of the Jetstar operation.'[4]

As Dixon had, Joyce would regularly point to Qantas's enduring culture and the richness of its history. Joyce was Dixon's equal in the area of personal grit, but he could come across as awkward, lacking the casual style, bonhomie and rugged good looks of his predecessor. Somehow, Dixon always managed to sound slightly tongue-in-cheek, and was ever ready with a quick riposte, which took the edge off what could often otherwise sound like platitudes.

Ultimately, the new CEO's strategic toolkit was vastly different from Dixon's. As his years in charge would confirm, it had to be. What Joyce might have lacked in spontaneity, he more than made up for in earnestness and sincerity. He was the rancher to Dixon's cowboy. Also, while equally hard-nosed when it came to business, Joyce sought to elevate diversity and diversification, while maintaining Dixon's mantra about competitiveness.

When he took over as CEO of Qantas, Joyce recalls, someone asked him what it felt like to be taking the reins in the midst of the GFC. He replied that there was no other airline in the world he'd rather lead than Qantas. It was, of course, a sensible answer in the circumstances, but he meant it.

At one of his first overseas speaking engagements after becoming CEO, Joyce said: 'We are a diverse company, reflecting Australia's great multicultural and merit-based society. I am well aware of my good fortune to lead Australia's iconic national airline. Few other countries would be so open to a newcomer.'[5]

This was true, and it was a theme he would revert to many times.

4

The Tipping Point

As the new century proceeded, the noose was tightening around Qantas's international operations to Europe. The airline had been privatised in 1995 as part of a movement towards government disinvestment in commercial business activities, like airlines and telecoms. This went hand in hand with growing consumer power and, in Australia's case, a surge in inbound tourism.

At first this rise was good for Qantas. Although there was increased competition for the European market from Singapore Airlines and other Asian airlines, the government was still protecting Qantas by limiting the number of seats these airlines could fly. But Canberra was starting to move away from the belief that 'what's good for Qantas is good for Australia'. Aussies wanted cheap fares, and so did inbound tourists.

To make matters worse, the Asian airlines were undermining the economics of the European airlines' Australian services, forcing them to cut back. Singapore was Qantas's de facto international hub, where flights from Australia's capital cities connected with the through service of QF1 from Sydney. And it was, of course, Singapore Airlines' hub. As the 1990s progressed, the Singapore route became a limiting factor, so Canberra made the important decision to open up another major intermediate gateway to the west. It was to prove a crucial change in Australian aviation policy, and one that would provoke radical changes inside Qantas. It didn't happen all at once, but the process was much like the apocryphal boiling frog, as the competition became so hot as to be nearly fatal.

It was this confluence of the government's change of policy and the remarkable growth of Emirates – followed soon after by Etihad and Qatar Airways – that created the intractable problem Joyce faced when he took over.

Emirates had two big factors on its side. First, the timing was right. As the 1990s dawned, international barriers to entry were coming down, with governments gradually moving to support the interests of consumers and the tourism industry. Secondly, aircraft technology was making it possible to fly commercially over very long distances, so that, as the new millennium approached, it became possible to link almost any two points in the world with a single stopover in Dubai. As the number of connections increased, the power of the hub operation improved exponentially.

There was nothing new about hub operations. The European majors connected their short-haul services onto flights to Asia and the Americas, while the South-East Asian airlines gathered local traffic to connect on to Europe and the Americas. That Emirates was able to stand out was due both to its geography and the drive and imagination of its leadership.

Contrary to popular myth, Emirates was not subsidised, nor was it protected from competition. Dubai maintained unconditional 'open skies', meaning anyone could fly there, with as many seats as they wished. Emirates did, however, have the advantage of superb facilities and a highly supportive government. It benefited from low airport charges and fuel costs too. The fact that other airlines which wanted to operate there received similar treatment was largely academic, because most of its competitors didn't.

By using Emirates as a tool to achieve a wider goal, Dubai made itself a global business centre and, eventually, a tourism destination in its own right.

The airline took off as a global force when the first of the game-changing twin-engined long-range 777s from Boeing hit the skies in 1995. Emirates had boldly ordered seven of the 777s back in 1992, as the world was recovering from the first Gulf War, which had stymied international aviation. As its new planes arrived in the second half of the 1990s, they became the go-to aircraft for Emirates. Thanks to their extra-long range and the superior economics of a twin-engined aircraft, they opened up a world of one-stop connections over its Dubai hub. Today, the airline operates some 250 widebody aircraft, including 116 A380s, and it has orders for 200 more aircraft.

In 2019, the most recent 'normal' year, the tiny emirate of Dubai had 17 million visitors; Australia that year, by way of comparison, had 9 million.

Emirates began flying to Melbourne in 1996, but to protect Qantas's domestic hub it was not until 2000 that it was allowed to fly to Sydney. By this time, Emirates' new aircraft, with glitzy service and entertainment programs, along with very competitive pricing, all helped along by a very aggressive marketing campaign (including sponsoring the Melbourne Cup from 2004 onwards), were devouring Qantas's lunch.

Over time, the Gulf carrier was allowed to increase its Australian flights and capacity. And it did so rapidly. The fact that Emirates could offer a one-stop service to so many points the world over gave it an enormous competitive advantage. Unlike Qantas, which focused mostly on its Sydney hub, the Gulf carriers and Singapore Airlines flew direct from several state capitals. This helped divert the valuable business travellers that Qantas had previously been able to capture almost at will. It also helped considerably that Emirates' cost base was about 20 per cent lower than that of Qantas.

In March 2007, Etihad came along as well, mirroring the Emirates model with a daily flight using new aircraft over the Abu Dhabi hub to access London and other European destinations.

And all the while, the South-East Asian airlines were also adding new flights.

The rise of the Gulf carriers and the growing presence of Singapore Airlines and other South-East Asian airlines in the Australia market was making it impossible for the 'end-of-the-line' carrier to operate profitably. By the time Dixon handed over to Joyce, there seemed no obvious way out.

They cast around for a 'silver bullet' solution. Qantas's only hope appeared to be a merger, as a larger market presence might propel the merged airlines into a more powerful position from which to fight back. But it wasn't that easy.

For most industries, there's a natural trend towards rationalisation that usually involves mergers. There are multinational banks and telecommunications organisations; most corporations are open to foreign ownership; airports can be foreign-owned. For decades, even the iconic Australian brand Vegemite was owned by a US company. Holden cars are owned by General Motors. Foreign ownership is the norm.

Not so the international airline business. Unusually, this most global of activities is constrained by a complex set of rules that prevents a foreign entity from owning and controlling another nation's international airline. The origins of the rule lie in protectionism. Partly, protecting the national airline helps maintain local skills, and supposedly provides a national uplift capability in case of emergency, although that is far from clear. Mostly, the rules are there today simply because they're there.

Some exceptions exist. Within Europe, limits on foreign ownership have largely been removed – but that applies to countries and flights inside its geography. Several countries within Latin America have found ways of avoiding the worst effects of the rules, while in East Asia, low-cost airline 'cross-border joint ventures' achieve much of the practical effect of foreign ownership without technically breaking the rules.

Unilaterally deciding to allow a foreign company to own your national airline is no solution, because then any other government can refuse entry to it on the grounds that it's not nationally 'owned'. Hard to believe, but that's the way it is.

The restriction is an almost direct cause of the sorry economics of international airlines. Consequently, the prospect of mergers has enormous attraction.

In the late 1990s, Air France and the Netherlands' KLM navigated a quasi-merger that avoided the restrictions, while Lufthansa bought several smaller European airlines. A little later again, British Airways, under Willie Walsh, made a similar move with Spain's Iberia and others, to form the International Airlines Group.

Walsh and Dixon – whose airlines had been cooperating for a decade, but within the traditional limits of ownership – came to the conclusion that a tipping point had been reached in the industry, and it was time for airlines and governments to bite the (silver) bullet.

The aviation world was under great stress and changing rapidly, and the future of aviation would not – and could not – look like the past. Before he retired, Dixon said: 'For Qantas, consolidation is highly desirable . . . It is in our interests to be at the leading edge of efforts to build a global airline grouping. This will be the way to preserve the best of Qantas, while providing an expanded network, delivering new avenues for revenue growth, and creating increased scale and sources of efficiency.'[1]

He believed the wave of industry consolidation sweeping the globe was also Qantas's destiny. Consolidation was already happening in Europe and in Latin America, while in the United States, as the major airlines went into Chapter 11 bankruptcy protection, amalgamation was rife. It was time for the practice to spread across the world.

Well, that was the logic, but in international aviation, nationalism still reigned.

The idea of a merger between British Airways and Qantas was revolutionary, but Dixon believed the timing was right.

He continued to act as a consultant on the matter after stepping down from the CEO's role, working with Joyce to cement the relationship with BA.

British Airways had held a minority share in Qantas from just before the Australian airline was privatised in the mid-1990s. Then, in 2004, as Sir Rod Eddington was looking under every rock he could find to ease BA's financial ills, he sold BA's then 18.25 per cent holding because it wasn't making a decent return. Now, Willie Walsh was in charge and equity holdings were back on the table. As he saw it, British Airways was under siege, and its longstanding international operation was threatened. It needed something radical – and urgently!

A merger with British Airways was, for Qantas, hardly the optimal solution, even if it could be achieved. If it was hoping to compete effectively with the Gulf carriers, which could offer a service from Australia to almost anywhere in Europe with just one stopover, it would fall far short. Any relationship with BA would mean flights from Australia would always have an additional stop in London, before backtracking to other European destinations.

But for the time being, the BA merger seemed the only available option. Pairing with Singapore Airlines would have enabled the entity to compete better with Emirates and co., but the ACCC would never accept that. It was already difficult enough to get approval for the much more limited joint-services agreement with British Airways, and a tie-up between Qantas and Singapore Airlines would be even more anti-competitive.

Just days after Dixon's farewell speech, and as media speculation rose, Qantas confirmed to the market that it was exploring the potential merger with British Airways PLC via a dual-listed company structure, and that a further announcement would be made in due course.

Although industry consolidation was highly desirable and a logical next evolutionary step, this move had limited prospects of success in the arcane world of aviation regulation. Even now, with two Irishmen at the head of the respective airlines, the odds were stacked against it happening. The Australian government expressed concerns, the unions were worried about giving away the shop to a more powerful UK entity, and analysts were concerned about the financial details.

Joyce had plenty of time to think about the merger strategy before taking the hot seat. As Jetstar CEO, he had worked closely with Dixon for several years, and in the months after the announcement of his appointment, he was being personally tutored to take over the controls. For Dixon, the 'next critical turning point for the company will be one for Alan Joyce, my successor', he said. The BA merger was critical!

All the while, a large part of the windscreen was filled with the pungent threat of Emirates' escalating strength in the Australian market – which was only magnified as the GFC intensified. Qantas's European operation was losing increasingly large amounts of money.

Joyce was undoubtedly influenced by Dixon's perceptions of the world outside, as well as the inside of Qantas. There was no doubt it was time for a change. Perhaps the economic havoc being wrought by the GFC would force some logic into the system.

Already in 2008, the international pressure on Qantas had become intolerable. The influx of new seats into Australia coincided unhappily with sluggish international traffic recovery, which was still subdued in the grip of the GFC.

The high-quality and multi-destination capabilities of the Dubai hub had become harder to compete with. Nor did Qantas's attempts to influence government policy to slow the rate of the Gulf carriers' incursions meet with any sympathy. For the new CEO, the usual recourse to Canberra for protection wasn't going to work. It was time for change – but Qantas just wasn't prepared for that.

With its market share shrinking, the timing couldn't have been much worse for the arrival at Qantas of eight super-jumbo A380s to join the fleet between 2008 and 2010, replacing its ageing 747s. These new craft – hub-to-hub giants specifically designed to carry over 500 passengers on trunk routes – weren't needed but just kept on coming.

Qantas had spent a small fortune retraining its senior pilots to fly the large Airbus aircraft. Until now, Qantas's long-haul pilots had only ever flown Boeing aircraft, from the 707 to the 747.

In order to differentiate the great leap to this new luxury, super-quiet aircraft, Qantas trained cabin crews specifically for the A380. And on the flight deck it was mostly the senior pilots who were given first dibs at retraining to fly the new equipment. This was an enormously expensive venture. Most senior pilots were on salaries of more than $250,000 and had to be taken offline for the intensive weeks of training, so it became a very costly process.

Then they came back to find that there weren't enough hours to fly, because Qantas was cutting back on the loss-making A380 operations. Pilots like to fly, and particularly so on this prestigious new aircraft for which they had worked so hard to prepare. Even when one or two were being paid over $500,000 for working fewer than twenty hours a month, not getting enough flight hours really rankled. Of course, it was all management's fault.

By 2009, Qantas was haemorrhaging money on its European routes. The US market had stabilised as the major US airlines went through a round of bankruptcies, pulling back on their trans-Pacific operations. But Europe was vital if Qantas was to maintain its international operations.

QF1, the Sydney–London route, was immutable. Not only for the history supporting it, but it was vital to Qantas's domestic network and the growth of its frequent-flyer program. It was a connector, an essential cog in the machine. And for the pilots, many of whom had been flying the route for decades, it was unthinkable that it could be threatened.

The A380 offered a very different experience from Qantas's trusty 747s. But flying the massive jet cost more than US$30,000 an hour in direct operating costs alone, so it had to generate large numbers of economy and premium travellers just to break even.

As Dixon handed over to Joyce, this massive storm was brewing, but they were powerless to do anything about it. Every political avenue had been explored to restrict the foreign competition, to no avail. Even with Qantas's marketing and sales departments working at full pace, the A380 flights just couldn't generate a profit.

All the pilots could see, however, were full planes, so everything seemed rosy. The passengers loved the A380 and it performed beautifully. Yet management was dragging its heels on ramping up the service, even delaying new deliveries. With Joyce in place, they reasoned, this could only be part of a plot to 'Jetstar-ise' Qantas and drive down their hefty incomes.

Step by step, management became encircled by threats, both external and from within. In 2008, the engineers' union, driven by concerns about heavy maintenance being moved offshore, had embarked on an industrial campaign, often suggesting safety standards were reduced; this provoked widespread delays. Ultimately there was reconciliation, but it cost the airline over $150 million. The TWU was rattling its sword too, and the pilots – who rarely undertook industrial action, and hadn't done so for half a century – were increasingly restive.

All the while, the red ink on Qantas's international services was spreading, as the Gulf carriers' capacity grew.

PART II

PUSHBACK

'For the leadership of any company, you have to
be that proverbial duck on the water . . . there
might be a lot going below the surface, but people
have to see a smooth, gliding approach.'

—Alan Joyce

5

Plotting the Future

Alan Joyce started as Qantas CEO on 28 November 2008. There was scant time for celebration. It was just sixty-seven days after the Lehman Brothers' bankruptcy, and extraordinary economic and financial upheaval was taking place. Like most airlines around the world, Qantas had already downgraded its profit expectations for the 2008/09 financial year, and was reducing its flying capacity and staffing levels in preparation for a rough ride.

As Joyce took over, there were fundamental strategic decisions to be made. If it really was a tipping point, British Airways would be part of Qantas's future; if not, it was a time for the new CEO and chair to reset the national airline's direction.

British Airways and Qantas had a long history together. In 1999, both had been founding members of the oneworld alliance, often uncharitably called 'the poor man's merger'. These alliances – there are two others, Star Alliance and SkyTeam – provide for mutual codesharing, so that each member can market services on the others' networks, giving the appearance of global coverage.

In one of his first public addresses as CEO, on 8 December 2008 to the Australia–Israel Chamber of Commerce, Joyce spoke of the long and storied history of Qantas, the unique two-brand strategy of Qantas and Jetstar, and of the power of the broader portfolio of Qantas Group businesses. But he also addressed the elephant in the room: the potential merger with BA. Joyce was circumspect with his audience, saying the carriers were still just talking and there was no guarantee that any deal would be concluded.

He predicted that the future aviation environment would resolve into three types of carriers: hub carriers, mega-carriers and niche carriers. And Qantas, he joked, being at the far end of the world, would never be a hub carrier 'unless Antarctica becomes the new Europe'.[1]

Qantas had the option to be a niche carrier, and a very strong and profitable one, but nevertheless would sit outside the major global groupings. 'And then there's the opportunity to participate fully in the globalisation of the industry through mergers,' he said. Consolidation, he acknowledged, gives airlines greater scale in what is a volatile and highly competitive industry. 'But if we are to step into a particular deal, it needs to be the right deal for us.' For Joyce, the right partner would need to exhibit a good brand fit, the right network reach, and attractive scale and economies.

There had been much fear and loathing in the media at the time about what participating in global consolidation might mean for Qantas – some believed it would represent a sellout of Qantas's international presence. There were always enough people feeling anxious about their future – rightly or wrongly – to keep the issue controversial.

But Joyce was adamant. 'What I can say to all Australians is this: whatever happens, Qantas will remain majority Australian-owned, the vast majority of our employees will always be Australian, and Australia will remain our headquarters.' For the most part, of course, these weren't choices for management to make, but it was important for Joyce to emphasise Qantas's perpetual Australianness.

While he was keeping his options open, Joyce for the time being still believed, like Dixon, that the future of aviation would be driven by consolidation, and that Qantas would be ready to participate, including with a significant ownership interest. Even if this merger didn't work, Joyce and the board were well aware that something had to give. The world's economy was crumbling as the GFC bedded in, and Qantas would never go back to business as it was in any case.

Ten days later, it was all over. Qantas and BA announced on 18 December 2008 that they had ended their talks about a potential merger. The parties had been unable to come to an agreement over the key terms. A big stumbling block was what to do with BA's £3 billion pension fund liability. But the airlines would continue to work together on their joint business between Australia and the United Kingdom, and as part of the oneworld alliance. There was to be no quick fix. It was time to move on.

The merger efforts had occupied a lot of time, and all the while the threat from Emirates and others had only grown stronger. For Qantas, there was really no way of combating an enemy that had far bigger firepower. Its only remaining strategy was to lobby the government to limit Emirates' access, but in Canberra the pleas were falling on deaf ears. The public interest demanded more seats and more choice. Qantas was not going to deliver that.

It would be almost another two years before the way became open for Qantas to refresh its model in a way that would be sustainable for the long term.

Alan Joyce, meanwhile, had to prepare his team for the future.

CFO Peter Gregg, who had felt himself the favourite to become CEO, submitted his resignation two weeks after the succession announcement. He left Qantas on 31 December 2008, to be replaced by his deputy, Colin Storrie. Gregg, who had been a key part of the APA bid, made no bones about his dissatisfaction with the selection process.

The senior management team was substantially reshaped. In late March 2009, the Qantas Group announced that ninety executive positions were to go – around 20 per cent of the senior management ranks – in what was a major head office restructure. Joyce was slimming the ranks and putting his imprint on the leadership team.

In quick time, the CEO had completed a review of the company's organisational structure, which he said was aimed at ensuring it would be better equipped to respond to commercial challenges. With the economy slowing fast, he also implemented a salary freeze and made a number of role changes for those managers who remained.

Joyce was signalling both that the future was going to need innovative thinking and that times were tough. Qantas needed to develop a leaner, faster-moving organisation, by moving to a structure that reduced the layers of management.

Many organisations that have been around for a long time develop what Joyce later referred to as a 'permafrost layer', which becomes a barrier to getting things done. 'Getting the culture change to make it really dynamic goes back to what that management structure looks like in the top 100 managers,' he says. 'And that took us a while to get there.'

This undoubtedly met with approval from the new chairman. Leigh Clifford had moved to shake up the management team even before the new CEO arrived, clearing the way for the Joyce's new broom. The mining executive from Melbourne's establishment saw eye-to-eye with the maths geek Irishman from the backblocks of Dublin.

Meanwhile, John Borghetti, the other main CEO candidate, continued running the Qantas brand. 'When I took over as CEO, Borghetti and I were working well together,' Joyce recalls.

In his speech to the Australia–Israel Chamber of Commerce, Joyce mentioned that Qantas had recently opened its Centre of Service Excellence, to bring the airline's service training under the one roof. 'The first person to join the training scheme will be the head of Qantas Airlines, John Borghetti,' he told the gathering.

Whether or not it was intended as a put-down of his former rival, it was probably not the best way to announce that Borghetti would be undergoing service training, whatever the reason.

With the BA merger shelved, other options were explored. In what was to be one of his final acts at Qantas, Borghetti unveiled a codeshare agreement with Abu Dhabi–based Etihad Airways in March 2009. The agreement, sealed with Etihad's CEO, Australian James Hogan, covered Etihad's services from Sydney, Brisbane and Melbourne to Abu Dhabi, and beyond to Amman in Jordan, Beirut in Lebanon and Bahrain. Etihad would codeshare on selected Qantas services between Australia and Auckland and on a range of Qantas domestic services.

It was no substitute for the BA merger – it didn't extend to Europe – but it was a foot in the door. Borghetti hailed the agreement as a 'significant strategic development for Qantas'.

Talk of safety in the airline industry is taboo. Suggesting an airline is unsafe is to undermine its very existence. Airlines themselves never use safety as a marketing ploy (well, hardly ever: Qantas does like to use Dustin Hoffman's line from *Rain Man* whenever possible). But when unions suggest to the public that the airline their employees work for is unsafe, airline management becomes very sensitive. That's not to say such claims are never valid, but more often than not they are blunt weapons, intended to influence management decisions.

An airline's safety record is contested in the court of public opinion. At Qantas, encouragement from disgruntled unions, concerned at possible offshoring of jobs, coupled with a sequence of incidents, was tarnishing the airline's reputation. Supported by an extended period of on-again, off-again industrial action that had caused delay to services earlier in the year, the image was being created of an airline whose safety standards were slipping.

Two potentially serious incidents had occurred. On QF30, over Manila, an oxygen tank exploded in flight, tearing a large hole in the aircraft's fuselage. And QF72 suddenly lost altitude before making an emergency landing at Learmonth, Western Australia. As a result, there were increasing numbers of media reporting of everyday occurrences, minor technical faults and aircraft substitutions around the world, 'quite ordinary events' that had received 'disproportionate and even alarmist coverage', according to Joyce.

Heightened media scrutiny is a regular aftermath of any safety incident. With millions of things that can go wrong in a large airline, multiple minor events occur every day, so whenever something relatively serious hits the news, social media users and journalists (and often unions with an axe to grind) focus on it for a while.

Joyce argued this had led to a vague but 'dangerous perception' that the rate of engineering issues at Qantas was increasing, that the carrier had been less careful on maintenance standards, and that it was because more maintenance work was being shifted offshore. When it was later shown that manufacturing and design faults had caused the QF30 and QF72 incidents, it became clear that the offshore maintenance argument had been a complete red herring – but the damage was done.

This became an issue that would not go away, despite Joyce's determination to work actively to bring the public's perceptions closer to the reality that he saw: that Qantas remained committed to safety, and that its engineering and maintenance standards were equal to the highest in the world.

Meanwhile, back in the world outside, Joyce watched helplessly as Qantas was buffeted by the global economic downturn and the volatility in currency and oil prices. The Australian dollar weakened by over 30 per cent against the US dollar in the half-year, an astonishing shift that really hurt, as many debts were denominated in US dollars. And premium and international travel numbers fell steeply, further hitting passenger revenues.

Qantas's profits were unravelling fast. The carrier had unveiled a big drop in interim profit before tax of $288 million for the half-year to 31 December 2008 – a 68.2 per cent decrease on the prior comparative period.

The Qantas share price dipped as low as $1.50 in early March 2009, and the International Air Transport Association (IATA) reported that some thirty-one carriers had gone broke around the world since the onset of the GFC. Oil prices had fallen as demand slackened in the soft economic conditions, but airline share values dropped as load factors (the proportion of seats sold) plummeted and freight volumes slumped. Many formerly strong airlines were reporting losses.

Fortunately, the Australian economy was better positioned than most. It was a major provider of commodities to growing markets like China's, which powered on through the GFC. Australia had also entered the downturn with relatively high interest rates and no central government debt, which provided room to stimulate economic growth both on the monetary and fiscal side.

That same month, Joyce travelled home to Ireland, and on his trip called into the Wings Club in Dublin, where he told the audience that Qantas had a range of strategic assets that made it uniquely different to other airlines. In full roadshow mode, he said, 'If we manage these assets wisely . . . Qantas would be very strongly positioned for the future.'[2]

The new boss was also focused on his portfolio of aviation and transport businesses and an 'unequalled ability to diversify our sources of income'. Diversification, in all its senses, would become a big theme of the Joyce era. Meanwhile, the core of the portfolio was the two brands of Qantas and Jetstar, which created an 'unmatched ability to meet the needs of a wide spectrum of customers'. Joyce was walking the fine line between talking up the airline for investors and not understating the concerns he held for the immediate future.

At the time, Qantas was one of only three airline groups in the world with an investment-grade credit rating (the other two were Southwest and Germany's heavily protected Lufthansa). All the others had junk bond status – an astonishing fact, given that so much of the world's trade and social connectivity depends on these companies.

Compared with much of the industry, Qantas had plenty of cash on hand, which was important in the 2009 environment as cash was king. Qantas had successfully completed a very timely $500 million equity capital raising in early February 2009, a vote of faith in the business by shareholders. (Joyce's team was to repeat this move when COVID reared its ugly head in 2020.) The airline was also retiring older aircraft and deferring lower-priority capital expenditure, as well as scouring the business to reduce costs – all aimed at bolstering its cash balances to ride out the storm.

Despite Joyce's efforts to get the airline into a solid position, by mid-April 2009 Qantas was in damage control. Trading conditions had taken a steep downturn in late March, forcing the airline to inform the market that it was sharply downgrading its 2008/09 full-year profit before tax outlook from around $500 million to between $100 million and $200 million.

Qantas's international routes and its freight services were bearing the brunt of the decline in economic conditions, with a damaging financial impact. Demand was slumping, particularly in premium classes, amid extensive sales and deep discounting by all carriers as they scrambled to raise cash. Premium air fares had dropped by between 40 and 50 per cent: return business-class fares to London had plummeted from $9500 pre-crisis to just over $5000.

Qantas further reduced passenger capacity by 5 per cent but did not yet withdraw from routes, always a last resort. Joyce grounded the equivalent of ten aircraft and made them available for sale, as well as deferring deliveries of four Airbus A380s and twelve much smaller Boeing 737-800 narrowbody aircraft. An additional 500 management positions were removed.

The economic conditions created an atmosphere of crisis, but it also helped to achieve the reductions that Joyce's management structure needed. He was the visible face of the measures, even if they coincided with the views of his chairman. The share price recovered to be back above $2 on the announcements, but Joyce tempered expectations by advising that he expected the volatility in operating conditions to continue for some time, making it difficult to provide forecasts.

Qantas sealed an important enterprise agreement breakthrough with about 1700 long-haul pilots in early May 2009. The negotiations had been aimed at capping pay rises at 3 per cent per annum across its unionised workforce. The long-running talks with the AIPA would result in pay rises of about 17 per cent over three years.

John Borghetti left Qantas on 6 May 2009, becoming the last of the Dixon-era chiefs to exit. Joyce denied suggestions Borghetti had been forced out amid the major changes to the senior management team. He said, with perhaps less generosity than Borghetti merited, 'while we are disappointed that he is leaving, we respect his view that 36 years with one employer definitely shows commitment over and above the norm'.[3]

The competition that had existed between the two men as Jetstar chewed into Qantas's domestic network was now becoming visible. Within a couple of years, it would have much greater significance for both the industry and the travelling public.

6

Reshuffle and Reset

As Borghetti left the building, Alan Joyce took the opportunity to reset his executive team. Rob Gurney, the sales and marketing boss, took over the role of group executive of Qantas Airlines commercial, while Lesley Grant became executive manager of customer and marketing.

Some investors and analysts expressed concern that the thinning ranks of experienced executives would hurt the airline's ability to navigate through the worst downturn in at least a decade. One fund manager said at the time, 'It's bloody ridiculous how they have turned over their senior management team.'

But Joyce had firm views on the type of person he wanted, and he went about the reorganisation in a disciplined and structured way.

First, he initiated detailed profiling of the senior and middle managers, to make sure there was the right culture fit, and to prepare the groundwork for succession at all levels. He wanted to get the most out of the highly talented team he'd assembled. That meant creating an atmosphere in which managers, experts in their specialty areas, felt free to express their opinions amid robust debate.

'Watching the ExCo [executive management committee] guys respectfully debate in front of Alan, trying to win the debate was really interesting,' observed one senior manager. 'The moment Alan entered the room, people were on their A game. And I don't think it was because people feared him. The tone of the conversation lifted because he was just so sharp and straight to the point. I never saw him belittle anyone, I never saw him being disrespectful.'

But if anyone came into a meeting unprepared, Joyce would let them have it. His easy command of numbers put him in a position where he could challenge just about any proposition.

One senior manager said Joyce had a piercing gaze. 'You know he's thinking, he's listening, and you just know he's a smart guy. His cogs are turning faster than yours. And you're looking at your notes and trying to get your key points in. And everyone's around the room trying to think, "What's Alan going to ask? What's Alan going to ask?" And the question was always on the mark.'

John Gissing, having moved up with Joyce from Jetstar, said he saw the CEO's commitment to diversity and inclusion in decision-making from day one, but it wasn't easy for many at first. 'It can be a bit confronting because, in the old structures, everybody had a role, and gathering [those] perspectives in a different way was a bit challenging sometimes. In the early days of gathering information, we had this fantastic capability within Qantas that we absolutely needed to tap into, but there was some stuff that wouldn't work. That had to change.'

There was more to resetting the culture than simply encouraging robust debate. Joyce wanted thoroughly to recraft the physical environment of the airline. This was one area where the Jetstar-isation would make a massive difference. The LCC's workspace, typically, was open plan, in contrast to the sprawling Qantas HQ, which was spread out across several ageing buildings. That arrangement was not only inconvenient, but it fanned the flames of that scourge of the airline business: work silos.

Joyce asked, 'How can we consolidate to be more efficient and bring those five or six disjointed buildings into one big facility? And how can you change the feel of the place and take executives from the top floor to level one and make the boardroom visible to everybody, not locked away in some corner?'

The numbers were crunched on a complete redevelopment and integration of the Mascot campus. The answer was to engage some talented architects and do a deal where the landlord would pay for the whole change in return for the company committing to a long-term lease. Eventually, this created an entirely different and open office environment. It complemented the culture of open discussion that Joyce was seeking to bring into the workplace.

There are so many specialisations within an airline group like Qantas that communicating laterally, across disciplines – or 'silos' – is innately difficult and leads to unhelpful bureaucracy. The walls of the silos can suppress lateral coordination, creating separate teams, which in turn can also feed empire building.

Take the example of reducing aircraft turnaround times. It sounds pretty simple: you land the plane, taxi, pull into a gate, perhaps log into an external auxiliary power plant, get a couple of hundred passengers and their baggage off, unload freight, clean the aircraft, change the flight and cabin crews, have an external aircraft inspection by one of the flight crew, refuel and restock, check any minor technical faults, reboard a new lot of passengers with their bags, load any freight, confirm your take-off slot and push back.

Before all that, of course, it's necessary to coordinate your landing and take-off slots, and your terminal, make sure they coincide with the respective slots at the other end of the route, contract with the various suppliers such as fuel companies and so on. And we've missed out a few items. Naturally, the airline wants to have all these tasks done as efficiently as possible.

Focusing on turnaround times might seem just a sideline for airline geeks. Yet shaving a few minutes off the time taken between landing and taking off again can constitute the airline's entire profits for the year. When LCCs first came on the scene, the average turnaround time for full-service airlines was about an hour. It was a leisurely process. On the Sydney–Melbourne route, for instance, that meant a single aircraft could perform four round trips in a day.

If that turnaround time could be reduced to thirty minutes, though, that aircraft could perform roughly another round trip each and every day. An airline with a fleet of twenty aircraft would be able to fly – and earn income from – twenty additional round trips. Alternatively, the efficient carrier could manage the same schedule as the full-service airline but with one fewer aircraft, which might mean an annual saving of perhaps $100 million.

That's why airlines today strive to cut even five or six or more minutes from their turnaround times. But a turnaround is a highly complex operation, involving considerable teamwork, and it becomes more and more complex as each minute is shaved off – always with primary attention given to maintaining safety standards.

John Gissing recalls a meeting in which aircraft turnaround times at an LCC were being compared with those of a premium carrier. 'There would be twenty people, each representing one of the Qantas verticals, in that discussion,' he says. 'I very quickly learned that if [Joyce] asked me a particular question about a problem, I would give him my view, but that he would be asking others as well. He'd be triangulating.' But he would also be ensuring everyone was on the same page and every stone was turned.

Then there was network planning, Joyce's forte. Rob Gurney says that before Joyce became CEO, this area 'was shrouded in mystery, a bit of a dark art, done in almost secrecy'. Joyce brought a very different approach to it, running workshops with the network planners, the revenue management, engineers, flight operations planning and other internal stakeholders.

'There would be thirty, forty people in a room,' Gurney says, 'because Alan realised that, with the network piece, you had to have everything else joined up. Instead of saying, "Well, here's the schedule, go and work with it," he had all those people engaged in the development process. There was no point planning the most beautiful schedule if you had two lines of flying out with heavy maintenance.'

Joyce recognised that another area needing an overhaul was Qantas's relationship with the media. His background was very different from Geoff Dixon's, whose innate marketing, PR and communications flair meant he had little use for professional in-house support. Joyce knew he needed someone to compensate for that.

He'd first attracted David Epstein, a former chief of staff to Prime Minister Kevin Rudd. Now another ambitious young executive entered the frame. Olivia Wirth, the executive director of the Tourism & Transport Forum (TTF), an industry lobby group, had applied for the role of Head of Corporate Affairs and Public Relations at Qantas.

Joyce had plenty of dealings with the media at Jetstar. 'But Qantas is different,' says Wirth. 'It attracts a different level of attention. It requires a different level of media management.'

Wirth came prepared for the interview having spoken with many editors and news directors about Qantas. They weren't particularly happy with how Qantas was operating and found it difficult to get commentary and the right level of access.

Joyce and Wirth had a very robust conversation – more of a debate than an interview. 'He had great energy and was very upfront and said, "I don't know what I don't know." I liked the honesty. I didn't go as far as saying I thought he needed to improve – I waited until I got inside to do that!'

Having won the role, Wirth began her own meteoric rise. A Qantas insider observed, 'She was pretty bloody effective, especially in some of those troubled times. As a leader, she certainly got results.'

As Joyce got to work, problems were raining down on the airline as the financial crisis worsened. Six months into the job, in late May 2009, he described the operating environment as the worst he'd seen in his twenty-one years in the airline business.

It was a global industry in crisis. The tally of airlines to have gone bust since the start of 2008 had risen to forty. The IATA had forecast US$9 billion in losses for the aviation industry in 2009.

Joyce needed new ways of protecting the farm – and his best option was to defer more of the aircraft that had been ordered during the Dixon era. There had been growing noise in pilot forums and the trade media that Qantas's leadership had erred back in 2000 and 2005 by committing the Group to the latest aircraft types in the A380s and the B787 Dreamliners – many felt they should have bought more tried-and-tested 777s.

Joyce defended the decisions. He would later say the company's greatness was based on being the first with the best aircraft. 'We were the first airline outside the US to fly the Boeing 707s and enter the jet age, and we're proud to be leading the way again today,' he said.[1] Brave words, but history has a way of foiling the best-laid plans. On the other hand, when it was necessary to delay deliveries, the manufacturers had little choice but to accept without complaint – or cost.

For now, those shiny big new toys would have to wait. Delivery dates for fifteen 787-8 aircraft due for delivery in 2014–15 were pushed back by four years, and orders for fifteen of the larger and longer-range B787-9s were cancelled. The ground-breaking Dreamliner had been plagued by design issues, so Boeing was easily persuaded to accept the delay requested by one of its better clients – especially one that was now dallying openly with its main competitor, Airbus. The A380s were new aircraft types too, and also suffered from chronic design and delivery problems. The delays and scaled-back orders gave Joyce some breathing space, reducing the Qantas Group's aircraft capital expenditure by US$3 billion, based on list prices.

Seeking every avenue to reduce costs, airlines around the world were taking the fight to the airports, which were still generating handsome profits. Joyce argued that the privatised Australian airports were making massive returns from their non-aviation revenues, such as car parking, duty-free sales and retail outlets, all of which depended on the airlines enticing the customers in through unsustainably low airfares. At the same time, some major airports outside Australia were reducing their landing fees to help their airline customers deal with the extraordinarily tough operating conditions.

The low – or even negative – operating margins at key airlines contrasted with the highly profitable margins of more than 60 per cent for the Sydney, Melbourne and Brisbane airports. Joyce decried the fact that no major airport in Australia had agreed to lower its charges to cooperate in stimulating passenger demand, while Qantas was still receiving demands by airports for substantial increases in leasing and staff carparking charges.

Skirmishes with the highly profitable, privatised major Australian airports would continue throughout the Joyce era – and they will surely not end with it.

At his earnings report in August 2009, Joyce soon had the ignominy of unveiling the carrier's worst annual result since it was privatised in 1995: a paltry net profit after tax of $123 million. This could not mean business as usual; further interventions by the CEO were needed.

A program called 'Q Future' was rolled out, the first of a series of major company-wide cost-cutting initiatives that would punctuate Joyce's first decade at the helm, targeting $1.5 billion in permanent savings over three years, starting from the 2009/10 financial year. With demand and revenues stalled, cost reduction was the only lever available to Joyce.

Operationally, the airline's dual-brand strategy was working well, and Joyce aimed to create an optimal balance of Qantas and Jetstar services. The two airlines already operated jointly on a number of key domestic routes, including the busy Sydney–Melbourne route, though for the time being Jetstar was confined to the small Avalon Airport, nearer to Geelong than Melbourne.

With Australia's domestic economic environment being slightly more forgiving than elsewhere, Qantas was one of the few airlines worldwide to produce a full-year profit. Even so, the mood was grim. There were more skirmishes breaking out at home, threatening Qantas's golden goose domestic operation.

Singapore-based Tiger Airways, which had established an Australian-based subsidiary in March 2007, was ramping up its low-cost service. Its owners – Singapore Airlines, Bill Franke's Indigo Partners, Tony Ryan's Irelandia Investments and Singapore's Temasek Holdings – had initially committed $10 million and five aircraft to the venture, launching flights on 20 November 2007 between Melbourne and the Gold Coast.

At first, Tiger avoided flying to Sydney, Brisbane and Adelaide as part of its strategy of keeping its costs low, but now that strategy was evolving. Tiger announced plans in April 2009 to enter the lucrative Melbourne–Sydney market, and in July increased its flights on the route to nine per day. More planes were arriving in late 2009, and Tiger announced it would launch into the Brisbane market that November.

Qantas responded, finally unleashing Jetstar on the Sydney–Melbourne (Tullamarine) route for the first time. Some analysts feared this would undermine the mainline Qantas business, but Joyce told the *Australian Financial Review* in August 2009 that the Group was seeing very little cannibalisation between Qantas and Jetstar; rather, Jetstar was penetrating the cost-sensitive end of the market. Acerbically, he added, 'If any carriers come into the Australian market and think Qantas is not going to be competitive, then they are surely mistaken.'[2]

As 2009 drew to a close, there were signs of an improvement in passenger volumes. Yields – the average fare per passenger kilometre flown – had started to stabilise, albeit at low levels. The airline announced its first increase to international fares in eighteen months.

Around the world, though, the painful economic conditions continued to wreak havoc. The world's airlines generated losses of almost US$10 billion in 2009, and the IATA estimated they would lose a further US$5.6 billion in 2010. But Qantas was emerging from the financial crisis as one of only two remaining passenger airlines in the world with an investment-grade credit rating, meaning Joyce had at least one feather in his cap after his first twelve months as CEO.

A rung further down the credit ratings ladder were Lufthansa and British Airways. BA had now agreed to a merger with Spanish carrier Iberia. Lufthansa had previously acquired stakes in Austrian Airlines, Brussels Airlines and BMI British Midland, while Air France-KLM, the pioneer of European consolidation, had taken a minority stake in Alitalia. Qantas remained on the merger sidelines looking on, despite rumours of a renewed push from Willie Walsh for a deal with BA.

Ultimately, Joyce recognised that the prerequisites for a cross-border merger – that is, relaxed ownership and control barriers – were not in place, and it would take years for change to come to Australia and the Asia-Pacific region. The aborted BA union was ultimately an eye-opening experience for Joyce. He later reflected that deals like that are extremely hard to do commercially, and very distracting for the management team. A different approach would be needed to fix Qantas's international business, and the options were worryingly limited.

*

In the wake of Joyce's cost-cutting measures, industrial unrest was growing. Ongoing action in 2009 by the ALAEA, protesting the offshoring of heavy maintenance, had resulted in a maintenance backlog that cost an estimated $130 million in additional expenses and lost revenue that financial year.

Another engineers' union, the Association of Professional Engineers, Scientists and Managers Australia (APESMA), announced industrial action in November 2009, as it battled with Qantas to reach the latest enterprise bargaining agreement. APESMA's claim – for a pay rise of some 26 per cent over three years – was rejected as unreasonable and unsustainable by Qantas management. Sporadic action by APESMA continued through December and presaged a difficult year ahead for Qantas's relationship with its organised labour.

Union concerns about jobs heading offshore were further stoked by Qantas management's continued lobbying in Canberra to ease ownership restrictions on the carrier, which were seen as attempts to remove jobs from the jurisdiction.

Just before Christmas 2009, the federal government released its National Aviation Policy Statement (White Paper), which eased ownership restrictions on Australian airlines. The government was relaxing foreign ownership restrictions specified in the *Qantas Sale Act* in 1992, which had laid out the terms for the airline's privatisation. Joyce saw it as a step forward, increasing the airline's flexibility in attracting capital. But the overall 49 per cent foreign ownership limit and requirements relating to Qantas's management, operational base and board composition remained in place.

This kept Qantas at a disadvantage, compared with Virgin Blue and any other Australian airline. It would not be the last debate around the *Qantas Sale Act*.

While welcome, this Christmas gift left Joyce under no illusions that Qantas was in for a smooth ride. In his first year in the top job, he'd been exposed to a wide range of challenges. He'd begun the process of reorganising internally, reducing management layers and creating the foundations for a more cohesive and structured team. Meanwhile, the problems with several unions were unresolved.

There was no solution in sight either to the question of how to improve the European international operation – in fact, that task was getting more difficult by the day. It was clear that Canberra wasn't going to provide any help in reducing the competitive heat. The external economic climate, too, was still gruesome; it was far too early to expect traffic to be recovering while the GFC played out. At least oil prices had come down from their terrifying levels of mid-2008, but by the end of 2009 they were heading back up towards US$100 a barrel again.

Thanks to reasonable strength in the domestic market, the Qantas share price had crept back up above $3 by the year's end. That, however, was a level it would not touch again until well into 2015. And the heat in the home market was about to increase, as Tiger Airways ramped up its incursions. More importantly, Virgin Blue was carving ever more aggressively into the share of its larger competitor.

In short, there wasn't a lot of good news in the wind – unless, that is, you enjoy a challenge. Fortunately, Joyce did.

7

QF32

In musical terms, a crescendo contains a phrase that starts softly and progressively becomes louder as the drama swells. Ravel's *Boléro* offers a good example: the steady backdrop drumbeat of daily life, overlaid with constant intrusions, leads with increasing intensity to its climax.

For Joyce, an ordinary Thursday in the late spring of 2010 would be the beginning of a crescendo that would endure for another year, yielding extraordinary levels of drama at the national carrier.

At 10.01 am, Singapore time, on 4 November 2010, just twenty-four days shy of the second anniversary of Joyce's appointment as CEO, a crisis was developing over the skies of Batam Island, Indonesia. That morning, VH-OQA, the *Nancy-Bird Walton*, the airline's first A380 to enter service, was operating QF32 through from London to Sydney.

One of Australia's most famed flying pioneers had loaned her name to the aircraft. The nineteen-year-old Nancy Bird took her first flying lesson in the spring of 1933, with no less an instructor than Charles Kingsford-Smith, renowned for achieving, with Charles Ulm, the first aerial crossing of the Pacific five years earlier.

Known as 'the Angel of the Outback', and the founder and patron of the Australian Women Pilots' Association, Nancy became an aviation inspiration for generations of female flyers. At the age of ninety-two, she was honoured in a ceremony held in Hangar 96 at the Qantas Jetbase, where the airline's first A380 was named after her. On 30 September 2008, as the Qantas choir sang, a Qantas captain cracked a bottle of champagne over the aircraft's nose, with Nancy characteristically admonishing him: 'You better not have scratched it!'

After numerous teething problems, this first of Qantas's A380s had arrived two years late, but the ceremony, led by then executive general manager John Borghetti, was one of those events that brought the company together. For an iconic airline, launching a unique new aircraft like the A380 was a moving moment. Some 3000 staff were present in the hangar, which could have been filled several times over.

As Borghetti said, 'I don't think there were too many dry eyes in the hangar that morning when the choir sang "I Still Call Australia Home" with the aircraft as a backdrop. It was quite an emotional moment for many people . . . The passion that Qantas staff have for the brand and the company comes out in situations like that, and it was a very proud moment for everyone.'[1]

Nancy died just four months later, but her name has since been immortalised in Sydney's new airport, due to be operational in 2026. The Western Sydney International (Nancy-Bird Walton) Airport will be a fitting companion to the existing Sydney Kingsford-Smith Airport across the other side of town, where she first learned to fly.

VH-OQA had departed Singapore Changi Airport on that fine, clear November morning, packed with 440 passengers and twenty-nine crew. There was nothing to suggest it was about to suffer a devastating uncontained failure in one of its four Rolls-Royce engines, resulting in multiple system failures midair. A steel disc in the number two engine (nearest the cabin on the port side) exploded, as it strained to lift the massive aircraft into the air.

If you are going to have a hero, he could hardly be better named than the captain on that flight, Richard Champion de Crespigny (who was later appointed a Member of the Order of Australia for his actions). He was fortunate in having four other senior airmen on the flight deck of the large A380. This was unusual, but proved helpful in addressing the wide range of problems the explosion created. Between them, the pilots had a combined flying experience of 71,000 hours, making them undoubtedly one of the most qualified crews ever to deal with an inflight incident.

Among them was a supervising check captain, David Evans, who was supervising another captain who was training to be a check captain, who in turn was performing a route check on Captain de Crespigny. The A380 had only been in service with Qantas for two years, so on-the-job training was still common. Additionally, the usual first and second officers were each extremely experienced.

In his book *QF32*, de Crespigny describes the first moments of the incident:

> At 10:01 am I was about to turn off the seatbelt sign when ... BOOM. I looked to my right to see if Matt [first officer Matt Hicks] had heard it too. BOOM! This one was louder than the first and the airframe shuddered ... The second boom was like nothing I'd experienced before.[2]

His instinctive reaction was to 'hit the "altitude hold" button, which told the autopilot to lower the nose and level the aircraft at the current altitude'. This dropped the nose (from its steep climb angle), reduced the engine thrust and eased the stress on the engines and airframe.

The aircraft circled for over an hour while the crew regained control and assessed the situation while preparing to land back at Changi Airport. The aircraft systems were sending a confusing 'avalanche of messages'. Normally, the pilot would have dumped the plane's large fuel supplies, as they were about 50 tonnes over the maximum landing weight, but the dumping system had failed following the explosion. They would have to land heavy – but how heavy was too heavy?

The fly-by-wire Airbus contained a performance app to calculate parameters in such events. But there were too many inputs and it refused to respond. After the pilots incrementally removed some of the less important inputs, finally it produced a touchdown speed of 165 knots. That would mean the craft would only have 130 metres of runway to spare after touching down.

The crew had lost the use of the leading edge slats, which have the effect of slowing the aircraft, meaning that the A380's approach speed was about 35 knots greater than normal. No small skill was required to make a safe landing. The extreme braking needed to contain the landing just before the end of the runway sent the temperature of the wing gear brakes to over 900 degrees Celsius.

This was in the early days of social media, and within minutes of a post of an engine cowling that had come off, suddenly Twitter was alive. Pictures showed a large, white aircraft part with a prominent Qantas kangaroo logo lying in a school playground in the city of Batam, south-east of Singapore. Once a local police chief had confirmed the debris sighting, conventional media were onto the story and the world was alerted to a crisis – even before the airline's management had any inkling of what had happened.

Newswires were quickly able to piece together the flight details and broke the story: a near-new Qantas A380 had crashed. The news reverberated around the world. This was the notoriously safe airline, flying a new model of the world's largest passenger jet. And it had crashed.

Once the mainstream media picked up the story, the frenzy began. At least one report emerged from a news agency within moments of the incident, stating that a Qantas aircraft had suffered a disaster. Other reports suggested that parts of the aircraft's wings had fallen off.

The instant nature of social media reporting meant that very little fact-checking was done by the mainstream media before going public. Rumours became facts, to be checked later. Reuters reported that 'Qantas told CNBC television that a plane that crashed near Singapore was an A380'; while perhaps someone from Qantas had agreed that the aircraft involved was an A380, they had certainly not told CNBC it had 'crashed'.

On the flight deck, amid the efforts to isolate the problems, the aircraft's satellite communications had been disabled, so no one on the aircraft could speak with head office. There was still air-to-ground communication with the Singapore tower, but the staff there had their hands full preparing for whatever the emergency might demand.

Back at Mascot, Olivia Wirth's phone rang. It was Alan Joyce. The Qantas CEO had received a phone call in the car in which he was travelling with his head of marketing. 'Why is the share price plummeting?' the caller had wanted to know. Had Wirth received any media calls?

As they spoke, Wirth's phone lit up. It was Bloomberg. The reporter told her they had evidence that a Qantas aircraft had gone down. Wirth said she knew nothing about that and would get back to them.

'I hung up and called Alan Milne, who was the head of our Integrated Operations Centre [IOC] at that stage,' Wirth recalls. 'I said, "I've heard this, can you confirm or deny what's going on?" And he said, "Let me go and speak to the Maintenance Operations Centre," because they could see all the [live] engine performance and see what's going on. And he said, "No, no, no – all the aircraft are still flying."'

Down the hall, Qantas's head of safety, John Gissing, had a knock on his door. 'My head of investigation appeared at my office door, ashen-faced, and said, "You've got to see this. There's a piece of our airplane on the ground in Batam in Indonesia." You don't forget that,' he notes. 'My first reaction: "What do you mean?" Then you see it on the screen and you imagine whatever worst-case scenarios might play out in your mind. And for me, that was a ninety seconds I'll never forget. That's how long it took for the IOC to answer the phone to tell me what the hell was going on with this. And they said, "It's all right, Gisso, the plane's in the air, just holding and offloading fuel."' As head of safety, Gissing immediately swung into his role as crisis centre chairman.

All the Qantas management knew was what was flashing around the world on social media. 'We went out as quickly as we could to the media and to the ASX, just to say, "There's been an incident, but the aircraft is still operating,"' says Wirth.

Joyce quickly returned to the crisis operations centre at Mascot. 'We had the chief engineer and the chief pilot of Qantas there and we were watching the TV screens from CNN, Fox News and Sky News of the aircraft pieces on the ground in Indonesia,' he later recalled. During the next couple of hours, the executive worked through the photographic evidence of what was on the ground to try to determine what had actually happened in the air.

If the incident occurred today, everyone would have been better prepared to handle the social media fallout. In 2010, though, the second-hand report had been the first sign of a problem – and a real-time demonstration of the new and dangerous power of the emerging medium. An aircraft accident like this, especially involving one of the new super-jumbos, was a major event in a world of instant reporting via twenty-four-hour news channels, ubiquitous social media and the associated fake news and misreporting.

'The engine had exploded, a piece of cowling with the logo on it fell to the ground, and a photo of it went on Twitter immediately and into the media. So we were chasing our tail with that,' Wirth recalls. 'The media reports went up because they had the footage of the cowling on the ground and so we quickly needed to get them to report correctly that the aircraft is still in the air, an engine had exploded shortly after take-off and it's going to have to dump fuel and circle before it can land.'

As it became clear that the aircraft was preparing for an emergency landing, the intensity of the immediate reporting dropped a little. Engine shutdowns are not uncommon in the industry. However, the original incomplete news continued to ricochet around the world's news platforms for several hours, fed by a tsunami of social and mainstream media, before the 'official' news was available to correct the facts.

The Reuters wire agency later corrected its original 'crash' reporting, stating that the aircraft had experienced engine trouble.

The *Nancy-Bird Walton* eventually made a successful emergency landing back in Singapore, where the extensive damage to the engines, wings and fuselage was immediately apparent to the waiting news cameras – and to a public armed with smartphones and social media connections.

After advising the stock exchange, that afternoon and evening Joyce took to the airwaves and television networks to calm a wary public, and to reinforce the decades-old messaging around Qantas's safety culture and record. 'As you'd expect, it was calm and collected in the [aircraft] cockpit,' he told many channels that afternoon, including the ABC.

After the landing, Captain de Crespigny reinforced the airline's brand by spending over an hour with all the passengers in the terminal, before they went out to face the media onslaught. Many were, understandably, traumatised. But the captain was a marketing gem, telling them, 'When you fly Qantas, you're flying with a premium airline – not a budget carrier – so you have every right to expect more with us.'

He even gave each of them his personal mobile phone number. He said, 'If Qantas doesn't treat you the way you expect to be treated, I want you to call me and tell me about it – or have a journalist making wild claims about the flight and you want to call me about it.' De Crespigny had done a similar thing a few months earlier on QF32 after an overnight delay, saying he'd felt the same need for information when he travelled with his family, and so he knew how the passengers would be feeling.

Following the 2010 incident, de Crespigny adopted the role of a brand ambassador – a communications representative – for Qantas. His book, *QF32*, was PR gold for both Qantas and Airbus. This was real-world evidence that the brand was not just about spin – there was real substance to it.

For Joyce, having the aircraft safely on the ground with no injuries to passengers or crew was a huge relief, but it also presented an opportunity for him to get on the front foot. The heroic actions of the flight crew allowed him to wrest back control of the narrative around Qantas's supposedly slipping safety standards.

And get on the front foot he did, adding colour to the narrative.

'Our pilots are probably some of the most experienced pilots in the world,' he said. 'They're trained for this event. Our pilots go through four simulator trainings every year and they practise engine failures. In the cabin, what would've occurred is the pilots actually would've identified at an early stage what they suspected would've occurred.

'One of the pilots worked on flying the aircraft. The other pilots then worked through the error messages that were occurring. The computer tells them that there are problems. They work through those error messages, and then the pilots would've landed the aircraft with immediate effect, which is what they did on this occasion. And the aircraft landed safely and . . . there were no injuries. Everybody was okay.'[3]

It was the most harrowing of events, but it was not the first crisis Qantas had faced in 2010. Recent experience between March and June of that year had given the crisis management team valuable opportunities to rehearse: the series of volcanic eruptions at Iceland's Eyjafjallajökull, and the resulting clouds of ash, had caused enormous disruption to air travel.

'We were able to look after our passengers [during the Icelandic events],' said Joyce. 'Passengers became our top priority. In this case, we're very much communicating to our passengers that safety is our number one concern, that we'll only put the aircraft back when we're absolutely sure of it despite the commercial implications for us.'[4]

These can be massively expensive events – Qantas estimated that the direct cost of the Iceland ash cloud alone was $46 million. But they also divert human resources at a time when operations in the rest of the world must continue as normal.

While the safety of the passengers and crew on QF32 was being established, three of Qantas's other A380s were boarding passengers, ready to depart within the hour. Executives at Qantas HQ knew there had been an explosion in one engine, but had little other information.

'QF32 was completely different – we'd never seen an engine like that,' says Gissing. 'When we saw the picture of the hole in the side of the engine, the sense of the un-containment of what was an exploding steel disc – that looked like something none of us had ever seen before. And in that context, how can you keep operating [the rest of the A380 fleet] until you at least have some inkling that you might know what's caused it?'

As Joyce recalls it, the crisis committee had a crucial decision to make. 'We knew there was a big engine problem that existed on the fleet,' he says. 'We had three A380 aircraft due to depart with over a thousand people on them. And we had to make a decision whether it was safe to operate those aircraft or to call them back to the gates and take people off them.

'From the little information we had, our chief engineer noticed something on the screen. He said, "I think we're going to have to ground the [A380] fleet." So we had a hypothesis that the aircraft wasn't safe to operate. And then, with the little information we had, we had to make a judgement call.'

Joyce triggered the immediate grounding of the rest of the airline's A380 fleet. It was the first time in Qantas's history that an entire aircraft type in its fleet was grounded. It was a big call. It meant stranding passengers in the United States and the

United Kingdom, fixing accommodation for them and rescheduling aircraft to fill the large hole left by the missing five A380s over more than a fortnight. Other airlines, meanwhile, had returned their Rolls-Royce-engined A380s back into the air. Qantas waited for clear reassurance before restoring the fleet to normal operations.

According to Gissing, 'A lot of the time you've immediately got some hypothesis, you've immediately got some sense of it. You can tap into history and information from lots of people with literally hundreds of years of experience when you put them together around a table and you can go, "Oh, it might be this or it might be that, or let's not react yet because we just need a few more facts." I was crisis management chair for that one, and when the crisis executive made the call to ground the A380 fleet, it was absolutely the right call.'

Joyce, always under fire on the safety front, was eager to dispel any suggestion of shortcomings on the airline's part. The crew had acted perfectly. After all, the A380 had landed safely, it had an all-star experienced flight deck team, passengers were treated highly professionally on the ground, and no one had been physically injured.

But it was vital, as well, to clarify that there had been no engineering fault on Qantas's part.

Rolls-Royce, whose share price had been hit hard, was reluctant to make public comment. Inevitably, it needed more information, and undoubtedly its lawyers were cautioning its management team to keep a low profile. Meanwhile, Qantas remained in the firing line. Joyce persistently implored Rolls-Royce's CEO, Sir John Rose, to go public. It was much like his own diminutive mother demanding a refund for the bad fish she'd been sold.

Wirth recalls 'having very difficult conversations with their head of corporate affairs at the time. I was saying, "This is your engine, you need to be able to speak." Because literally we were the only ones out there. And we made sure that we filled that vacuum, because Airbus was much slower to . . . respond. And Rolls-Royce did not want to participate.'

It soon became clear that the incident was caused by an engine defect and was nothing to do with Qantas maintenance anyway. In any case, Qantas's A380 engine contract with Rolls-Royce required that all maintenance be performed by the engine manufacturer, not the airline. But these were subtleties that escaped the public's attention.

Despite this, for days Rolls-Royce made no announcement. When, after intensive analysis, the engine maker finally admitted fault, Qantas initiated legal action for compensation in the Federal Court, moving to pre-empt any effort by Rolls-Royce to ensure the matter was dealt with in the UK court system.

An investigation ensued, led by Rolls-Royce and Airbus, working with Qantas and the Australian Transport Safety Bureau (ATSB). The cause was eventually determined to be an oil fire in an engine structure cavity. The fire, in turn, was the result of a faulty oil pipe fracturing in the engine, resulting in the fracture of a turbine disc. Shrapnel from the subsequent explosion punctured the wing, cutting fuel and hydraulic lines and controls to the landing flaps.

Qantas's executives would learn countless lessons from this and other airline incidents. Making on-the-spot decisions in the glare of the public eye, especially on matters that can involve life and death, engages many components: personality, instinct and training. It's easy to overthink this, but, under pressure, it's a person's character that shines through. That's the rudder, and most of the remainder depends on their education – in the broadest sense – and training.

Well-trained soldiers can override personal factors when put under severe pressure; they're drilled to respond to most situations. But there are a few who stand out because they are able to call on their humanity to deal with complex situations, where even the best of programming leaves them short.

For an airline CEO, the most dreaded event is losing an aircraft, with loss of life. It's a tragedy on a human level and it also exposes the heart of an airline. Every staff member feels the impact. Sadly, one predictable reaction is to allocate blame – and with social media as well as conventional outlets, these days that often begins immediately. The pressure is intense. Crisis also provides a soft opportunity for any disaffected elements to emphasise safety concerns. Inevitably, the CEO is in the firing line.

Thankfully, serious aircraft accidents are extremely rare. Every airline has meticulous emergency plans that swing into action as soon as any major event is triggered – a hijacking, a missing aircraft, a major incident on board. Every conceivable scenario is workshopped and planned for. There is intense cooperation across the entire industry on safety issues, but each individual airline must develop its own specific procedures.

In the case of QF32, given the nature and scope of the explosion, it was a near miracle that more severe damage was not suffered by the aircraft – or by passengers. The calmness and competence of the flight crew played an enormous role in getting the aircraft down safely.

For Joyce, it offered a lesson in how to operate effectively as the person on whose desk the buck stops. He would later recall, as CEO, 'You try to operate at 35,000 feet. That gives you this perspective to see everything that's going on, all of the risks, all of the opportunities. Then, occasionally, you do need to get down to five feet . . . Did we [the Qantas executives and board] get into the details of [A380] engines? Absolutely! I needed to. The board needed to. And we were operating at five feet, because we had to make the decision to put the aircraft back in the air.'

Unfortunately, though, 'Dealing with the business world means you often don't have perfect information. In that case, it's important to have a hypothesis, get the information you have to help you inform if that decision is right, and then get on and make the decision.'

Significantly, the QF32 incident reshaped the airline's media strategy for the future.

'That afternoon started a month of rolling updates, essentially,' says Olivia Wirth. 'At one stage we were doing three updates a day and we would bring Alan out, but only when there was a major announcement or something significant to talk about, such as the decision to ground the fleet. But then we worked with the pilots to do commentary about it, and Alan Milne, who is a great communicator, so we could give as much commentary and colour to the media as possible.'

Qantas did not have a social media presence at that stage. The airline used Facebook and Twitter as a means of monitoring what was going on, but didn't participate. 'That was a real learning to say, "Right, we need to get our own channels. We need to make sure we do have ongoing effective monitoring in place that you can respond to in real time,' Wirth says.

With the initial QF32 diagnosis complete, the Qantas A380 fleet re-entered service after eighteen days on the ground.

'But once we got back up, we then had this challenge around the A380 being a pretty new aircraft,' Wirth recalls. 'How do we rebuild the customer's faith in this new, magnificent piece of aircraft technology? How do we give them comfort that everything's okay? So we did a lot of work around that. Alan went on the first flight. We did *Four Corners* and did *60 Minutes* on this, to show we didn't have anything to hide.

'We went into a huge amount of detail, which was quite different for Qantas. And that was something that was actually discussed at the board level. So it was a different approach around understanding that we needed to own it, be transparent, use the media and work with our media partners to try and help the customers feel okay about it.

'We did some consumer research at the time that showed there was genuine customer concern, but it wasn't off the charts. Ultimately, the episode built back the strength of our brand around safety before anything else – and that we never compromise on safety, that our pilots are phenomenal and well trained and incredibly disciplined.'

The aircraft involved in QF32, VH-OQA, remained grounded for almost eighteen months, as one of the most extensive – and expensive – aircraft repairs was conducted in a dedicated hangar at Changi Airport.

On 21 April 2012, the same crew who'd flown QF32 some 536 days earlier, led by captains Richard de Crespigny and David Evans, received the aircraft's logbooks, signifying the end of the $139 million repair job. They piloted the A380, with newly modified engines, from Singapore to Sydney with top Qantas executives and guests on board. Over fifty technicians from Airbus, Qantas and Singapore Engineering had been involved in some 87,000 hours of repair work on the aircraft itself, plus 5000 hours of design work. Some 6.1 kilometres of wiring in the aircraft was replaced.

The *Nancy-Bird Walton* was the first Qantas A380, and it remains in service today, although on 28 March 2020 it was grounded again during the COVID pandemic. In June it was ferried to the Victorville boneyard in the Nevada Desert for storage, but exited on 24 September, to undergo maintenance and re-enter service with Qantas. She's a tough old bird.

Joyce later admitted that Qantas QF32 was the closest the airline has come to losing a jet aircraft, creating 'huge concerns around the brand at that stage . . . But it's a very robust brand – and we rebounded.'[5] The incident was ultimately an exercise in a special sort of crisis management: to maintain the safety record and, as always, to protect and defend the Qantas brand.

It also put the airline on a massive learning curve regarding its communications and media strategy, especially in the emerging social media.

'What absolutely works is you keep it simple in terms of the key messages that need to come out [to the public],' says Joyce. 'And you provide a lot of background material for people to read. Some people have a different bent and a different interest and [want to] get into the details, so you make sure you provide that need and that requirement. For the layperson and someone that just wants to get the key messages, give them the key ideas so that they can relate to them. And I think, if you can get the balance right, you get the perfect outcome.'

Joyce remains robust in his response to suggestions of reduced safety standards at Qantas. As maintenance needs and industry practices evolved in the 2000s, centralising heavy maintenance in specialist facilities became the industry norm. And the economics of these centres only worked if they were able to attract 'third-party' work – that is, jobs from other airlines. Few airlines were willing to fly their aircraft all the way to Australia for maintenance, so it became impossible for an Australian carrier to support the capital and labour costs required if it were to service its own maintenance needs.

The transition from the days of doing everything in-house was doubtless an uncomfortable one, and the engineers' unions understandably pushed back. However, the indiscriminate suggestions that Qantas's safety standards were declining as a result were unfounded.

In October 2008, two months before Joyce became Qantas CEO, the Australian Manufacturing Workers Union (AMWU) conducted a survey of 200 Qantas workers across facilities in Sydney and Brisbane, and at Tullamarine and Avalon airports in Victoria. It found that a majority of workers believed 'corners were getting cut' at the airline. It was hardly an impartial assessment, of course, but it represented the union's view.

Now, as the QF32 drama unfolded, those voices again accused Qantas of cutting corners. The AMWU said Qantas's move to offshore some of its maintenance tasks had required Australian-based crews to routinely recheck and completely redo the work.

Joyce immediately went on the attack, telling the ABC's *7.30 Report* on the evening of the QF32 incident that it was an engine issue, and that the engine in question had been maintained by the manufacturer, Rolls-Royce. The aircraft was relatively new to the fleet, he said, having flown just 8533 hours at the time of the accident. It was in no way anything to do with Qantas's maintenance standards.

Joyce said he was very disappointed with the statements by the engineers' union. 'They've been making a number of outrageous claims in the past that have proven not to be true, and Qantas still stands on the safety record,' he said. 'We've got the best safety record of any major airline in the world, and the issue is when it comes to engine failures, we have less engine failures than any other airline. It's proven – the statistics are there – and yet the engineers' union keeps on making false claims, and I think it's outrageous.'

Joyce's outrage at the unions would simmer in the months that followed. But the safety rumblings had many more months to run, as the tempo of the drama steadily increased.

8

The Slow Bake

In early 2011, Joyce outlined the 'grave challenges' faced by Qantas International, and announced he was undertaking a wholesale review. Joyce shocked the market – and many within Qantas – by publicly criticising the 'underperforming' international business.

In bargaining mode, the AIPA immediately hit back, saying Qantas pilots' job security was under threat. Industrial action loomed as negotiations for a new enterprise bargaining agreement for international pilots continued through the first quarter of that year.

Qantas maintained there was no threat to the job security of its pilots, and added that the overall wage claim from AIPA was not 2.5 per cent, as the union had suggested, but rather 26 per cent over three years – equivalent to an 8.15 per cent increase year on year, when factoring in the combined effect of the wage claim, classification table and travel claims submitted by AIPA. If agreed to, the wage rises would 'put the real job security of many thousands of Qantas Group employees at risk', according to the carrier.

For Joyce, it was crucial that the Qantas Group could grow and find new revenue sources. The expansion of Jetstar in Asia was seen as the key to providing earnings and job stability to the wider Group. But that strategy was diametrically opposed to the views of unions representing the Qantas-branded pilots, engineers and ground staff. They were concerned that expansion in Asia via the Jetstar brand would leave them choosing between diminished conditions, being sidelined from career progression at a shrinking mainline Qantas, or – worse – out of a job altogether.

On 19 April 2011, in a lunchtime speech to the Australian Institute of Company Directors in Sydney, Joyce was confrontational. Hitting out at the AIPA, as well as at the engineering and transport workers' unions, he said that while he understood why staff wanted job security, it was no more in his power to guarantee jobs in writing 'than to promise that Santa will swing by on December 24'. 'The truth,' he said, 'is the wolf is not only inside the door, it's gnawing on our legs.'

The 'wolf' of Joyce's metaphor was partly the price of jet fuel, which had shot up by more than 40 per cent over the previous six months.

Qantas International was now losing an estimated $200 million a year.

The Qantas Group's commercial executive, Rob Gurney, says Joyce felt the need to make stakeholders aware that the international business 'was not only loss-making, but it was a long way from coming close to even the most optimistic projections of meeting its cost of capital on the way it was configured at that time. And I think that left him very open for out-of-the-box kind of options as to how to address it.'

Joyce went on: 'I will never accept that Qantas has no right to explore all options available in a modern, globalised economy, because that would mean condemning Qantas to inevitable decline.'

Across Australia's private sector at the time, just 15 per cent of the workforce were union members. With its roots in government ownership, some three-quarters of Qantas's 35,000-strong workforce were members of fourteen different unions, covered by over fifty collective agreements that required renegotiation every three years. This brought with it a level of inertia, a powerful force towards maintenance of the status quo that was out of step with the disruption that was reshaping the industry more broadly.

'The demands being put forward by the union leadership are so extreme, and so damaging to Qantas, that I cannot in all conscience accept them,' Joyce told his audience.

Captain Barry Jackson, a Qantas A380 pilot and the head of AIPA, said the discussions on job security weren't about jobs for life, but about efficiencies. In return, however, the pilots were seeking a guarantee that they would have access to the growth. 'Alan doesn't want to agree to these things because he wants to grow the airline outside the country,' he said. 'There's a huge amount of experienced pilots sitting at home on leave while foreign bases are being grown through the Jetstar network.'[1]

From the pilots' point of view, this seemed a credible complaint, although it did avoid addressing the mounting losses the international services were suffering. In reality, two issues were being conflated, magnifying the discord.

First, the growth market was Asia – that was beyond dispute. Equally, the low-yielding shape of that growth meant that an airline with Jetstar's costs could exploit it profitably, while Qantas's premium product was neither appropriate nor cost-effective. Then there was Qantas's existing international network, which was obviously unprofitable and in need of care. It had little prospect of growth and was making heavy losses. That was a fact of life, unpalatable though it was.

Joyce's problems were multiplying – and it was at this time that he experienced his frightening episode with prostate cancer, when for a time it appeared as if his battles with various unions might well be academic. That helped put many things in perspective for him, as well as increasing his resolve to protect the Qantas brand.

The ALAEA, representing some 1600 licensed engineers, had meanwhile, on 9 May 2011, halted conciliation talks on its enterprise bargaining agreement, for which talks had been underway since September 2010. The ALAEA announced that industrial action would begin four days later. According to Qantas, the cost of the union's claim was 28.6 per cent over three years, 'with further increased costs being incurred in subsequent years bringing the real cost to above 36 per cent, which would damage Qantas, restrict our business and jeopardise the jobs of their members and all other Qantas employees'.[2]

There was a brief reprieve when the ALAEA called off further planned industrial action later in the month, but Qantas management complained that the union's tactics – threatening a strike action and then cancelling it at the last minute – were causing uncertainty for passengers and affecting bookings. Later that month, however, Fair Work Australia approved a ballot allowing long-haul pilots to vote on taking industrial action. It would be the first time in forty-five years that such action was even contemplated.

Joyce went on *The 7.30 Report* to say the continuous threats of industrial action were attempts to further damage the brand. 'Unfortunately, this is the way some of these rogue union leaders think,' the CEO said, adding that the demands 'will result in job losses in this company . . . and endanger the survival of the company'.[3]

Reconciliation now seemed a vanishingly small prospect.

Joyce believed that culling unprofitable overseas routes and investing in the higher-growth, lower-cost Jetstar made more sense than continuing to invest, for now, in the inefficient international business unit. Setting up a new premium subsidiary airline in Asia, about which rumours were starting to circulate, was also in Joyce's playbook. Like the other parts of the Asian strategy, this was about growth rather than substitution, but it wasn't going to satisfy the Qantas pilots.

In June, the ALAEA introduced rolling two-hour work

stoppages, undertook one-minute strikes, banned workers from using screwdrivers with their right hands, and held work stoppages with only one staff member – all apparently small actions that caused significant disruption.

In July, the engineers' union organised strikes over the school holidays, but cancelled them after Joyce wrote to the union requesting they be called off in the national interest, following the grounding of Tiger Airways by the Civil Aviation Safety Authority (CASA) due to safety concerns.

Next, the AIPA threatened to take industrial action that would cause further disruptions to Australian travellers. Qantas called the union demands 'excessive and unsustainable'. They included a 2.5 per cent pay increase each year for three years, in itself a seemingly modest request. But the AIPA was also seeking two free international economy flights each year (upgradeable to first class), on top of existing staff discounts. It didn't seem a lot, but it added to a heavy weight on what was already a loss-making service.

One claim the pilots were making was that the international business couldn't possibly be losing money because it was subsidising the other Qantas businesses, such as the loyalty business and the domestic airline. Insofar as the systems were interconnected, this contained a grain of truth. On that reasoning, everything rose or failed together.

More substantive, and more contentious – as well as vastly more damaging – was a union demand that pilots on all Qantas airlines, including Jetstar and Jetconnect (a New Zealand–based subsidiary set up to operate trans-Tasman services), be paid the same rates as Qantas pilots. The AIPA also sought a new classification table that would lock in pay rates for flying aircraft that were not yet part of the Qantas fleet, and discounted Qantas Club membership for pilots and their families. Qantas responded that the claim was designed to damage the viability of Jetstar and other subsidiaries, 'in the naive belief that this will lead to increased activity in Qantas'.

The AIPA's action commenced later that month, including union announcements to passengers over the inflight public address system, work bans and wearing unauthorised (non-uniform) ties. The pilots were much more moderate in their disruptive measures, but it all added up, and the public had alternatives, especially when it came to international flights.

Qantas was not alone in facing troubled times with unions. Australian employers were facing the worst period of industrial unrest in decades, with disputes affecting mines, ports and airlines alike – and employees were feeling pain.

In the midst of this public debate, and as the union action built relentlessly, Joyce unveiled a new strategy, titled 'Building a Stronger Qantas', on 16 August 2011. Its purpose was to address the weakness in the airline's international operation.

Joyce's 'five-year transformation plan', effective immediately, set about fixing 'a steadily fading business, suffering big financial losses and a substantial decline in market share. Qantas International's issues are neither cyclical nor temporary,' he said. As the CEO saw things, fixing that arm of the business was not optional.

The high fuel prices were badly impacting international business, and the high Australian dollar – it had now exceeded parity with the US dollar – had driven a 50 per cent increase in Qantas's cost base since the GFC. While it reduced the cost of servicing debt, the high dollar (and therefore salaries, which made up about a third of the company's total costs) made Qantas less competitive in international markets. 'We have to put in place a plan to make sure that Qantas does adapt to the current market situations: the high fuel price and the high Australian dollar. We have to adapt to that,' Joyce said.

The board was becoming restless too. Chairman Leigh Clifford told shareholders that, 'quite simply, the International business is unsustainable, particularly considering the capital it uses, and needs to change'.[4]

Said Joyce, 'We do believe that the International business is a key part of what we do. It links to domestic, it links to frequent flyer. Those businesses do need a strong international operation. But there's no silver bullet to fix International. It means a lot of hard work.'

It was hard work because, unlike its US rivals, Qantas undertook its transformation process without the advantages of a Chapter 11 bankruptcy reorganisation process, whereby contracts could be relaxed through the court process. Qantas had to do it outside that framework, and it established more than 250 projects to achieve its aims.

'We worked closely with our people on everything that we were doing,' Joyce says. 'We asked our people from all parts of the organisation their ideas, we got their buy-in, got their support, got them keen on making the transformation because the future of the organisation was dependent on it. And they came with us on that journey. They helped us implement it.'

Many US carriers that went through a Chapter 11 bankruptcy process lost the engagement of staff and customers along the way. 'Unlike a lot of Chapter 11 process in the US, we are achieving what we call "the trifecta",' Joyce says. 'We're getting record customer satisfaction, record financial performance and record employee engagement, simultaneously. That is unique – it is a phenomenal thing. So this mechanism, while a lot harder in terms of changing the contracts and the terms . . . does give you other benefits to customer satisfaction and people engagement.'[5]

Joyce was confident from prior experience that the international business could be fixed. A decade earlier, he pointed out, the same dire projections had been made about the domestic operations.

He later recounted, 'I remember when people saw the low-cost carriers coming in. They said, "Why are you persisting with this domestic business?" The low-cost carriers everywhere else in the world have dominated, and they've killed the full-service carriers. Qantas is going to be dead domestically within ten years.

But ten years later, our low-cost competitor has changed its strategy on its head, it's walked away. The only market in the world where the low-cost carrier's walked away from its strategy into a full-service strategy, because it couldn't compete against Qantas.'[6]

In 2011, with Jetstar by now ring-fencing Virgin Blue, Qantas's domestic operation was in relatively good shape, giving Joyce the platform to attack the international arm's problem. 'One of the things that makes our business very different from a lot of airlines around the world is the structural advantages of our domestic operation,' Joyce said. 'We have 62 per cent of the domestic market, we have 90 per cent of the domestic profit pools, and it's been consistent like that for over seven years. If anything, it's improving.'

It just needed innovation – and determination. Meanwhile, Qantas's domestic market share contrasted starkly with the international business, which had shrunk to just 18 per cent, not including Jetstar International. Unlike in the domestic arena, Qantas had little power to shape the market.

Most of its routes, primarily to Asia and Europe, were loss-making, with no improvement in sight. Joyce explained that competitors had been 'piling in, many with substantial foreign government backing'. Foremost among them were the Middle Eastern and Asian carriers, with their well-positioned hubs.

Emirates, in particular, was circling the wounded Qantas International, ready to fill any route and capacity vacancy left by the Australian carrier's withdrawal. It announced plans to increase its weekly flights out of Australia from sixty-three to seventy when it moved to a three-times-daily service between Sydney and Dubai on 1 October. There was more: Emirates still held authority for fourteen additional weekly slots and would exercise those rights, and would deploy larger A380s instead of 777s if it saw an opportunity.

Joyce estimated Qantas International's cost base to be around 20 per cent higher than its key competitors; it gobbled up

38 per cent of the Qantas Group's invested capital. He decided to cut investment in the loss-making division until it returned its cost of capital.

The five-year plan was signed off by shareholders at the annual general meeting that October. It had two main objectives: to return Qantas International to profitability in the short term, and to exceed the cost of capital on a sustainable basis of both the domestic and international flying businesses combined within five years. Among other things, this heralded a new approach to assessing financial performance: against the cost of capital. If a business area didn't return the investment cost plus a profit margin, it was underperforming.

There are billions of dollars in capital tied up in owning (or leasing) 150 or so aircraft. Most successful businesses make consistent returns of at least 10 per cent on the capital they have invested. The global airline industry, by contrast, had never made back the cost of all this capital. That meant airline investors would have been far better off putting their money in the bank, with virtually no risk. Airlines are highly risky and should really be making a much higher margin than less risky businesses. Being 'sustainable' means attracting investors and lenders who have other options – less risky places to put their money.

If the airline doesn't make a sufficient return, several things happen. The riskier it becomes, the more its credit rating goes down, meaning it has to pay more to borrow money, which impacts profits and investor returns.

A new marketing program was devised to accompany the turnaround plan for Qantas International. Dubbed 'A New Spirit of Australia', it had a slick video and soundtrack, and made the case that the recovery was aimed at four broad goals:

- Opening gateways to the world;
- Growing with Asia;
- Being best for global travellers; and
- Building a strong, viable business to create shareholder value.

The 'gateway' strategy was built on an expanded network of alliance relationships, namely with American Airlines for North America and LAN in South America.

It still had a serious weakness. The Americas routes were not where the biggest losses were piling up. Those were to the north (Asia) and to the west (where Emirates was so strong), where foreign airline competition was fierce and getting fiercer. Joyce's August 2011 solution was lukewarm, and he knew it.

The partners who could help Qantas westbound were limited in number. It relied mainly on 'looking at new opportunities to work with Malaysia Airlines', a second-tier carrier and chronic loss-maker itself. At the time, Malaysian was still not a full member of the oneworld alliance, which Qantas had helped form. The plan also envisioned an expansion of the partnership with British Airways, a carrier with its own substantial financial challenges. This remained a weak link.

The key piece of the puzzle remained missing. As Joyce acknowledged, 'We are negotiating further opportunities to advance our "gateway" strategy.'

As it turned out, that puzzle piece was just around the corner.

9

At the End of the Line

In 2004, Jetstar was created in response to an existential threat: the fact that Qantas's domestic market was being disrupted – destroyed, really – by a rampant Virgin Blue, whose costs were vastly lower and whose business plan was tailored to the modern marketplace. The move had succeeded better than could possibly have been hoped.

As a key strategist and CEO of the new airline, Joyce had much to do with that, with his focus on costs and efficiency. From the start, his bottom-up approach to building an airline to fit the new conditions represented a challenge to the status quo. And Joyce was that challenge personified, particularly for the unions whose noses were out of joint over the lower pay rates and conditions that had been negotiated.

While Jetstar may have saved the domestic operation, it became the trigger for a long-lasting antagonism to any change in Qantas's mainline activities. For years the pilots' unions persisted with a string of legal actions designed to reverse the changes, and other operational unions watched every move to reduce costs with trepidation. When Joyce was made Qantas CEO, these concerns escalated to a new level, as the threat of 'Jetstar-ising' the national carrier seemed to be becoming reality. When Jetstar itself morphed into an international operation, the distrust redoubled: it now appeared that Jetstar was the means for moving the entire Qantas Group offshore.

In reality, there were several strains to Jetstar's and Qantas's Asian moves. They weren't aimed at 'offshoring' the business; rather, they sought to tap into growth markets that otherwise wouldn't have been accessible. Rather than evading a threat, as had happened with Virgin Blue, Qantas's international operations in Asia were all about exploiting opportunities.

With his insider knowledge of Jetstar, and having now peered deep into the inner workings of the rest of the Qantas Group, Joyce decided to focus on integrating Jetstar into the Group strategy early in his tenure as the CEO. It was his baby, though, so he was very conscious of concerns that he'd be favouring Jetstar. The optics as well as the practicalities were important.

'He was accused many times by the unions of all sorts of skulduggery where that's concerned,' said one Qantas manager. 'But the reality was, he was very balanced about it.'

Jetstar was now surging ahead, stimulated by the delivery of fourteen A320s in 2010. It now had a fleet of fifty aircraft.

As the new century progressed, Australia's economic future had become inextricably tied to Asia. By 2010, six of Australia's top ten trading partners were in the region. The most important was China. Qantas Group was keen to follow the trade routes and secure its share of the action.

Given the low-yielding profile of much of the new growth traffic, Jetstar – now helmed by Bruce Buchanan – was the obvious vehicle for much of this expansion, and an aggressive pan-Asia strategy was laid out for it. Buchanan enthusiastically expanded into Asia, surfing the wave created by the expansion into Thailand and Indonesia of Tony Fernandes' AirAsia.

Jetstar International was mainly concerned with servicing outbound Australian leisure travellers. It performed a valuable role in substituting for Qantas on some routes where the mainline carrier's high costs made the operation uneconomic.

Where Jetstar did fly in parallel with the main brand, it was to segment the market in much the same skilful way that the network planners had achieved with the Australian domestic routes.

Then there were the Jetstar subsidiaries – the cross-border joint ventures. These were mainly domestic operations within Japan and Vietnam, while the Singapore-based Jetstar Asia played multiple roles, offering onward Asian connections to Aussies flying beyond Qantas's Singapore services, as well as tapping into the valuable routes onwards from Singapore into and from Asia.

By March 2011, Jetstar Asia was flying from Singapore to twenty-five destinations in thirteen countries, including seven airports in Greater China. In Vietnam's high-growth domestic economy of 87 million people, Jetstar Pacific serviced seven destinations. Jetstar Japan was already in the late planning stages, set to launch in July 2012 as the country pursued its own low-cost revolution.

The 'Growing with Asia' part of Joyce's August 2011 international transformation plan had another feature that would see Qantas contemplate the riskier move of establishing a new premium carrier in Asia, later dubbed RedQ. Provocatively, to Qantas's unions, the new airline was to be established in Singapore or Kuala Lumpur, and aimed to deploy up to twenty-four A320s within its first few years of operation.

The aim of establishing RedQ, with its not-so-subtle link to Qantas, was to help the airline attract business travellers back to the Group. The branding was a delicate issue. Although South-East Asian governments were by now tacitly willing to permit foreign low-cost airline joint ventures involving foreign companies (such as the Singapore-based Jetstar Asia), the same did not apply to 'flag carriers'. There was simply no way any Asian government would allow Qantas to establish a joint venture there in its own name.

Joyce told the *Australian Financial Review* that the plan was for the carrier to have 'an exclusive jet-feel to it – it will be perceived as the best product to Asia there is'.[1] The typical 180-seat layout was to be halved, both to ensure comfort and to bolster the range of the aircraft, so they could reach points in China, India and North Asia. This would mean a major perception shift in the region, as Qantas had long had a reputation as a cheap product, often using older aircraft.

The international transformation plan also included proposals for up to 110 Airbus A320 aircraft to be acquired, to support Qantas Group capacity growth and expansion into new markets. This included aircraft for Jetstar Japan and RedQ.

The aircraft orders kicked off a capital-intensive period for Jetstar's short-haul expansion. The Group went on to invest $1.9 billion in new aircraft in the 2011 and 2012 financial years, helping bring the average fleet age down to the lowest level it had been for some time at just 8.3 years. In true low-cost form, this simplified the fleet and helped reduce costs.

Of very specific concern to the operations staff, the five-year plan also involved deferring the delivery of Qantas's final six A380s by up to six years, and retiring four Boeing 747s. There were network changes, more efficient practices were introduced, along with approximately 1000 redundancies, which would come from management positions, pilots, cabin crew and engineering. As long as it seemed there was no prospect of westbound international services recovering, there was no point in flogging the dead horse – the losses had to be reduced. Joyce said he expected the majority of these redundancies would be voluntary. But the move inflamed already tense relationships with labour groups.

A level of distrust had developed, which made what Joyce saw as perfectly 'logical' international moves seem like a threat to the Qantas/Jetstar operation at home. It was an opportunistic strategy to chase the high-growth Asian markets and generate new business, but reducing the losses on failed routes was also a no-brainer.

*

To give the Asian joint venture strategy a boost, something occurred that was to create a fortuitous opening for the Qantas Group's Asia strategy. The previous year, on 19 January 2010, after several government bailouts, the heavyweight – and overweight – oneworld member Japan Airlines (JAL) filed for bankruptcy.

Japan is a major Asian market, with high levels of valuable business travel. With a population of 128 million people – more than five times Australia's then 22 million – Japan was a temptingly large market. It had been a very conservative international market, dominated by JAL until the government gave privately owned domestic airline All Nippon Airways (ANA) the right to go international in the late 1980s.

ANA was much more aggressively competitive and had a stranglehold on the large domestic market. Almost unknown outside Japan, it had become the largest airline in the world, measured by available seat numbers. JAL, which had previously been government-owned, was much more bureaucratic, and with a smaller domestic network was simply unable to keep up.

It was early days for the budding oneworld alliance, which had been formed by Qantas, BA and American Airlines, and JAL represented an important gateway to the valuable Japanese market, which included plenty of premium travel to the United States.

The longer-established Star Alliance had already tied up ANA as a member. That had left the newer SkyTeam alliance – led by Delta and Air France – with no partner in what Delta saw as a key market. Having previously acquired Northwest Airlines, which had gained a ubiquitous presence in North Asia, Delta saw JAL as the jewel it needed to give it dominance in the region over the other US airlines.

Seeing an opportunity now that JAL had to reorganise, Delta moved to lure it away from oneworld. Delta had emerged from Chapter 11 bankruptcy three years earlier and was cashed up and keen to expand. It made some juicy offers: the potential for cost cuts and increased revenue from its SkyTeam alliance through

Delta's extensive presence in North Asia. To sweeten the pill, it offered US$500 million in equity, and a further US$500 million in guarantees and loans.

Delta was offering just what JAL needed to get off to a speedy start as it emerged from bankruptcy, and although many of the remaining JAL executives felt a familiarity with and loyalty to oneworld, management leaned heavily towards accepting the lucrative offer.

Oneworld's team of American and Qantas fought from a position of weakness. American had been struggling to avoid bankruptcy, while Qantas was not equipped either to be offering large investments. Cathay Pacific, also in oneworld, was luke-warm about helping, as it saw nearby JAL as a competitor. It came down to a head-to-head battle between two of the United States' major airlines, and American was on the brink of losing.

American Airlines' chief commercial officer, who had been heading the negotiations in Japan, phoned Rob Gurney late one afternoon and implored him to fly to Tokyo that night. Things were looking desperate. They were about to lose JAL, and with it the highly prized access to the Japan market. To lose JAL at that time would have been a great setback for oneworld.

Gurney called Joyce, who promptly agreed. 'The last thing Alan said to me was, "Look, Rob, I trust your judgement to do whatever you think is necessary from a Qantas perspective, but just don't commit to any equity because we don't have any money at the moment,' Gurney recalls. But Joyce did send along Tino La Spina, then deputy chief financial officer, to accompany Gurney and keep an eye on him. The Qantas executives were hopeful but did not expect much.

Qantas's pitch was that it would help JAL set up Jetstar Japan, 'and we would bring all of the IP into that market and actually invest in it', Gurney explains. 'And that, I think, resonated very strongly – that we were prepared to put in capital and help JAL do something quite transformative across their group. So iron-ically, we actually did invest, but in a very different way.'

The mission was successful and JAL remained in oneworld. The deal had been sealed largely thanks to a unique asset of the Qantas Group: Jetstar. It was an unexpected benefit produced by the dual-brand strategy, but no less valuable for that.

JAL was a high-cost operator by world standards, even after emerging from bankruptcy, but it was aware that the low-fare market was finally taking off in North Asia. ANA was, at this time, working through a long-winded process to set up its own domestic LCC, Peach, and was preparing to move. JAL didn't have the in-house skills to establish its own subsidiary, so the prospect of a joint venture with the world's leading low-cost subsidiary was attractive. Jetstar Japan was conceived.

What was to become the new JAL low-cost subsidiary wasn't the only sweetener – and, as Gurney says, the Qantas Group did end up investing equity in that joint venture. But it helped save JAL as a bilateral and oneworld partner, which would prove enormously helpful to Qantas, American and British Airways, as well as Cathay Pacific.

On 16 August 2011, the launch of Jetstar Japan was formally announced – the same day as Alan Joyce's five-year international transformation plan. Among the shareholders were JAL, Mitsubishi and Qantas, and operations launched on 3 July 2012.

Jetstar Japan has not been an unqualified success in its own right. But to the extent that it contributed to keeping Japan Airlines in the oneworld fold, it has been priceless. When the American Airlines executive made the urgent call to Australia that day, JAL was on the point of signing with Delta, which would have excluded oneworld airlines from any partnership in the Japanese market.

In fact, the repercussions could have been even more damaging for Qantas, had Delta succeeded in persuading JAL into the SkyTeam fold. A month later, Virgin Blue concluded a Pacific joint venture with Delta. With this sizeable partner, Virgin Australia could have gained a significant advantage over a partner-less Qantas in the Japanese market.

The initial enthusiasm for Jetstar's offshore ventures eventually waned as the entities struggled for profitability. The concept of cross-border joint ventures in a restrictive regulatory framework meant that nothing was easy, especially as Jetstar could have only a minority share. There were other cultural and legal hurdles too.

In Vietnam, there had been a shocking setback in 2010. The previous year, management of the Jetstar Pacific joint venture with Vietnam Airlines had entered a substantial fuel-hedging program, a common practice elsewhere but not in Vietnam. When oil prices went the wrong way, the airline was left with booked losses of over $30 million, with nothing to show for them. The former CEO, a Vietnamese citizen, was detained and the Australian chief operating officer and chief financial officer were not permitted to leave the country while corruption charges were considered. They were only freed after a very stressful six months of uncertainty.

Any negative news about the offshore Jetstar operations only served to make its expansion plans more controversial. And, while the Asian expansion strategy was unfolding, union resistance to Joyce's plans was intensifying, conflating concerns about Qantas's international cutbacks with the assumption that Jetstar's expansion was a direct corollary.

The secretary of the powerful Australian Council of Trade Unions (ACTU), Jeff Lawrence, said that 16 August 2011 was one of the darkest days in the history of Qantas, as the airline's management had 'turned its back on Australia and on Australian jobs to head down the path of a race to the bottom'.[2] Lawrence announced that the unions would investigate all regulatory and legislative options to ensure Qantas remained an Australian company.

On behalf of the international pilots, the AIPA's Barry Jackson said, 'Strip away the spin . . . and what's left is exactly what Qantas pilots have been warning of for months: a shift of Australian Qantas operations into Asia to start employing people working to Asian conditions and standards.'³ The ALAEA flagged it would push ahead with industrial action, while the TWU announced it would seek support for industrial action.

Joyce responded that Qantas was 'not offshoring a single job'. There was a misinformation when it came to Qantas's plans, he added. 'We're actually creating *new* businesses in Japan and in Asia that we believe will be profitable and will give us profitability that will return here to Australia. The jobs that are lost today are as a result of our poorly performing international business. We're cutting back services to London. Those jobs are just gone. They're not really being replaced with any jobs in Asia. And unless Qantas changes, we will not see a Qantas going into the future,' he told *ABC News*.

'We need the union leaders to realise that change is needed. If they keep on resisting change and Qantas stays as an inefficient carrier competing against the Middle Eastern carriers and the Asian carriers, we won't have a Qantas, like we don't have an Ansett. We're coming up to the tenth anniversary of Ansett's collapse. It's very important for us to recognise the mistakes of the past and that great brands can disappear. If great brands do not change, they will no longer be around, and they have no right to existence.'⁴

Reports surfaced that the unions would seek support from Qantas shareholders for a no-confidence motion against the CEO and chairman at the annual general meeting in October. The growing unease of 2011 hurt Qantas's share price, which had dropped to a two-and-a-half-year low of around $1.50 by mid-August. Shareholders were already voting with their wallets.

Less than two weeks after unveiling Jetstar Japan and the five-year international transformation plan, Joyce unveiled a 46 per cent increase in underlying profit before tax of $552 million for the twelve months to 30 June 2011, as revenue rose 8 per cent to $14.9 billion. Joyce described it as 'our best performance since the global financial crisis', achieved despite a number of challenges facing Qantas International and the global aviation industry.⁵

By the end of August 2011, the TWU had joined the engineers and pilots in a series of coordinated actions. The TWU had started negotiating with the airline in late 2010 and was seeking a 15 per cent pay increase over the next three years, which Qantas said was 'just not sustainable in the current economic climate and when these employees are already the highest paid in the Australian aviation industry'.[6] (For the calendar year 2011, Australia's inflation rate was 3.1 per cent.)

According to Qantas, the TWU had recently negotiated a new deal with Virgin, at rates 12 per cent lower than they were demanding of Qantas, and including a wage freeze and a lower pay scale for new starters, 'giving Virgin a competitive advantage over Qantas'.[7] Additionally, the TWU was making a job security claim, requiring Qantas contractors to be paid the same rates as staff members. This became the biggest sticking point in negotiations.

Next, the TWU and the ALAEA announced strike action during the spring school holidays, on the eve of the major football codes' grand finals – a peak time for Qantas. The action affected the travel plans of some 8500 domestic and international Qantas passengers, taking the total to over 25,000 passengers affected by cancelled and delayed flights. The airline did what it could to minimise the disruption, even deploying Australian-based Qantas management as baggage handlers and in other frontline roles. In September, Qantas issued the first of several apologies to passengers for the delays and disruption, expressing its concern that three unions were working together to attack Qantas in a coordinated campaign.

'It was a very challenging industrial relations environment, and it was putting a lot of pressure on the operation and the customer delivery. But by the time the withdrawal notice had gone, you'd already cancelled flights and notified customers and these things,' one Qantas executive says of the time.

Other union deals, meanwhile, were continuing to fall into place. In early October, after six months of negotiations, the

airline reached an in-principle agreement with the union representing short-haul cabin crew, the Flight Attendants' Association
of Australia (FAAA), which included a 3 per cent pay increase
and a $500 lump sum payment each year for three years. That
deal was later finalised in mid-December. Qantas had also struck
a deal with 360 storeworkers represented by the National Union
of Workers.

But for the three holdout unions – the AIPA, the TWU and the
ALAEA – the increasingly high-stakes game continued.

The conflict was about more than just pay – lots more. Something
more sinister was developing. The drumbeat that had been intensifying over the past eighteen months was now approaching its
crescendo.

The unions at the coalface – the operational parts of the
business – felt themselves to be most at risk from Qantas's new
initiatives. They also had the greatest power to disrupt operations. Yet they did not always see eye to eye with the remainder
of the workforce.

On 4 October, as the temperature rose, Joyce sent a memo
to the entire Qantas workforce outlining threats made against
employees after they declined to take strike action against the
airline in support of the other unions; some had also had their
homes damaged and car windows smashed. Joyce and his senior management had received several threatening letters in May
2011, and now more emails with the subject line 'death threats'
had appeared.

Joyce wrote to staff:

I have become aware of acts of bullying and intimidation
within Qantas. Qantas workers who are union members
have been subject to violence against their property after
they declined to take strike action. Members of Qantas management who stepped in to support business have received

menacing correspondence, including to their homes. These acts are abhorrent and illegal.

Those who are in the business of using threats, violence and intimidation to obtain their industrial ends should know this: these tactics are cowardly and deplorable. They will not work. Anyone who is caught will face the full consequences.

The next day, *The Daily Telegraph* reported that Joyce himself had received death threats, which he referred to the Australian Federal Police and New South Wales police to investigate. A typed letter sent to Joyce reportedly read in part: 'It's coming soon Paddy. You can't even see it! The Unions will fight you . . . Qantas is our airline, started & staffed by Australians, not foreign filth like you. All your evil plans . . . will come back to you very swiftly, & kick you . . . out of the country.' The *Telegraph* added that Olivia Wirth had also received a death threat letter sent to her home, as had other managers who took part in contingency plans during a recent strike.[8]

The industrial action escalated in October, driving the number of passengers impacted since unions commenced their strike action six weeks earlier to 46,500 passengers, from 348 cancelled or delayed flights.

The TWU and ALAEA would plan strike action and then call it off again that month, disrupting operations and exasperating management. The airline described the moves as 'cynical games from the union', adding: 'While we would like to reinstate services, it's too late – you can't just turn an airline on and off.'[9] Qantas said ALAEA had provided the airline with written notification that it would keep the ban on overtime and the 'go-slow' in place until Christmas.

By 13 October, Joyce had had enough. Fronting the media, he said: 'The first thing I want to do is apologise to our customers once again. This industrial action is clearly hurting Qantas and our brand. It is having an impact on our costs and on forward bookings. But it is not just Qantas and our customers that are affected. The broader Australian community and economy is hurting as well.'

He announced a reduction in domestic flying operations to help reduce the workload bottleneck in engineering and to make the remaining operation more reliable. This included grounding four 737s (out of the then fleet of fifty-four) and one widebody 767 (out of twenty-five). Two more 767s were grounded the following week.

The business community was getting restless and starting to leave Qantas. They now had a domestic alternative. By mid-October, Qantas estimated, some 60,000 customers had been affected by the disruptions. Qantas was being starved of cash and losing customers to a resurgent Virgin Australia, who the previous year had appointed John Borghetti as CEO. The dispute was perfect timing for Borghetti, as he chased the corporate market and racked up leisure travellers anxious that their holiday plans wouldn't be disrupted.

An increasingly irritated Joyce said, 'Not only are the [three unions] seeking pay and conditions that would put us even further beyond our competitors, they want the right to control key elements of how we run the company. Quite simply, these three unions are not representative of the broader union movement. Effectively they are trying to dictate how we run Qantas!'[10]

As was his practice, Joyce sifted through the different possible scenarios. For him, there was an entirely obvious and unavoidable outcome – although few aside from those very close to him, including the board, had any idea of the measures he was formulating.

'We had three options when it came to this,' he later told a University of New South Wales 'Meet the CEO' event. 'We could capitulate to the unions, and in my mind, that would've endangered the long-term survival of Qantas. Qantas would not be around in ten years' time if we had given in to their outrageous demands. We could have kept on going the way we were going, which would've been death by a thousand cuts, and the unions said it was a "slow bake" that would've lasted another year. Or we could take action available to us under Fair Work Australia, to bring it to an end.

'So we knew the counterfactual of not doing something was going to be a lot worse in terms of us making the recovery, and that was important. And for the shareholders, anybody will tell you the biggest thing you can do for shareholders is take away uncertainty. And the uncertainty of this lasting for another year, and the potential damage that could cause, was going to be a real problem.'[11]

By mid-October 2011, Joyce had decided how he was going to ensure certainty.

10

Grounding the Fleet

An emergency board meeting was called at 10.30 am on Saturday, 29 October 2011, just a day after the annual general meeting. Qantas chairman Leigh Clifford was at a wedding ceremony, and conducted the whole conversation standing under a tree outside the church. He asked the directors if they agreed and supported Joyce in his decision to ground the entire Qantas fleet. By midday, it was approved.

'It was the only time Clifford had called for a vote from the directors,' Joyce says. 'It was unanimous. He didn't have to do that, but he wanted to make sure that the board was clear, everybody was behind me and the management team's [decision], and that we didn't have to worry about board support on any of these things. And he's always been very good at that.'

When the small group of unions began the 'slow bake' of Qantas in pursuit of their pay and conditions claims, the board had shared the CEO's frustration, watching on as bookings for the vital Christmas period dried up. Short of caving in to the unions' demands – which all agreed would have undermined the airline's very existence – something had to be done. And it had to be definitive.

At the company's annual general meeting the day before, union members, bosses and employees had hurled abuse at Joyce, executives and board members, insulting them with profanities, calling them dictators and associating them with the recently deceased Libyan leader Muammar Gaddafi. There are many victims in public life, caught in the crossfire of dramatic events, and it's easy to overlook the personal pain this can inflict.

Late on that Saturday afternoon, Qantas announced, to widespread shock, that, from 8 pm on Monday, 31 October 2011, it would lock out all employees covered by the industrial agreements currently being negotiated with the ALAEA, the TWU and the AIPA. The scale of the lockout made it necessary for all Qantas aircraft to be grounded, to avoid the possibility of malicious actions, or key staff simply walking off the job. For precautionary reasons, this would take place immediately – from 5 pm. Any aircraft currently in the sky would complete the sector they were operating.

'Our risk assessment was pretty clear,' explains John Gissing, 'that if there is a decision to lock out, there was a belief that it could cause distraction. So it would have to be simultaneous with a grounding of the fleet, to do that safely and consistently.'

Qantas announced that the financial impact of the industrial action taken to date had cost $68 million – some $15 million per week. By the end of October, nearly 70,000 passengers had been affected from more than 500 cancelled flights. Forward bookings were down between 10 and 25 per cent, depending on the sector.

'The easiest thing for me to do, the easiest thing for the board to do, the easiest thing for managers to do is to agree to [the union] demands,' said Joyce. 'But that will kick the can down the street. It will create problems for Qantas eventually.'[1]

The financial impact of grounding the airline was massive, estimated at $20 million each day. But Joyce was adamant that the grounding would continue until the ALAEA, the TWU and the AIPA dropped their 'extreme demands'. 'If this action continues, as the unions have promised,' he said, 'we will have no choice but to close down Qantas part by part . . . Killing Qantas slowly would be a tragedy for Qantas and our employees. But it would also have a terrible domino effect right across Australia, affecting businesses large and small, tourism, freight and families. We have got to achieve a resolution to this crisis. I am using the only effective avenue at my disposal to bring about peace and certainty.'[2]

Qantas advised customers booked on Qantas flights not to go to the airport until further notice, and offered a full refund to any customer who chose to cancel their flight because of the grounding. (Jetstar flights, QantasLink flights and Qantas flights across the Tasman operated by Jetconnect would continue, as would Express Freighters Australia and Atlas Freighters.)

Key members of the federal government had been advised of Qantas's decision that afternoon. Joyce had called the transport minister, Anthony Albanese, at 2 pm; the future prime minister was playing tennis at the time. He was not amused, and nor were other members of the cabinet as they were progressively informed.

Albanese was already well aware that a flashpoint had been reached; the previous Wednesday, he had summoned both Joyce and TWU leader Tony Sheldon to a meeting after the management-level talks failed. Most of the issues were resolved, but Sheldon wanted non-Qantas contractors to be included in the enterprise bargaining agreement along with Qantas's TWU employees, something Joyce argued was not possible under the *Fair Work Act*. The talks had ended in acrimony.

Albanese now said the government would apply to Fair Work Australia to make a determination on the industrial action and the actions of Qantas management. 'The government is extremely concerned about the future of Qantas, its workforce, but also the travelling public,' he announced.[3]

The move had caught almost everyone outside the Qantas management team by surprise. Opinion was divided within politics, within industry and across the country. It was excruciatingly embarrassing for the federal Labor government. Prime Minister Julia Gillard was not amused. The PM was in Perth for the annual Commonwealth Heads of Government Meeting (CHOGM), hosting leaders from around the world. It was a showcase of Australia's important role in the Commonwealth, and a golden opportunity for Gillard to occupy the diplomatic spotlight. And the national flag carrier had chosen *this* moment to ground its fleet and lock out its union workforce.

Gillard's official pronouncement was probably more moderate than her private thoughts: 'The government overall was concerned about the extreme action taken by Qantas that had stranded tens of thousands of passengers far away from home.' She was able to return to Canberra on her government jet, but the foreign minister, Kevin Rudd, who was due to leave Perth on a Qantas flight, was stuck. Other national leaders made their own arrangements.

Treasurer Wayne Swan was at pains to assure the public that no federal ministers had known in advance that Joyce was contemplating the 'extreme action' of grounding the airline.

The damage to the relationship between Joyce and the three unions, in particular, was now irreparable. TWU boss Sheldon was scathing. 'This was a reckless and unnecessary decision, but a decision that had been well planned,' he fumed. 'Who believes in fairy tales, that he woke up Saturday morning and just had a brain snap? A brain snap that costs this country the shutdown of its airline . . . that caused enormous disruption to passengers and the economy. Why did he not advise shareholders [at the previous day's annual general meeting] of his plan to ruin the airline and wreck employee relations for years to come?'[4]

The AIPA's vice-president, Richard Woodward, described the grounding as 'a knife to the nation's throat'.[5]

The online comments section of *The Age* went into overdrive, and it was clear where the general sentiment lay:

Extreme executive salaries attract executives who take extreme actions. *KC*

Alan Joyce has shown us the face of corporate terrorism and we are all his hostages. *HP*

Alan Joyce, the Sol Trujillo of the airline industry. May he suffer a similar fate, and quickly. *BM*

Alan, you're paid $5 million a year to run an airline, not ruin an airline. *CB*

Another case of the 1 per cent gouging the 99 per cent. Bonuses all around too, I should imagine. Rest in peace, Qantas. *AR*

If Joyce cannot sort out his company's problems, why is he being paid $5 million a year? *AP*

Qantas – the lying kangaroo? *NC*

Is this a world record? A $2 million pay rise for a job well done on Friday, and close the company down on Saturday. Well done, Alan, on behalf of all Qantas shareholders. *LB*

With a bit of luck we'll have no Joyce in the matter. *JC*

Alan Joyce is looking more and more like the love child of Maggie Thatcher. *JP*

One Qantas worker said: 'Joyce showed just how mercenary he was prepared to be: throwing the biggest dummy spit in Australian corporate history.'[6]

The next day, a Sunday, Fair Work Australia convened at 2 pm to consider the federal government's urgent application for a termination or suspension of the industrial disputes between Qantas and the three unions.

Early on the Monday morning, Fair Work Australia granted the government's application to terminate all industrial action by the unions, clearing the way for the progressive resumption of Qantas flights by midafternoon that day, subject to approval from the CASA, which was duly granted. The intervention was made on the grounds that it was needed to prevent further damage to the national economy, particularly in the tourism and mining sectors.

As operations recommenced on the Monday afternoon, with a full resumption to come the next day, 1 November, staff were not locked out, pay was not withheld and the only week-day the very important corporate market was disrupted was on 1 November. This just happened to be on the very same day as 'the race that stops the nation', the Melbourne Cup, which was a public holiday in Victoria in any case.

The grounding lit up social media – and the federal parliament – all that week, and soon reverberated around the nation and across the world. Industry responses were roundly supportive of Qantas, in contrast to the popular reaction. AirAsia CEO Tony Fernandes was one who backed the move on Twitter, offering a broader perspective: 'You have to salute Alan Joyce for doing what he's doing. This is not about workers versus management. It's about survival in the modern world.'

At the end of that week, on Friday, 4 November, Joyce fronted up in Canberra for a grilling by a Senate inquiry. In the interven-ing days, he had attempted to smooth relations with Gillard, and Albanese. The government was still furious, and its relationship with the national carrier had become toxic.

A bill that had been proposed before the grounding by inde-pendent senator Nick Xenophon and Greens leader Bob Brown, which aimed to rein in Qantas's aggressive Asian expansion plans, took on added significance following the shock move. Joyce was challenged in detail about whether his decision to ground the airline had been made before the Saturday.

The CEO offered a spirited defence of his conduct. In a fiery exchange, Joyce said: 'I'm not running away from this. I'm absolutely here talking about the decision I've made, why I've made the decision, why I feel passionate about the decision I've made. And I'm happy to defend that and talk about that under any form or anywhere, because it was the right call.'

Labor's Senator Doug Cameron – a former national secretary of the AMWU – fired back: 'I think you've got a lot of explaining to do as to why you're a rogue employer. Because this is one of the biggest calls that have been made by corporate Australia: to actually destroy parts of the economy to get your way.'

Senator Brown chimed in: 'You're very obscure and devious about the fact that you are aiming at a lockout.'

'Sorry, Senator, I think that's absolutely inappropriate to say,' Joyce retorted. 'We were very clear on our approach all the way through.'

Cameron fired back: 'You're a bit like Richard Nixon at the moment. You're just trying to talk your way out of this. Don't do it, please.'

Joyce, resolute, responded: 'This is a bit like a McCarthy trial!'

It was intense political theatre.

'It was the last resort, and it will always be the last resort,' Joyce continued. 'Grounding an airline like Qantas is a huge decision, and it's a decision done because we had nowhere else to go.' He said the airline hadn't advised anybody on either side of politics about a lockout.

The senators probed further about the source of the decision:

Alan Joyce:	The decision was a board endorsement. It was my decision.
Senator Xenophon:	You made a decision on your own?
Joyce:	Yes.
Xenophon:	Using your discretion?
Joyce:	Yes.
Xenophon:	Using your delegated authority?
Joyce:	Yes.
Xenophon:	So, for a momentous decision to ground the entire fleet?
Joyce:	Yep.
Xenophon:	To stand down 27,000 employees, that was all on your head?
Joyce:	That was my decision, absolutely.

For the mathematician Joyce, he'd analysed the risks and it paid off. For him it was, quite simply, the right thing to do. And he wasn't shirking his responsibility. He was buoyed by the unstinting support he had received from his chairman and board throughout the saga.

'The board has been phenomenal,' he later recalled. 'There wasn't one stage where I thought there was a single director that wasn't behind what we were doing. They were very much supportive of everything.'[7]

Crucially, for Qantas and its passengers, under the orders issued by Fair Work Australia, there were to be up to twenty-one days of negotiations between the parties, during which time no industrial action could take place. If no agreement was reached during this period, binding arbitration would take place under the control of Fair Work Australia.

Joyce said the decision was a good outcome and would provide certainty for Qantas's passengers and employees. The airline was, however, unable to reach a new agreement with the unions by 21 November. It had taken over fifteen months, and some fifty meetings, but now it was time to let the independent umpire resolve the dispute.

Three days later, the Fair Work Australia Commission terminated all industrial action by the pilots' union, the licensed engineers' union and the transport workers' union for up to four years, allowing passengers to book with 'absolute confidence and certainty'. The new workplace agreements for all three unions would be determined by the independent umpire.

On 23 November, New South Wales police suspended their investigations into the alleged death threats against Joyce and other senior Qantas managers. No charges had been laid and there were no new leads forthcoming.

The TWU said it was a predictable ending to what it had always regarded as a 'stunt' from the beginning. 'It is a disgraceful diversion of police resources,' Tony Sheldon said. 'The truth is now out. The next issue is for the truth to come out on the dodgy claim that Alan Joyce only decided to shut down the aviation industry on October 29. That's where the real investigation is needed.'[8]

Later in November, Qantas estimated that the industrial action and subsequent lockout and grounding had cost the carrier $194 million. Joyce had prevailed, but the financial scars – and the trauma for staff – had cut deep.

Qantas's grounding was a dramatic move, but clinical in its execution. Elsewhere in the world, measures were being taken that were far messier and ultimately more painful for staff, creditors and shareholders alike. This was a global airline industry in turmoil.

In the United States, Qantas's key oneworld partner American Airlines filed for Chapter 11 bankruptcy protection in November 2011, becoming the last of the 'big three' US carriers to take that path; both United Airlines and Delta had filed for bankruptcy protection in the years following the 2001 terrorist attacks. American's parent, the AMR Corporation, said the decision was made to reorganise 'in order to achieve a cost and debt structure that is industry competitive and thereby assure its long-term viability'. The airline said labour contract rules were forcing it to spend at least US$600 million more than rival airlines – an echo of Qantas's problems.

If Australians thought the Qantas grounding was tough – and, although brief, it was – it was a stroll in the park compared with the damage wrought by an airline company going through Chapter 11; the destruction of equity and indiscriminate staff retrenchment were an ugly alternative. Employment at US airlines had peaked in 2000 at just above 750,000 jobs, but almost a quarter had vanished over the ensuing decade.

Virgin Australia, meanwhile, was basking in the glow of the Qantas meltdown. Demand was strong and Virgin won corporate accounts, helping it swing from a $67 million underlying loss in the 2011 financial year to a $83 million profit in 2012. That would be the only time Virgin was in the black that decade.

*

Joyce's preoccupation with cost reduction constantly came under fire – and reasonably enough, because it often meant people were being fired, since wages accounted for a third of all the airline's costs. They were also very much the only ones management could control. Reducing the next-largest outgoing cost – fuel – meant flying less, which had not always been a sound strategy. Reducing aircraft numbers meant ceding vital routes and market share to rivals.

During his time at Aer Lingus and at Jetstar, Joyce learned to have a cost focus 'because you don't know what's going to hit you next in the aviation industry', he says, and because the pressure on margins is ever-present. Hence one of Joyce's mantras: 'Cost is certain, revenue isn't.'

Joyce expressed another common refrain to an interviewer in December 2011.

'Many people criticise your strategy,' the interviewer began, 'saying you've gone down the cost-cutting route when you should be going the revenue-building route – what do you say?'

'Well, I think you have to chew gum and walk at the same time,' Joyce replied. 'I don't think you can pick one of those strategies, and say that they're unique. We have never done that. We think that you have to be efficient. If you've got a 25 per cent cost disadvantage against Singapore Airlines and Emirates . . . you've got a problem. You have to get your service levels right to be able to compete against them [and] at the same time getting the cost down. You have to do both. If Qantas doesn't focus on both, it's not going to be a business that survives.'[8]

Following the Fair Work Australia decision, Qantas started on the comeback trail. The termination of industrial action brought greater operational certainty, and by late November 2011 bookings had recovered well, particularly in the domestic market. Qantas's on-time performance was the best of any major domestic airline in December, allowing it to retain crucial major corporate accounts, as well as winning back some business. Its brand and customer satisfaction ratings – by now a key measure of the brand's performance – had improved significantly.

On 19 December, Qantas and the ALAEA reached a three-year draft agreement, which was submitted to Fair Work Australia for authorisation. It covered a 3 per cent per annum pay increase, new licensing arrangements, changes that eased restrictions on extended-hours rosters and arrangements for the transition to retirement for licensed engineers – which gave the airline most of what it had wanted at the outset. The agreement was endorsed by Fair Work Australia just over a month later.

Most importantly, for Joyce, the ALAEA dropped its demands for stronger job security clauses, and its insistence that maintenance on Qantas's A380s be performed in Australia. Other clauses designed to prevent the airline from establishing a new airline in Kuala Lumpur or Singapore were also dropped, although that option was never ultimately exercised when new opportunities emerged.

Things were taking longer with the TWU. Tony Sheldon kept up his attacks on Joyce, labelling him a 'disaster' for Qantas. 'He's overseen the destruction of thousands of Australian jobs and outsourced work to Asia,' he said.[9] It wasn't until well into the following year that matters with the TWU were finally resolved. In early August 2012, Fair Work Australia, using its arbitration powers, ruled that Qantas was entitled to run its business free from TWU control.

The outcome provided a pay rise for 3800 baggage handlers, airport ground staff, catering, freight and other transport employees, and precluded the TWU from taking industrial action for at least the next two years. It was the first time since enterprise bargaining had begun almost twenty years previously that Qantas was forced into arbitration to resolve a pay dispute.

Resolving the pilots' claims took even longer. Finally, in January 2013, the Fair Work Commission (as Fair Work Australia had been renamed) completed the arbitration case with the AIPA, again endorsing Qantas's right to manage its business. The union was unsuccessful in its original claim that Qantas terms and conditions would in effect apply to other Qantas Group entities, including Jetstar. Qantas achieved a number of productivity improvements and flexibilities; the pilots received pay rises.

Joyce's desire for control over decision-making and strategy had been restored. As one analyst put it, exaggerating only a little, the dispute was never about the numbers, but about issues of management control. Reducing costs and keeping them down was essential, but caving in to job security and offshore hiring demands would have had long-term management impacts, which would also have had cost implications.

As the hugely turbulent 2011 drew to a close, serious cracks had appeared in Joyce's controversial plans for RedQ, the premium start-up in Asia. He had originally looked at both Singapore and Kuala Lumpur as potential hubs, but the latter was now the focus, yet it was a much inferior location. What's more, Qantas was no longer considering the capital-intensive option of deploying its own aircraft, and was now considering using Malaysia Airlines aircraft instead.

Joyce told an investor day, held to inform the investment community, that Qantas wanted to position itself within South-East Asia ahead of expected liberalisation of access in the region.

'We want to capture those premium customers who have been frustrated with our lack of frequencies,' he said. 'In five years, we plan to have a hub in the world's fastest-growing aviation region, feeding traffic into both our Qantas and Jetstar networks. This is how we will end the disadvantage of being an end-of-the-line carrier.'[10]

For now, Qantas was staring down the barrel of being only a 'niche' operator – but in the turbulent and never boring airline business, there was to be another vital development. Together with the respite on the industrial front, it would be an enormous step towards turning around Qantas's international business. Joyce had explored a British Airways merger and a South-East Asian hub; he wasn't about to stop trying to escape the niche role.

Behind the scenes, the prospect was emerging of a solution so revolutionary that few, even in the Qantas boardroom or executive team, could have imagined it.

11

Escaping the Niche

Through 2012, Qantas's international business continued to haemorrhage money. Its domestic troubles were intensifying too, as Virgin scrambled to take a larger toehold in the market, supported by its strong foreign airline equity partners.

In Europe, Willie Walsh had devised an innovative formula to allow British Airways to merge with the Spanish flag carrier, Iberia. Encouraged by this success, Walsh again opened the door to a merger with Qantas, telling the *Financial Times* he 'could look again' at the Australian airline.[1] But the shortcomings of a BA deal remained, and it offered the same Europe product that was always going to be inferior when competing with the Gulf carriers.

Meanwhile, RedQ had been scuttled. In March 2012, Joyce said the project had been dropped after failing to strike a deal with Malaysia Airlines. Malaysian was having its own financial crisis, racking up US$780 million in losses the previous year, and was unwilling to take on more risk. In reality, RedQ was never going to be a viable entity for Qantas once discussions shifted from the premium Singapore hub to second-tier Kuala Lumpur, especially with no Qantas aircraft being flown.

For Qantas, it seemed to be one step forward and two steps back in the tough international market. The ideas were good but the reality wasn't. But better news was on the horizon. At Virgin Australia, John Borghetti had made a move two years prior that opened the door to a game-changing outcome for Qantas.

The Qantas codesharing agreement with Etihad deteriorated after Borghetti's departure. There was no chemistry between Joyce and Etihad CEO James Hogan. At that time, Qantas's plans for the Gulf, if any, involved using Jetstar, which was never a suitable partner for Etihad anyway.

Shortly after taking up the CEO role at Virgin in 2010, Borghetti received a call from Hogan. Did he want to talk about a commercial tie-up? Borghetti did. A week later, the two, along with their executive teams, met in Singapore and did the deal 'in a matter of hours'.[2]

In February 2012, and almost two years into his capital-intensive transformation of Virgin, Borghetti made a structural adjustment to address the airline's capital limitations. A reorganisation left its Australian and international arms under discrete ownership, freeing the domestic arm to attract foreign capital. The international arm remained majority Australian-owned to comply with international rules, but the domestic arm could be up to 100 per cent foreign-owned. Borghetti had invested in new fit-outs for the aircraft and in lounges that would attract business travellers, putting the airline in a position to aggressively target corporate accounts.

James Hogan was in town the following month, fresh from snapping up equity stakes in Air Berlin and Air Seychelles, to address the National Aviation Press Club in Sydney. He announced that Etihad was continuing to look for more 'low-risk, high-return equity partners', adding: 'We think there could be one or two more deals we can do ... in America, Europe, in India or even here in Australia.' He also lauded Borghetti for his 'outstanding' work in repositioning the Virgin brand and product.

Hogan and Borghetti saw eye to eye, and Etihad had bottomless pockets. Based in the UAE's capital, Abu Dhabi, Etihad had been set up to mirror the airline industry success of neighbouring emirate Dubai, an hour's drive at speed down the straight fourteen-lane Sheikh Zayed Road. Unlike Dubai, which had no natural assets, Abu Dhabi sat on one-sixth of the world's oil resources.

During May 2012, Etihad quietly acquired a 3.96 per cent stake in Virgin Australia for $35.6 million via market purchases, joining Air New Zealand on the share roster (the Kiwi carrier owned a 19.9 per cent stake). For Virgin, having a solid partner like Etihad brought with it both financial stability and a stairway to an instant European network.

Hogan told Reuters: 'At a point in time, we would like to take the stake to a minimum of 10%, if we get the necessary approvals.' He added that Etihad would play a long game, and this was 'just step by step building'.[3]

Etihad's investment was a wake-up call for Joyce. His immediate response was to start lobbying Canberra to prevent Etihad from raising its investment in Virgin.

From his nearly four decades at Qantas, Borghetti knew its strengths and weaknesses, its valuable assets and how they could be used. Progressively, he now looked to encircle Qantas on each front, international, domestic and regional, and to capture a share of the corporate market. Internationally, Borghetti had moved remarkably quickly to establish a virtual route network covering most of the world: with Etihad through Abu Dhabi to Europe and Africa; with Singapore Airlines through Singapore to Asia, Europe and beyond; and codesharing with Delta through its network in the United States and (in combination with Air New Zealand) across the Tasman, and domestically in the latter country. This near-global coverage was vital for customer connectivity and for growing Virgin's frequent-flyer program.

But another party had been miffed at not being made aware until the last minute what was in the wind between Virgin and Etihad. In 2006, Virgin Blue (as it then was) had sealed a code-share agreement with Emirates, giving it entry to the Australian domestic market. When he took over, Borghetti saw this as an

unequal partnership in which Emirates gained most of the value –
and anyway, Emirates was not in the business of making equity
investments. CEO Tim Clark had previously been burned by
a troubled investment venture in Sri Lanka's national airline,
selling Emirates' shareholding at a loss in 2010.

With the Etihad investment in Virgin, Emirates' Australian
traffic 'feed' was suddenly endangered, and it was without a partner in its most valuable single market. And there was no way it
would be part of a three-way tie-up if it involved Etihad.

Now, both Qantas and Emirates had a neat reciprocal problem. Qantas wanted a profitable means of servicing the Europe
market, while Emirates needed better access behind its Australian
gateway entry ports.

'Frankfurt was losing $70 million a year,' Joyce recalls. 'And
then we pulled Paris because it was only three a week but it was
losing $30 million a year. They were taking up a huge amount of
aircraft and we just couldn't make it work. We knew we needed
London, but with the BA arrangement it wasn't working as effectively as before.'

What he needed was someone to build the bridge.

Joyce and other members of his senior team had spent the
better part of the previous three years mounting an aggressive
onslaught against Emirates, as it encroached ever further into
Qantas's territory. Occasionally the language bordered on hys-
terical abuse; one Qantas executive was accused of suggesting
Emirates' lower costs relied on slave labour.

The lack of any market protection from Canberra meant the
public rhetoric would have to continue, to try to influence public opinion, but Joyce could already see that battle was effectively
lost. Emirates would continue to threaten the existence of Qantas
as a serious international player. The other large Gulf carrier,
Etihad, was chewing away at Qantas's other leg, by supporting
Virgin in the domestic market.

*

If Barry Brown is known at all to the Australian public, it is as the shiny head who for several years presented the Emirates Melbourne Cup at Flemington Racecourse on the first Tuesday in November, after making a suitably short speech. That was one of his less demanding roles as Emirates' go-to man in Australia and New Zealand.

Brown had been part of the country's airline establishment for decades, starting out representing the private French airline UTA in Australia, with – inevitably – a spell at Qantas, along with others in various countries. So, by 2011, he had frequently bumped into his Qantas counterpart, the personable commercial executive Rob Gurney. Without the knowledge of his boss, Brown had phoned Gurney one autumn afternoon to suggest they catch up for a drink at Sydney's Sofitel Hotel on Phillip Street. Formerly the Wentworth, this was Sydney's first five-star hotel, built by Qantas in 1966 to provide suitable quarters for its interstate and overseas visitors. Both men enjoy white wine, and although Brown prefers sauvignon blanc to Gurney's chardonnay, it seemed there was room for compromise.

After securing Gurney's agreement to complete confidentiality, Brown soon came to the point. How would Qantas feel about a partnership? After a gulp, Gurney took the suggestion back to his boss.

For Joyce, it was time to grasp the nettle. As he describes it, the relationship quickly blossomed. 'There was an interest from both sides, and it was fascinating because I didn't know Tim [Emirates CEO Sir Tim Clark] at all well at the time. I'd probably seen him in the news a bit. Maybe met him at an IATA conference, but didn't know him.'

The pair were very different people. Clark was already an industry legend, while Joyce was a young CEO of just four years' standing as the head of Qantas, with an undistinguished record and with a propensity for making rude remarks about Emirates. But they did have some things in common, and they got on well personally. Both had started their airline careers in the network planning area and were deeply passionate about aviation. Both were battle-hardened, and Joyce had shown he was capable of making big calls when the chips were down.

Their commercial DNA, too, was very similar, says Gurney. 'Network planners really think about how to create a competitive advantage through a new network offering, and what you can bring that others can't,' he observes. For both airlines, the network advantages were significant. But the chemistry needed to work.

'Tim could recount the Emirates network. He actually had it in his head, he was that immersed in it,' says Gurney. 'And Alan was not dissimilar in that sense.' (Gurney would soon after leave Qantas for a stint as CEO of Helloworld, the former Jetset Travelworld Group, and Emirates would later appoint him as its regional head, based in Australia.)

Clark and Joyce genuinely connected, says Olivia Wirth. 'Perhaps on paper they were an odd couple, but when you understand what they're deeply passionate about, they are actually surprisingly similar in that regard,' she agrees.

Joyce created a top-secret internal strategy team to analyse the risks and benefits of a partnership, and to examine the options. Qantas was hardly in a strong negotiating position, having publicly and loudly broadcast the harm being done to it by Emirates for years, all the way back to Geoff Dixon's days as CEO.

Those were still real concerns, and they would linger for a long time, fed by doubters who believed Qantas would be giving Emirates the keys to the bullion room. There were understandable fears too, from the operations teams, that Qantas would cut back substantially on flying its own metal, simply becoming a virtual airline to the west – much like Virgin, which only operated a handful of weekly services westbound to Abu Dhabi. But that belied the critical position the Australian flag carrier was in, and how limited its other options were – if it had any at all. It also downplayed the potential upside of the substantial network expansion a partnership would deliver Qantas.

After some preliminary discussions between the respective executive teams, Clark and Joyce agreed to a weekend retreat in May 2012. Each CEO brought five executives to the Wolgan Valley resort in the Blue Mountains, the luxury resort Emirates had built in 2009. It was a favourite of Clark's, created to develop the airline's exclusive image. The resort's 1830s-era homestead had once been visited by Charles Darwin; for this reason, the Emirates discussion was dubbed 'Project Darwin'.

'What Tim did was superb,' Joyce recalls. 'He said, "We're not going to talk about business, we're just going to get our teams to know each other. If the chemistry works, we'll know it's a goer. If the chemistry doesn't, we just shake hands and wish each other all the best."'

To their alarm, they discovered that there was a travel agents' gathering that weekend at Wolgan Valley, but although Joyce was surely recognisable to many of them, fortunately none seemed to know Clark or discern the meeting's significance, so the secret didn't leak out.

'We spent the days just having a few drinks, having meals, chatting,' says Joyce. 'There's an outdoor fire area. Tim has his cigar and we're sitting out in the bloody cold at the very end of it and he said, "I think the chemistry works, your team's great." And I said, "I think it works as well."'

Olivia Wirth agrees. 'The personal relationships really drove the business outcome,' she recalls. 'It was really about us sitting across the table, determining if we could genuinely work together. Because there was no point signing a contract if we couldn't execute it.'

The Qantas leadership team had many debates around this. Emirates had not been in partnership with anyone else, whereas partnerships were deeply embedded in the Qantas corporate psyche. 'Firstly, we had to work with Jetstar and Qantas internally, let alone the partnerships we'd forged since day one with other international players,' says Wirth. 'We have lots of experience, lots of scars and lots of wins in the partnership space. It was absolutely fundamental that we could say honestly that we could get along culturally.

'At the heart of it, the real questions were, "Is it a *true* partnership? Will there be give and take on both sides? Are they going to be prepared to compromise?" Because that's what you have to do in a partnership. So there was a real question around whether they could actually execute on a partnership. There had to be trust.'

While the talks were proceeding, Qantas's fortunes were receding. By early June 2012, the share price stood at record lows, slumping below the crucial $1 level; over $1 billion in market value had been wiped off in less than a week. Qantas had just issued guidance for a $400 million loss in its international division.

Joyce was unfazed. The day after a 19 per cent rout on the stock market, he said: 'I would not trade this job for any other job in the world.' The *Australian Financial Review*'s 'Rear Window' column quipped, rather pointedly: 'Really? What about the CEO of Guinness? It's a great drop and, Alan should know, Dublin's a great town.'[4]

But Joyce was en route to Beijing, to chair the IATA's management board at the association's annual general meeting. It would prove a busy but pivotal time for Joyce – and Qantas. Following the meeting, Joyce and Clark stayed on for a full day to thrash out details of the agreement. Once they had agreed to go ahead, they set a deadline of 6 September to seal a deal – a tight target, but doable.

On the sidelines of the IATA annual general meeting, *Sydney Morning Herald* journalist Matt O'Sullivan unearthed some gems. He spoke to Tim Clark, who, rather than denying the whole deal, categorically ruled out taking a cornerstone stake in Qantas, but added that any potential tie-up would be limited to a codeshare deal at most. 'We are looking at all sorts of things and possibly we will engage with Qantas at some point to talk about a codeshare,' he said, adding: 'We are running a whole load of negotiations and looking at other ways of expanding our operations but no equity, no establishment of foreign hubs.'[5]

Joyce and Clark met again in Dubai a few weeks later, and subsequently had multiple weekly calls. Meanwhile, Joyce let his old mate Willie Walsh know that Qantas's on-again, off-again romance with British Airways was over. Qantas had a new pal, and one likely to solve many problems.

On 26 July 2012, seven weeks after the IATA meeting in Beijing, the *Australian Financial Review* broke the story that Qantas was discussing a comprehensive tie-up with the world's largest international airline, Emirates. The report said Qantas was edging closer to a 'transformational alliance' with the Dubai-owned carrier, and speculated that a deal would 'almost certainly precipitate the end of Qantas's long-standing joint venture with British Airways on the Kangaroo Route to London and into Europe'.[6]

In a statement to the ASX, Qantas confirmed it was in discussions with a number of airlines about potential alliances, including Emirates. The share price bounced almost 9 per cent by the close of trade.

The news was met with shock and awe, even – perhaps especially – within Qantas. One insider said, 'It stunned a lot of people that we would tie ourselves that closely to an airline like Emirates and move the hub to the Middle East. [But] it was also exciting for people. It was like, "Wow, there's an alternative way to think about our network and our growth, to try to get International back to profitability."'

Says Olivia Wirth, with a hint of understatement: 'In some ways, given the longstanding partnership role that we play in the oneworld alliance, forming a strategic relationship with Emirates would have seemed at odds. But from our perspective, it was absolutely critical to connect us to Europe.'

PART III

WHEELS UP

*'As with everything, you have to be bold.
Incremental deals, I have always found,
are probably not the way to go.'*

—Alan Joyce

12

Seismic Events

In August 2012, just eight months after the grounding, Qantas unveiled a 2012 financial year underlying profit before tax of $95 million, aided by the strength of three of the Qantas Group's four businesses (Jetstar, domestic and the frequent-flyer program). The net result was dragged down by almost $400 million in one-off costs as the Group implemented its five-year international transformation plan 'and addressed its legacy cost base', resulting in a net loss of $244 million.

But that was now in the rear-view mirror. The future was opening up. Joyce was emboldened by the positive trajectory with Emirates and by his October 2011 grounding decision – the latter reflected in customer data, which he closely monitored. It showed the CEO that customer loyalty to the premium Qantas brand had returned to historically strong levels.

'The brand is as healthy as it's ever been,' Joyce told 7.30's Leigh Sales in late August 2012. 'It's actually recovered better from the industrial action this year than it did in 2008' – when industrial action by the ALAEA had caused mass cancellations and delays to passengers, costing the airline over $130 million. Joyce was also buoyed by the response of corporate Australia to the grounding. The carrier at that stage enjoyed an 88 per cent share of the corporate market, and had enjoyed 'massive' retention rates of existing corporate business. 'Over 177 corporate accounts renewed and we have forty-eight new corporate accounts signed up, nine of which came back from the competition and we lost three,' said Joyce.

In a dig at his old sparring partner Borghetti, he added: 'They tried the competition, didn't like it, wasn't the right product, wasn't the right network and have come back to Qantas. We've been very competitive in price, because the capacity has been added, but we don't undercut our competition in terms of what we're offering for the premium traffic.'

Being 'very competitive in price' meant unheard-of discounts for corporates. Qantas was paying a high price to keep its company accounts, but keeping them was much easier than winning them back once they were lost to the opposition.

After lobbying vigorously against the Gulf carriers' growing access to Australia and the threat to national pride, the deal with Emirates was done. It had only taken a 180-degree turnabout. On 6 September 2012, Qantas and Emirates announced their new global aviation partnership, under which Qantas moved its hub for European flights to Dubai and the airlines entered an extensive commercial relationship, slated to commence in April 2013.

Qantas and Emirates each flew an A380 aircraft side-by-side over Sydney Harbour to mark the agreement, with the flights codenamed 'Seismic 1' and 'Seismic 2'.

The challenge now was getting the deal approved by the federal government. It had only been a year since the shutdown, which had stranded many senior politicians and government officials in Perth. 'We were meeting with [Prime Minister] Gillard's chief of staff, Ben Hubbard, for long periods of time, trying to get them comfortable,' says Wirth. 'And the ACCC – that was a process in itself as well.'

The ten-year partnership included integration of networks, with coordinated pricing, sales and scheduling, as well as a benefit-sharing model. It stopped short of either airline taking equity in the other, but the deal offered so much more than Qantas's dalliances with British Airways.

The ACCC gave its interim approval in December 2012, and this was swiftly followed by a statement from federal tourism minister Martin Ferguson lauding the competition authority's decision. Ferguson said the tourism industry would benefit from the stability the alliance gave Qantas and would help create air links vital to attracting long-haul passengers.

Final approval to the partnership came from the ACCC on 26 March 2013, just days before the first Qantas flight was due to transit through Dubai. The deal was sanctioned for an initial five years, which was later extended to the full term. Under the partnership, Qantas launched daily A380 services from both Sydney and Melbourne to London via Dubai, meaning that, together, Emirates and Qantas would offer ninety-eight services between Australia and Dubai each week.

Joyce described the partnership with Emirates as the most significant in Qantas's history and a partnership of equals. It was 'an integrated commercial arrangement that will give our customers a global network, world class travel experiences and extensive frequent flyer benefits'.[1]

Some commentators, and no doubt a few Qantas managers, were concerned that Emirates would gain too much access to Qantas's frequent flyers, and would plunder the membership for its own benefit.

'I never really saw it that way,' says Rob Gurney. 'We felt that Emirates had a very good product and our customers were flying with them anyway. What Emirates would've struggled with was seriously penetrating the large, managed Australian corporate travel accounts in a big way. They would've had some business from them, but Qantas was very strong in that area. That was probably the big opportunity for Emirates, to gain access to that market in a way where it wasn't forced, as a partner of Qantas . . . It added a completely different dimension to it for them.'

Most importantly, the deal revitalised Qantas International on the fiercely competitive Kangaroo Route, allowing Qantas to offer one-stop access from Australia to more than seventy destinations in Europe, the Middle East and Africa. Equally, it allowed Qantas the breathing room to recalibrate its Asian network to cater better for its business travellers.

In the space of less than a year, Joyce had made what would be two of his most influential decisions in reshaping Qantas's future. In one move, Qantas had gained access to effectively all the routes beyond Dubai that Emirates operated, where previously it had whittled back its European network to London and Frankfurt. Ten years earlier, Qantas had run one-third of its international capacity to Europe, one-third to Asia and one-third essentially to the Americas. By the time of the Emirates deal, capacity to Europe was less than 8 per cent of the network, over 50 per cent went into Asia, and the remainder to the rest of the world, dominated by the United States.

For Emirates' customers, the deal opened up Qantas's Australian domestic network of more than fifty destinations and 5000 weekly flights. The carriers also agreed to coordinate their services between Australia and New Zealand, and between Australia and South-East Asia. The Emirates and Qantas frequent-flyer programs would be aligned, expanding the opportunities for customers to earn and redeem points.

Joyce said – without a hint of irony, after years of working so hard to block the airline – 'Emirates is the ideal partner for Qantas. It has a wonderful brand, a modern fleet, an uncompromising approach to quality and it flies to the A-list of international destinations. This is the most significant partnership the Qantas Group has ever formed with another airline, moving past the traditional alliance model to a new level. It will deliver benefits to all parts of the Group.'

Respect and mutual confidence were essential, Joyce continued. 'I've always made it clear we would not form any new partnership until we found the partner that was absolutely right for us, our customers and our business. Tim Clark is an aviation visionary with a meticulous eye for detail, combined with an understated management style. He commands respect, and he has made this partnership possible. Qantas alone can't take passengers everywhere – but together Qantas and Emirates can take Australians just about anywhere.'[2]

It was a strategic masterstroke, delivering on all four pillars of the international strategy that Joyce had unveiled a year prior. As part of its network recalibration, Qantas increased dedicated capacity between Australia and Singapore, having 'de-hubbed' it from the Kangaroo Route. Now flights to Singapore and Hong Kong were rescheduled to enable more same-day connections across Asia. Qantas also withdrew from the Singapore–Frankfurt route, its last remaining European service.

The Emirates deal sounded the death knell for Qantas's joint business agreement with British Airways, which had been active since 1995. Willie Walsh said the agreement ended on amicable terms, adding that 'the world has changed'.

According to Leigh Clifford, when Qantas first decided in late 2008 that the merger with British Airways was not going to work, 'we said, "Well, what are the options for us to fix this international business?" Out of that came the Emirates deal, and frankly, that was fantastic.'

Rerouting can take time, even for network planners, and there were some wrinkles. Getting together with Emirates called into question the value of the branded global airline alliances, including oneworld – but all that could be worked out later. The biggest threat to Qantas's international operations had been solved. It now had a better network than ever and, quietly and without fuss, had dodged losing hundreds of millions of dollars annually. Even the international pilots were more or less satisfied, after a while.

A massive piece of the long-term sustainability puzzle had been set in place.

The blockbuster deal between Qantas and Emirates was a poke in the eye for Virgin. Minutes after Joyce's press conference with Sir Tim Clark ended, Virgin reportedly fired off an angry email to Dubai, cancelling a reciprocal staff travel agreement.

The *Australian Financial Review* wise-cracked: 'Clark surely would have been tempted to axe John Borghetti from the Christmas card list in response, 'cept Santa doesn't stop in the United Arab Emirates. It's too bloody hot for reindeer.'[3]

In September, almost simultaneously with the Emirates announcement, Etihad increased its stake in Virgin to 10 per cent. A month later, Singapore Airlines bought an initial 10 per cent stake for $105 million. There was never a dull moment.

John Borghetti also raised the stakes. In October, Virgin announced plans to buy a 60 per cent controlling holding in Tiger Airways for $35 million, to mirror Qantas's budget market strategy with Jetstar. As Virgin's unit costs had risen, it was losing touch with the low end of the market.

Virgin also sought 100 per cent control of regional airline Skywest for $47 million so it might attack the lucrative West Australian regional routes, which Qantas had all but monopolised following Ansett's demise. The Singapore-listed Skywest provided lucrative fly-in, fly-out services for the mining sector.

Joyce knew that there would be a time lag before these investments returned any benefits, so Qantas moved aggressively to maintain its near 90 per cent hold on the corporate market, reportedly being willing to reduce prices – in some cases by as much as 40 to 50 per cent – to persuade clients not to move to Virgin.

Partnering with Emirates meant some new network opportunities were available to Qantas internationally, which made the corporate product even more attractive. With the Emirates partnership signed, the way ahead looked a lot smoother.

Virgin was, step by step, turning up the heat, but there were two magic ingredients of Qantas's offering that were hard to compete with.

One was the allure of the Chairman's Lounge. The pulling power of this cannot be overstated for corporate contracts. Established by Qantas in the late 1970s, this exclusive club is priceless for those doing business as they travel and make contacts for their next role. It is also handy for upgrades when a customer travels privately. Chairman's Lounge members receive a black membership card but pay no annual fee. Entry to the club is via unmarked doors and members are greeted by name, with personal reminders when their flight is leaving. Once inside, they enjoy high-end furnishings, five-star shower suites and top-shelf food and liquor, as well as the cocooning effect of complete separation from the masses. No thongs or boardshorts in here.

Members of the federal parliament and other politicians are gifted with membership. Outside that, invitations are understood to be based on flight expenditure over celebrity. Many chief executives are members, but not all. It's well known as a key incentive in any corporate travel contract. If a company drops Qantas for the opposition, the CEO soon finds that his or her black card has stopped working. One corporate travel buyer for a very large Australian company said he would save millions if they could switch to Virgin, but his chairman insisted it was vital for the company that he maintained his access to the Chairman's Lounge. It's unlikely to be an isolated tale in the corporate world.

There's no public record of how many members there are in total, or of who selects them and for how long membership is valid. But what is clear is that the Chairman's Lounge is an enormous drawcard – and the Qantas CEO has a lot to do with the membership decisions. At Virgin, John Borghetti tried hard to imitate it, without much success.

The other great drawcard for Qantas is its massive frequent-flyer program, which attacts leisure travellers as well as corporates. The larger Qantas network and the higher frequencies of its flights helped keep many business customers in the fold, while the Chairman's Lounge was a huge barrier to leaving. All in all, Qantas was a formidable proposition.

Despite this, Borghetti was making inroads. The large investment in Virgin by Etihad and Singapore Airlines, with a leaner Air New Zealand also on the share register, now seemed likely to provide a funding buffer that would make Virgin a continuing challenger.

A capacity and fare war seemed inevitable.

13

Line in the Sand

The confrontation over the premium market had been brewing ever since Borghetti left Qantas to seek other pastures. In retrospect, it was almost inevitable that he would move to Virgin, as the former LCC looked to attack Qantas in the higher-yield market segments – grist to Borghetti's mill.

Joyce and Borghetti had much in common. Both came from less than privileged backgrounds and had to get where they were by relying on their own resources. Each had a strong sense of responsibility, coupled with a belief that they had what it took as a leader – although in Borghetti's case, the latter came more gradually.

Arriving from Italy at the age of seven with his parents, Borghetti worked three jobs from a young age – and even after he started work in the Qantas Empire Airways mailroom at the age of seventeen, thanks to a friend of his father's who was a Qantas employee. Borghetti was highly conscientious. At sixteen, he'd run his father's restaurant while Dad went back to Italy for a holiday. School was an ordeal for the young man, as a migrant in a tough suburb in Melbourne, and he couldn't wait to escape and get to work. Maths was his least favourite class.

Joyce too, as the oldest of four brothers from a working-class home in Dublin, felt the weight of responsibility when money was tight, which was most of the time. And although he followed an academic path, it was his instinctive skills, born of a tough upbringing, that often carried him through in his business career.

At Qantas, each man had plenty of opportunity to see how the other worked, as they bumped up against each other as Joyce's Jetstar began to intrude on Borghetti's premium-brand network. For Borghetti, the low-cost brand was a threat to yields. Having Jetstar aircraft flying in the domestic network, the LCC threatened his patch, but he was shrewd enough to realise that at least a little cannibalisation was needed.

For four years the dual-brand strategy continued – first domestically, as Jetstar grew rapidly, and then internationally (and mostly successfully) at a time when the premium brand was suffering. Joyce was receiving the plaudits and expanding, while Borghetti was often fighting a rearguard action to protect the international brand from attack.

When Geoff Dixon announced his departure from Qantas, Borghetti felt he was the CEO's preferred candidate. Although he put on a brave face when the baby-faced Irishman was chosen over him, he'd very much wanted to lead Australia's national icon. It would have been the ultimate feather in the cap for an industrious and diligent executive in a career spanning more than three decades.

Despite losing the Qantas race, Borghetti knew he had more to contribute. 'I'm certainly not going into retirement,' he told the *Australian Financial Review* at the time. 'My ambition is to remain in executive life and I am in a position where I could contribute to a CEO role.'[1]

After several years of competitive tension at Qantas, then, there was plenty of history between Joyce and Borghetti when the latter began leading Virgin Blue in 2010. It was the older man's chance to show that the Qantas board's decision had been wrong. He was fired up, with an ambitious new airline at his disposal.

Joyce, meanwhile, had been undergoing his baptism by fire, confronting restive unions and taking difficult decisions as the international market became ever more challenging. The Qantas share price was in the doldrums and sinking steadily, with no signs of improvement.

A brutal capacity and fare war was about to erupt in the domestic market, one that would persist for three years. It was to prove devastating for Virgin, and would provoke a fundamental review by Joyce of what Qantas needed to do to establish a firm basis for the future.

The origins of the battle stretched all the way back to the start of the century, when Virgin Blue burst onto the scene in 2000.

After the collapse of Ansett in 2001, Virgin founder Sir Richard Branson made several bold claims about his upstart Aussie carrier. One was that it could ultimately secure a 50 per cent share of the domestic market. For a small airline with only a handful of aircraft, that seemed like typical Branson bluster, yet within four years the LCC, with its much lower cost base, had a fleet of over forty planes. A 50 per cent share was well in sight.

But Virgin's rise provoked a response from the incumbent. Two years later, Geoff Dixon outlined for the first time his 65 per cent 'line in the sand' market-share target – a veiled threat to the new entrant not to menace Qantas's position. That percentage was also the tipping point at which, according to some marketing and sales theories, returns became disproportionately larger.

As a reference point, in the much larger US market there are four airlines – American Airlines, United Airlines, Delta and Southwest – that together control a 65 per cent market share. Qantas's market dominance in its internal market is unusually high. In other substantial domestic markets, only a tiny few, including Turkish Airlines and Lufthansa, enjoy a larger market share.

When Qantas launched Jetstar in 2004, aiming to squeeze the new competitor in a pincer movement, Virgin's meteoric growth was stopped in its tracks within the year.

Andrew David was Virgin Blue's chief operating officer at the time. He confirms that Virgin genuinely held aspirations to grow to 50 per cent of the market. 'We had such a low cost base, and clearly there was a market here for an LCC,' he says. 'We had grown to forty-plus aircraft in about three years . . . [and] we would have got [to a 50 per cent share] if it wasn't for Alan and Jetstar.'

Virgin Blue, under its founding CEO, Brett Godfrey, was forced to look around for new ways to expand profitably.

'I watched Brett react to Jetstar and the light bulbs went on,' David continues. 'He said, "We've got to rethink this business." To Brett's credit, he worked out that SME [small to medium-sized enterprises] was a good hunting ground, and if we could improve the service levels and add some product, like the lounges, then we were a viable alternative.'

The Jetstar response had been so successful that Virgin had been forced to look for new sources of customers. So long as it remained a no-frills airline, it had little chance of picking up valuable business travellers, who paid higher fares and flew more frequently. In 2005, Godfrey recast Virgin as a self-styled 'New World Carrier'.

With generous incentives from the Queensland government, Virgin Blue had established its headquarters in Brisbane. To help ensure its viability, the state government had committed that its government members and bureaucrats would fly Virgin. Not all of the elected representatives were keen; there were no Qantas frequent-flyer points, the lounges weren't swish like Qantas's, and there was no business class. And they now had no chance to rub shoulders with the other great minds in the Chairman's Lounge.

One Queensland state politician excused himself from flying Virgin by arguing that there was not enough room for him to open his laptop, in the one-size-fits-all seating configuration, preventing him from working. A Virgin executive quietly noted that, even if he did manage to open it, he wouldn't know how to turn it on.

But the protest vividly illustrated that Virgin had a problem and needed to change. The refreshed 'New World Carrier' would allow customers to enjoy low prices but would also compete for premium passengers, offering the frills needed to lure business travellers and corporate accounts. It's a dangerous tactic for a low-cost airline, adding costs in search of higher yields. For one thing, the costs had to go up before the fares could, but it also risked sending mixed messages to Virgin staff and the public. Was it no longer the low-fares airline?

The move also involved ceding a large proportion of the low-priced end of the market to Jetstar, although there was little choice in that regard. Even if Jetstar's costs were no lower, the group airline was in a position to lean on its big brother, getting better deals on its purchases like fuel where Qantas had more market clout.

Virgin Blue was now a substantial force with over fifty 737s, and it was morphing *Matrix*-like to reappear in new competitive forms. In early 2007, such was the profile shift as Tiger Airways entered the domestic market that Godfrey had even publicly floated, and then rejected, the idea of an ultra-low-cost subsidiary.

Virgin was adding frills and promoting them loudly. 'We're now more of a traditional airline in many respects,' Godfrey told Bloomberg at the airline's results announcement in September 2007, although it was still a work in progress. But the subtle moves were having an impact. Thanks to the new direction, average yield for the year was up 9 per cent, and profit had nearly doubled.

Godfrey announced plans to commence long-haul international flights on the lucrative US route in late 2008, using seven widebody 777s the airline had ordered. This was a massive pragmatic shift, but Godfrey was targeting the cherry in Qantas's international network. On US routes, Qantas was able to charge 40 per cent higher prices per kilometre, compared with the more competitive European routes. Jetstar had severely wounded Virgin Blue, but Godfrey was showing just how versatile Virgin could be.

The timing seemed just right for Borghetti, with his deep understanding of the business and corporate markets, to drive the New World Carrier into its next era of higher yields.

Adapting to change incrementally has its dangers. But taking big steps can also be hazardous. The risk with incrementalism is that, in bringing every stakeholder along with you on each step of the way, you may never adapt fast enough to meet the external threats. Yet the crash-through-or-crash approach can be catastrophic. Over the years, Joyce would attempt both approaches, and a few others in between. Right now he was feeling encircled.

By 2009, competition was ramping up on every front. At the same time, there was the GFC's impact on travel demand. The only slightly good news was that almost everyone else was feeling the pain too.

No one had seen the GFC coming. For most parts of the world, it was preceded by a time of economic and political stability. China was growing fast and becoming a massive market for Australia's exports. The financial masters of the universe had things so well under control that the conventional wisdom was that Millennials and the new Generation Z would never experience an economic downturn. Little did anyone know that the masters had been laying a minefield. When things blew up, the airline business was hit hard, and long. The next few years were not the ideal time for a fare war, even if Australia's domestic economy had held up better than most.

Borghetti's appointment as Virgin CEO in March 2010 sent shockwaves through Qantas, who reportedly fired the responsible executive search firm, Heidrick & Struggles, from further work at the flag carrier. At the same time, an anonymous executive spoke to the *Australian Financial Review* to lament a complete 'brain drain' at Qantas; another recently departed executive said the place was 'run by consultants now'.[2]

Over at Virgin, however, things were not so rosy either. At the start of May 2010, just before Godfrey retired, the airline had advised the ASX it was expecting to post a pre-tax profit of $80 million; but by the end of that month, after Borghetti had taken a look at the figures on commencing as CEO, Virgin issued a profit warning, declaring the figure could be as low as $20 million.

Shortly before the move was confirmed, amid media speculation that Borghetti was going to take the Virgin role, Joyce was asked by one of his executives what he thought. He replied, 'Well, I hope that he gets it because we know exactly what he's going to do. Load it up with cost and product and basically make it an easy target.'

Borghetti's commencement at Virgin prompted more high-profile executive departures from Qantas as he set about building his team. Jane McKeon, the head of government and international relations, left Qantas in June 2010 before joining Virgin Blue, as did Qantas's head of domestic pricing and yield, Will Owens.

Joyce saw Virgin's move to the centre as high-risk. 'The middle-of-the-road strategy is not a great strategy,' he had said to an aviation conference in July 2010. 'You could end up as roadkill,' he added provocatively, noting it would be very hard for Virgin to penetrate the corporate market.[3]

The differences in views of the marketplace were striking. Shortly after leaving Qantas, Borghetti had said, with a mild dig at Joyce, 'I don't believe that aviation is all about costs. Yes, costs are important but it is really a margin game. It means the revenue line is equally important. The premium you can get on the revenue line is just as important as getting your costs down.'[4]

As the incoming CEO, he told Virgin's annual general meeting in November 2010 that the corporate market was controlled by a single player with a higher cost base, and which was ripe for competition. Jetstar could compete with Virgin Blue for the cheap end of the market but, he argued, Qantas's costs were too high to compete with Virgin when it came to the higher-fare traffic. But, he said, his airline would need more business-friendly flight timings and a broader network.

When Godfrey had conceived the New World model, he planned to offer a premium economy product, not the much more costly business class. Borghetti, who had long been familiar with (and largely responsible for) Qantas's premium product, believed he could make the full product work.

He had some distractions, though. In January 2011, Air New Zealand launched a surprise raid on Virgin stock, initially buying up a 14.9 per cent stake to gain more influence over the strategy and alliance moves of Australia's second airline and to provide a growth option. The equity stake accompanied a codeshare and revenue-sharing agreement.

Air New Zealand's own growth plans had been stymied because its order for the troubled 787 Dreamliner, like that of Qantas, was delayed. That put the brakes on Jetstar's international ambitions in Asia – and in Europe – and led to costly alternatives for airlines needing capacity, such as leasing or buying Airbus A330s, or delaying the retirement of older, less-efficient craft, such as Qantas's domestic fleet of older 767s.

Borghetti's decision to lease widebody A330 planes for the domestic market meant it would soon be offering a full business-class product with reclining seats, which would raise the competitive stakes with Qantas on transcontinental routes between Australia's east coast and Perth. The new planes were able to carry at least fifty more passengers than the narrow-body 737s, even with an international-style business-class section; with their two aisles, they were also a more attractive product.

A three-times-daily Sydney–Perth service commenced on 26 May 2011. For the first time since the demise of Ansett over a decade earlier, two airlines were providing business class on flights across the Nullarbor. The move coincided with Virgin Blue's rebranding as Virgin Australia, which was clearly targeted at attracting Qantas's premium customers. With an upmarket ad campaign, Virgin was no longer the upstart low-cost carrier. Borghetti felt he had the equipment to target the business community much more effectively.

Qantas responded immediately, introducing more firepower. It upped capacity on the key east-coast routes, bringing an internationally configured 747 jumbo and several A330 aircraft into service between Perth and the east coast. Virgin saw this as an overreaction. And indeed, Joyce couldn't have been accused of taking the new threat for granted. If it was reminiscent of David and Goliath, this time Goliath was taking no chances.

Borghetti later suggested he believed Qantas had underestimated Virgin's ability to take corporate market share away. He told the *AFR Weekend* magazine, 'I always knew we had a short period of time to make the changes we had to make, as we had a very good competitor, [but] what I didn't realise was that we [had] more time than I had expected, and that helped us a lot.'[5]

The dual-brand strategy had become central to the Qantas Group. It gave Qantas access to a much broader range of customers, and provided it with great flexibility in managing routes that were becoming marginal or unprofitable at the higher price point, but solidly profitable for Jetstar, with its lower cost base.

Following the global financial crisis, Joyce considered Jetstar and Qantas with a fresh strategic eye, attempting to work out how best to use the brands in tandem. Joyce knew he needed to better understand how the business and premium segments worked in the Australian market.

Joyce commissioned work from consultants Bain to figure out how the two brands should coexist, and to better understand what the post-GFC market looked like. Would business travel bounce back, or would video conferencing take away some of the high-yielding traffic? Should Qantas be investing in things like NextGen check-in? Would the product on the ground – that is, the lounges – be more important than the product in the air? And, crucially, how should Jetstar and Qantas play in the market? How do you segment customers and markets and routes in such a way that the two brands are not competing?

Jetstar had been operating for several years now, but, in a constantly changing marketplace, Joyce was consistently searching for the dynamic equilibrium, and all the time learning more about how the market worked. 'The brand premium is there over Virgin, and over Jetstar,' he recalls. 'On Melbourne–Sydney, you could get a $39 airfare with Jetstar and people will pay over $100 for the leading airfare on Qantas. There is a brand premium that's there for this amazing brand. And that brand premium domestically is such that it covers the cost base differential, because Qantas's cost base on domestic is also above [that of] Jetstar and Virgin.'

The CEO's attention to detail and constant inquisitiveness kept his team on their toes. Every time Qantas could leverage its brand in this way, the airline achieved higher margins. This was not finger-in-the-wind pricing; it became increasingly sophisticated, and lucrative. The lure of frequent-flyer and status points were an important ingredient, leading, in effect, to a 'triple-brand' strategy.

In similar fashion, Qantas bolstered capacity on major business routes to defend against Borghetti's planned move on the segment, while Jetstar added capacity on leisure routes, from which Virgin was shifting away. The resulting double-digit growth in capacity was aimed at maintaining the Qantas Group's 65 per cent profit-maximising market share.

It was no-holds-barred warfare. The public loved it, and the business community nailed down corporate deals they had never seen before.

14

Juggling with Chainsaws

As 2012 progressed, Alan Joyce must have felt a bit like a juggler, on stage, with new balls of all shapes and sizes being added, and the occasional live chainsaw thrown in. New threats and challenges emerged from all angles, morphing, mutating and generally creating an air of uncertainty that defied any rational planning.

No sooner had the union disruptions been (mostly) quelled by the fleet grounding when Virgin, with its new partners, became a more real and present threat. Joyce could handle the personally directed backlash following the grounding; he believed in his heart that he had taken the only practical course available. But there were still so many unpredictable and unmanageable challenges in the air.

The international arm of Qantas was troubling. The Asian Jetstar strategy was faltering, with battles on different fronts. The share price seemed to plumb new depths daily. Oil prices were edging north again. The Australian dollar was uncomfortably high, well above the 'Goldilocks zone' around the 70 US cents range. Joyce's former mate Geoff Dixon was sniping from the sidelines.

One option Joyce had was to set up a new management framework, to prepare for an environment that he felt would improve if he was given the time. His confidence to undertake this change came from the support he continued to receive from his chairman and board, who well understood the complex realities of the airline world.

Joyce also gained resolve from his lengthy talks with the industry elder statesman Tim Clark, a man who had seen everything and weathered many storms. Winning the professional and personal respect of Clark gave Joyce an enormous confidence boost, along with an education that money couldn't buy. Added to that, the real prospect of a spectacular solution to the financial sinkhole of international operations underpinned many of the bold decisions that were to come.

In May 2012, Joyce announced a restructure of the business and changes to his executive team. Qantas International and Qantas Domestic – until then combined as 'Qantas Airlines' – were henceforth to be managed as two distinct businesses, each with its own CEO, operational and commercial functions. From 1 July 2012, their financial results would be reported separately.

Formally splitting the international and domestic arms would ensure Qantas could run each business according to its specific priorities and market conditions. Qantas International's finances would no longer be obscured by the successful domestic operation. It was time to bring it out into the open.

The head of the increasingly successful frequent-flyer program, Simon Hickey, was appointed CEO of Qantas International, with a brief to fix what Joyce described as 'a great airline with a rich history, but a loss-maker and incapable of delivering sustainable returns'.[1]

The reorganisation coincided with the successful Wolgan Valley meeting with Emirates, and was announced a few weeks before the formal agreement with the Gulf carrier was reached. From the moment Hickey took over as international CEO, his primary mission was getting the Emirates deal done.

Other winners in Qantas's 2012 restructure included rising star Jayne Hrdlicka. She took over as CEO of the Jetstar Group from Bruce Buchanan, who had resigned. Hrdlicka joined Qantas from Bain & Company in August 2010, taking on the role of Group Executive, Strategy and Technology, where she played a key role in devising a formula for cooperating with Emirates, as well as helping Joyce with key cultural change initiatives.

Joyce had worked with Hrdlicka in his Ansett days, and at both Jetstar and Qantas, where she was working as a consultant. 'It took a bit of persuading for her to come back into the aviation industry full-time and take the job,' he recalls.

Lesley Grant, one of the architects of Qantas's new international strategy, took on Simon Hickey's role as CEO of Qantas Frequent Flyer, which would later be renamed Qantas Loyalty. Lyell Strambi shifted from Group Executive, Qantas Airlines Operations to focus purely on the local operations as CEO of Qantas Domestic. Among the other executives to move were Gareth Evans (to chief financial officer) and Olivia Wirth (who became Group Executive for Government and Corporate Affairs). Wirth would stay in the role for just twelve months before becoming Group Executive for Brand, Marketing & Corporate Affairs. This was the team that would lead Qantas through its major revamp in the coming months.

There were also ructions in union land. Paul Howes, the national secretary of the 140,000-member AWU, launched legal action against the 3200-member ALAEA's boss, Steve Purvinas. Howes claimed he was humiliated and 'gravely injured in his feelings' by the aircraft engineers' union chief: Purvinas had allegedly earlier sent an email with the subject line 'problems with the AWU' to members of the ACTU executive, which Howes saw as being part of a campaign by the ALAEA to poach Qantas workers from the AWU.

The AWU and the ALAEA had long been at loggerheads over which union was entitled to represent Qantas aircraft engineers. The skirmish followed a jibe in May from Howes, who accused Purvinas of waging a 'one-man jihad' against Qantas. Purvinas's email accused Howes of 'swanning around with politicians and leaders of industry in the Qantas Chairman's Lounge as he prepares to clear for himself a safe Labor seat in the Federal Parliament'.

An initial directions hearing was set in the Victorian Supreme Court on 28 September 2012, but the two union bosses smoked the peace pipe under talks brokered by TWU national secretary Tony Sheldon, and Howes dropped the action in mid-October. According to a report in *The Australian*, the pair conceded that their very public disagreement was undermining unity in the fight against 'vicious attacks' by employers. After signing the peace deal, Howes and Purvinas reportedly went and talked 'over a beer', with Howes declaring: 'Despite our relationship having many ups and downs, I have always respected him.'[2]

Meanwhile, investor land was also fomenting. After revelations back in August 2011 that Dixon's investor group was positioning itself to acquire a strategic stake in Qantas as the share price tanked, Joyce moved to establish a defence team of senior executives and bankers to monitor the airline's share register for signs of unusual trading activity.

It kicked off a painful episode for Joyce and Dixon, who were also neighbours. Dixon, who after leaving Qantas had become chairman of Tourism Australia in 2009, had bought an apartment in The Rocks in Sydney for $7.75 million, just a short walk from Joyce's digs, for which he had paid $4.575 million in 2008.

Transport Minister Anthony Albanese had stated publicly later that month that any private equity bid for Qantas was not in the national interest. The Airline Partners Australia investment group had quietly abandoned their plans over concerns about global instability, but their interest continued to percolate. By October 2012, Dixon and his investor group had built an almost 2 per cent stake in Qantas. The bid had one unlikely backer. In delicious irony, engineering union boss Steve Purvinas was strongly supportive of the Dixon-led play.

The group had been talking Qantas down for months, calling for change to the airline's strategy. Dixon wanted nothing to do with Emirates. He had never been a fan of Middle East–based carriers, and he didn't believe the tie-up would eliminate a strong competitor or offer new growth opportunities. As chairman of Tourism Australia, he also said it was bad news for inbound tourism.

In an interview with *The Australian* in May 2012, Dixon argued that Qantas had 'lost its way' under Joyce and that there was a 'lack of strategy' at the airline. He criticised the decision to form the partnership with Emirates, saying that it was a 'step backwards' and that Qantas should have pursued a partnership with a major Asian airline instead.[3]

A few months later, Dixon confirmed he had been involved in the private equity group, but argued that it 'wasn't about regime change'. 'I am very supportive of the way Alan and his management team are running it,' he said. 'And I am still very good friends with quite a few of the board members.' He added that his investment group was still active, but if Qantas 'settles down well, the share price may get to the point where there is no longer the value there'. Dixon and his co-investors, he said, could simply see value in Qantas's beaten-down share price.[4]

Joyce was more than miffed. In late November 2012, he announced that Qantas was severing its ties with long-time partner Tourism Australia and suspended the airline's $44 million funding package. He cited Dixon's 'clear conflict of interest' as part of the 'APA Mk 2' consortium, which was 'very much out there briefing against the company'.[5]

Tim Clark also weighed in, saying Joyce was addressing the legacies of his predecessors. Dixon remained chairman of Tourism Australia, which fell under the purview of tourism minister Martin Ferguson; the pair were close, almost matey, according to reports. But Ferguson understood the business well and had been supportive of Qantas's agreement with Emirates.

By late November, there was still no offer on the table from the group for shareholders to consider, and the stalemate continued into the new year. In late January 2013, reports emerged that the Dixon group had quietly sold their stake in the airline on 22 January 2013, with the share price back above $1.50 – they reportedly netted a profit of about $18 million. But the play caused a rift between Joyce and Dixon that would take years to patch up.

With his new management structure in place, and with the destabilising threat of Dixon and APA Mk 2 now in the rear-view mirror, Joyce set about getting off to a good start in 2013.

He was upbeat about his business's fundamentals. 'Qantas Domestic, Jetstar and Qantas Frequent Flyer are all benefiting from Australians' healthy demand for domestic, business and leisure travel,' he said as the economy started bubbling along in the post-GFC recovery phase.[6]

But Joyce's good mood cooled on 30 January 2013, when Prime Minister Julia Gillard made a surprise announcement that the federal election would be held more than seven months later, on 14 September 2013. Elections typically have a dampening effect on air travel; it was clear a campaign of such extended duration would not be good for business. The embattled Gillard said the September timetable would end speculation about the timing, and 'give shape and order to the year'.

In February, Qantas unveiled an underlying profit before tax of $223 million for the first half of the financial year, up 10 per cent. Losses had been reduced at Qantas International by 65 per cent as the transformation plan kicked in.

Yet equity investors were becoming uneasy. The shine was beginning to come off the golden child, Qantas Domestic, as Virgin Australia lifted its profile. Despite investments in new lounges and check-in technology, rising capacity levels hit Qantas's domestic earnings hard: they had slipped by a third in the period to $218 million.

'We have seen elevated levels of capacity growth from competitors attempting to claim market share from Qantas Domestic,' Joyce said. 'This has put pressure on yield for all airlines.'[7]

Qantas was keeping its stranglehold on the vital business travellers, maintaining its 84 per cent share of the corporate market. Despite this, there were plans to expand domestic capacity by 5–7 per cent in the first six months of 2013.

Gillard was ousted by Kevin Rudd in a leadership ballot in June 2013, and he promptly abandoned his predecessor's election date commitment, creating yet more uncertainty for the travelling public. It wasn't the politicians' finest hour.

Virgin Australia reported in early August that trading in the April–June quarter had been 'very soft'. Joyce sensed blood in the water. In a speech to the American Chamber of Commerce, he said that if there was a domestic aviation war, then the Qantas Group was 'winning it on all fronts'. That month, Joyce said, the airline was seeing a trend of corporate customers coming back after trying the alternative. He spoke about big new corporate accounts, such as Fortescue Metals Group and the Roy Hill charter contract.

When it reported, Virgin had tapped the markets to raise over $800 million of debt against much of its aircraft fleet, and its cash balance had dwindled to $327 million at the end of the financial year. Qantas, meanwhile, had $2.8 billion of cash on its balance sheet, and Transport Minister Anthony Albanese had written letters of comfort to the ratings agencies to shore up its investment-grade credit rating, to restore the level playing field.

Joyce even had a dig at Etihad, contrasting it as a bicycle to Emirates' BMW, as he reflected at an industry conference on Qantas's groundbreaking alliance with Emirates. He had outmanoeuvred Borghetti – or so he thought.

Rudd by now had set the federal election for 7 September, a week earlier than Gillard's date, and the campaign was creating even more turbulence for the airlines than usual. In the end, it resulted in a landslide victory for Tony Abbott and the Coalition, ending six years of the increasingly tumultuous Rudd/Gillard/ Rudd Labor government. It marked the start of a nine-year stretch of Coalition rule, although the revolving door of prime ministers would continue to spin.

Despite Joyce's efforts, by election day the Qantas Group had fallen below its 'line in the sand' of 65 per cent domestic market share. Virgin had grown by 18 per cent over the previous two years, while Qantas had expanded its capacity by 8 per cent. There were simply too many seats chasing too few passengers. Virgin claimed its mainline operations now accounted for 30 per cent of Australian domestic capacity, versus 42 per cent for Qantas.

Qantas's annual general meeting in October 2013 brought more sombre news, with Clifford noting that the tough domestic market conditions were 'unlikely to ease in the short term, with growth coming into the market at the same time as weak underlying demand'. Qantas issued a profit warning, citing falling domestic and international yields, and Joyce told shareholders the airline had to be realistic about the challenges it faced: 'A volatile economy, an uncertain exchange rate, high fuel prices and intense competition on domestic and international routes.'

Joyce elaborated: 'We are a national carrier operating in one of the most liberalised aviation markets in the world . . . The domestic market is still absorbing capacity growth that has been double the long-run average. And this growth has come at the same time as weak underlying demand across the market, from the leisure to corporate segments.'[8]

Then, just weeks later, Virgin launched a $350 million equity raising and signalled its intention to continue its aggressive capacity strategy.

It was a devastating blow for Joyce and Qantas. The CEO wrote to the deputy prime minister and transport minister, Warren Truss, expressing his concerns, and cited the *Qantas Sale Act* restrictions as a major contributor to his airline's troubles.

Joyce knew that Labor and Greens opposition in the Senate meant his chances of having the Act amended were negligible. A different short-term solution, like a debt guarantee, could help. However, the new Coalition government was keen to demonstrate it was putting an end to industry protections.

Virgin's equity raising would be supported by Air New Zealand, Singapore Airlines and Etihad Airways, each with government shareholders. Furthermore, Virgin, which had long been reluctant to offer board seats to the foreign airlines, changed its tune: directors would be appointed by each of the three carriers.

The trading conditions deteriorated markedly in November, and passenger loads and yields dipped below the already negative trends for the year to date. Domestic demand had fallen off a small cliff, exacerbating the weakness evident before and after September's election. Credit Suisse estimated Virgin's cost base to be around 24.5 per cent lower than Qantas's in the domestic market, meaning it could better absorb the fare discounting.

Qantas had hit rock bottom. It was generating net losses well in excess of $1 million a day. Joyce gave a market update in early December and announced he was conducting a top-down structural review, the results of which would be announced at the interim results in February 2014. He blamed 'fundamentally changed market conditions' as he unveiled expectations of an underlying loss before tax in the range of $250 million to $300 million for the six months to 31 December 2013. Accelerated cost reductions would be sought across all areas of the business, to achieve targeted cost savings of an eye-popping $2 billion over three years. Capital expenditure would shrink, Joyce's own pay was to be cut, along with the board members', and pay freezes would be enacted for other executives.

With the exception of the closure of Qantas International, which was going through its own transformation plan, all options were on the table as part of the strategic review. Moves could include selling stakes of up to 10 per cent in the frequent-flyer business or Jetstar, to allow Qantas to pay down its debt and protect its credit rating. Joyce also flagged that another 1000 jobs would go as part of the cost-cutting.

On 10 December 2013, the Qantas share price closed at its lowest level since its 1995 privatisation, continuing its downward spiral after the company's profit warning the week prior. The stock fell 3 per cent and closed the day at 96.5 cents – half a cent below its previous record low in June 2012 – and hit an all-time intra-day low of 95.5 cents during the session.

The next day, ratings agency Standard & Poor's stripped Qantas of its investment-grade credit rating, noting there had been a structural shift in the domestic market that had eroded the airline's yield. Moody's Investors Service placed Qantas on review for a possible downgrade to its investment-grade rating because of its deteriorating financial situation, and downgraded it shortly after New Year 2014.

The loss of its prized investment-grade credit rating – and the associated funding advantages of cheaper debt – stung Qantas. Chief financial officer Gareth Evans said the downgrade underlined the importance of taking decisive action to address an extremely difficult operating environment.

On 13 December, Air New Zealand, Singapore Airlines and Etihad Airways lifted their combined stakes in Virgin Australia Holdings from 63 per cent to 67 per cent under the carrier's $350 million capital raising, after only one-quarter of retail shareholders took up their entitlements. Richard Branson's Virgin Group kept its 10 per cent stake in the group. Joyce was livid; the lobbying of Canberra for some form of assistance was set to intensify.

The curtains came down on an intense year – 2013 had brought a perfect storm of rampant domestic and international competition and sky-high oil prices. And the outlook for 2014 seemed no better.

Surely, for Joyce, the only way was up – or out.

15

The Capacity Wars Turn Nasty

Understandably, Qantas was keen to prevent a new assault on its premium market by a revamped Virgin Australia, and Joyce pulled out all the stops to stall the offensive. But the airline's goal of providing 65 per cent of the total seats in the market was questioned by many observers. Perhaps it should have been 50 per cent? Perhaps there shouldn't be a line in the sand at all?

At a Qantas investor day in December 2011, a graph of the 'S-curve theory' was displayed, showing that a higher share of capacity led to a superior share of revenues. S-curve theories have been around for a long time, but they're far from universally accepted. Even so, they have been used by network planners around the world for decades to express the revenue premium that comes when a dominant airline hoards the landing slots at major hub airports.

The optimum profit-maximising position for the Qantas Group on the curve was at 65 per cent. Given the structural peculiarities of its domestic and international business, a 65 per cent market share translated into a stranglehold of 80 per cent of the $1 billion domestic market profit pool.

Even Geoff Dixon and his friends, during their destabilising campaign for change in the second half of 2012, had said the

65 per cent 'line in the sand' was so important that they were willing to sell stakes in Jetstar and the frequent-flyer program to maintain it. And Alan Joyce clung to his former boss's strategy tenaciously.

Surrendering any of its 65 per cent share to salvage short-term profitability was simply not an option. If Qantas relented in the capacity war, Joyce feared, it would lose the price premium it enjoyed as a result of its superior network, frequencies and loyalty. And, Joyce argued, you give up that advantage 'at your peril', because 'you can never get back at both ends of the market'.[1]

Qantas CFO Gareth Evans leant his shoulder to the debate, explaining that the strategy was about scale, and 'part of the premium service we offer and the fares we sell'. Evans added that it gave Qantas a very real competitive advantage that allowed it to maximise earnings in even the toughest market conditions. 'Stepping back from the 65 per cent would effectively be waving the white flag,' he said.[2]

Qantas feared that Virgin, if given the space to grow to an equal share of the market, would not stop at 50 per cent. With its offshore backers, it would surely target becoming the dominant domestic protagonist, moving to its own 65 per cent profit-maximising position.

The whole debate left many analysts scratching their heads. One said the capacity wars were 'possibly the dumbest thing I have ever seen in a domestic duopoly. There was no winner, both sets of shareholders were major losers.'

If the numerous academic studies on the S-curve were equivocal about its validity, there was common agreement that whenever airlines applied the strategy, it almost invariably led to an excess of capacity.

In 2013, various analysts and commentators were arguing that Qantas was either lazy or stupid. Some in the finance community were questioning the wisdom of maintaining the 65 per cent target in the face of Virgin's persistence. If Qantas and Virgin each held 50 per cent of the domestic market, they argued, the carriers could be rational actors in a duopoly and maximise returns, benefiting shareholders – although that would come at the expense of consumers, who were currently enjoying the fruits of the battle.

Even if the theory was flawed, some argued, Virgin could only have so much appetite – and capability – for losses, meaning it could ultimately be bullied into submission. That fallback position went out the window once its foreign airline shareholders showed a willingness to put up their cash to support the strategy.

The result of the capacity increases was to shrink the total domestic profit pool from more than $700 million in the 2012 financial year to less than $100 million in the final six months of 2013. The S-curve had a sting in its tail.

The start of 2014 had brought more heartburn for Qantas when Virgin, like a frill-necked lizard, reared its head threateningly.

As Joyce completed his structural review, first Etihad CEO James Hogan and then Air New Zealand CEO Christopher Luxon announced almost simultaneously that they would join the Virgin board. For now, Singapore Airlines remained quiet on its choice of board member, who was expected to be a substitute for CEO Goh Choon Phong.

It looked a formidable line-up, although the board members had sometimes overlapping and often conflicting interests. For Borghetti, it would be a difficult equation. Virgin chairman Neil Chatfield would be the lion-tamer.

Borghetti himself was also in the news, lobbing more salvos in his first sit-down interview since the row had erupted in 2013 over airline ownership rules. Borghetti likened the Qantas stoush to a nuclear war. 'The trouble with a nuclear war is you get collateral damage,' he added. 'Usually the collateral damage affects the guy that is the largest, because he has more to lose.'[3]

Joyce fired back with his 'level playing field' argument. 'Since early 2012, there has also been an unprecedented distortion of the Australian domestic market, with Virgin Australia's strategy to seek majority ownership and massive financial backing from foreign government-owned airlines,' he said. 'This foreign government capital has been used to finance dramatic increases in domestic capacity, with profound implications for the future of Australia's aviation industry.'

He then took aim at Virgin's aggressive capacity strategy, which he claimed was backed by cash injections from its foreign owners and designed to weaken Qantas in the domestic market. 'The uneven playing field in Australian aviation is being tilted further,' he argued, 'and Qantas cannot and will not stand still in these extraordinary circumstances.'[4] Joyce wanted to ensure that Virgin did not receive any unfair advantage through apparently unlimited injections of cash from its foreign, government-owned shareholders.

To 'level the playing field', Qantas began talks with the government about a standby debt facility backed by a government guarantee – a safety net of sorts. That would make Qantas a government-related entity for the purposes of the ratings agencies, and help bolster its credit rating, in turn lowering the price Qantas paid for debt. Air New Zealand had a similar arrangement with its government (although with the difference that the flag carrier was 51 per cent government-owned).

The talks dragged on for weeks while the government considered a range of options, including a debt guarantee – similar to what the banking sector had received during the global financial crisis – or an unsecured loan. Treasurer Joe Hockey made some encouraging comments and was open to a discussion about supporting Qantas.

Joyce argued that the *Qantas Sale Act* limited the airline's financial options and added cost to the business. Over the long term, he said, repealing it was essential to 'remove the distortions in our aviation system'.[5] But Prime Minister Tony Abbott led a government that had refused to bail out several struggling Australian companies: General Motors Holden, Toyota and SPC Ardmona. He wasn't convinced Qantas should get special treatment, even if it was a national icon.

Frustration over the provisions of the *Qantas Sale Act* was nothing new. Dixon had lashed out at it in his final speech as CEO in 2008, calling it a concession to the 'fearful opponents of privatisation' which limits foreign investment, particularly foreign airline investment, in Qantas. 'Now more than ever it is clear that the act is out of date,' Dixon had said.[6]

By 2014, the handicap was magnified because of Virgin's equity moves. 'Late last year, these three foreign-airline shareholders invested more than $300 million in Virgin Australia at a time when it was losing money,' Joyce said. 'That capital injection has supported continued domestic capacity growth by Virgin Australia despite its growing losses.'[7]

Richard Branson shot back, saying it would be unfair for the federal government to provide financial assistance to Qantas. 'It would be incredulous [*sic*] if the government can hand over money to [Joyce] and they don't hand over money to Virgin Australia . . . Every company in Australia will come begging to the government if they allowed that to happen,' Branson told *Arabian Business* magazine.[8]

Prime Minister Tony Abbott, speaking in parliament, finally ruled out the prospect of providing the airline with a standby credit facility aimed at restoring its investment-grade credit rating. The Abbott government's preferred approach was to seek to modify the *Qantas Sale Act*. It was an unwelcome rebuke for Joyce and Clifford, who had spoken at length with Abbott in the lead-up.

The rebuke only strengthened Joyce's determination to push ahead with his business reorganisation and the deep cuts to his workforce. He was at pains to clarify later that Qantas had never approached the government for a handout or subsidy, calling such moves 'self-defeating'.

Clifford, meanwhile, was pragmatic as ever. 'We didn't reach agreement on it [with the government], so life went on. There was no one coming to save us so we had to do it ourselves,' he later recalled.

In the end, there was bipartisan agreement to remove the foreign ownership provisions from the *Qantas Sale Act*, but the 51 per cent local ownership restriction remained.

Still the domestic capacity war dragged on. It seemed Virgin now had access to unlimited funds, meaning a full-frontal attack by Qantas was unlikely to be successful. This was not where Joyce wanted to be. He had to front his investors and the media to announce the half-year results for the six months to 31 December 2013. It wasn't going to be pretty.

He unveiled the company's first half-year result, a $235 million loss, the first in the nearly twenty years since Qantas moved out of government ownership.

International was still underperforming, as the Emirates partnership was taking a while to gain traction. The Jetstar strategy excursions into Asia with its local joint ventures were struggling too. Those alone lost $262 million in the half-year.

CFO Evans agreed the strategy was 'taking some time to grow into'. Establishment was expensive, and the LCC model had been badly hit by the record high fuel prices. With its lower overall cost base, fuel was accounting for around 50 per cent of costs for Jetstar operations, nullifying its marginal cost advantage over the full-service airlines.

In the Australian international market, the number of seats flown – mostly not by Qantas – had increased by one-half since Joyce became CEO. Over the same period, the number of international passengers Qantas carried had remained almost stagnant, although adding in Australian-based Jetstar International increased the group numbers by over 40 per cent.

The big new issue, though, was the frightening domestic

decline. Until now it had been propping up the poorer-performing segments. The capacity war had taken a heavy toll.

Later the same week, Virgin Australia reported that it actually made a loss in the domestic arena, while its international performance suffered badly as it struggled to establish the Pacific route. Borghetti's news was received much more positively, though, perhaps with a dose of sympathy for the underdog.

Joyce had been well aware this bad news was coming. He had completed his strategic review and was ready to take action. It would be radical action, and highly controversial.

Now a new, three-year 'Accelerated Transformation Plan' that he'd flagged in December 2013 was formally announced. This plan would permanently reduce costs by $2 billion in all parts of the Qantas Group through to the 2017 financial year. Despite Joyce's previous warnings, the share price fell 9 per cent on the day.

Why $2 billion? That, according to Joyce, was the scale of reform needed to ensure that Qantas was permanently and sustainably profitable. It dwarfed the scale of the international transformation plan launched two and a half years earlier. By comparison, that one had been almost timid. It hadn't got Qantas to a sufficiently tight position.

The Qantas Group's workforce was to be slashed by 15 per cent, or 5000 full-time-equivalent positions, over the three-year period. These reductions included removing some 1500 management and non-operational roles, as well as operational positions affected by fleet and network changes. Line maintenance operations would be restructured, and the Avalon Airport maintenance base closed – moves sure to be particularly unpopular with the engineers, and vindication of their concerns about job losses.

The Accelerated Transformation Plan also involved consolidating business activities, introducing new technology and procurement savings (by renegotiating contracts). Planned capital expenditure in the following two financial years was to be slashed by $1 billion. The Brisbane Airport terminal was sold and leased back, to generate cash. Every detail was covered, from faster aircraft turnarounds to saving fuel by optimising routes. No stone was left unturned.

The executive wages freeze was extended and broadened to cover all Qantas Group employees. Qantas board fees were cut and Joyce's take-home pay reduced by 36 per cent. There would be no pay rises or bonuses until Qantas was profitable again.

More than fifty aircraft deliveries were deferred, including eight A380s, or sold. Boeing 747s were retired ahead of schedule and replaced by smaller, more efficient two-engined A330-200s. Schedules were changed and unprofitable routes were dropped.

Joyce was at pains to stress that Qantas was up against 'some of the toughest market conditions it had ever faced . . . The market Qantas operates in has changed, with structural economic shifts exacerbated by an uneven playing field in Australian aviation policy.'[9]

No one in the industry would have argued with that – but was his action reasonable?

Not everyone thought so. ACTU secretary Dave Oliver demanded an independent audit of the financial situation and to 'identify potential alternatives to job cuts'. There was a lively meeting with the major Qantas unions later that week.[10]

Linda White, national secretary of the Australian Services Union, argued: 'We are very concerned at the level of cuts that are proposed and how that will impact on those left behind to pick up the pieces and keep the airline running.'[11]

Steve Purvinas of the ALAEA pulled out the safety card, saying the travelling public was being put at risk by the airline management's decisions to send more maintenance offshore. 'Finances are coming before safety,' he said.[12]

Billionaire Clive Palmer, keen for publicity for his Palmer United political party, tweeted that if jobs had to go at Qantas, the 'first should be CEO and the board of directors for failures which wiped billions off market value'.[13] Prime Minister Abbott obliquely observed Qantas could be 'very profitable' under good management.[14]

Rumours were swirling that Joyce's days – and those of his chairman, Leigh Clifford – were numbered. With losses mounting and Qantas's core market share falling, the dual-brand strategy in open question, the airline's credit rating downgraded to junk and hopes for government assistance in tatters, Joyce's credibility had drained away.

A report in the *Australian Financial Review* said 'the Irish chief executive had exhausted his bag of tricks to turn around the ailing national flag carrier, and the board of the airline is understood to be split in support of him and the strategy'.[15]

Joyce had to face the music. Every breakfast and news show wanted him on. This was news that attracted the widest of audiences – it was like a traffic accident, and everyone wanted to stickybeak. All the leading unionists were speaking out against the CEO; there were tales from staff who were being sacked. The media empathised with the thousands of staff about to lose their jobs; why was this sort of dramatic action necessary? Virgin wasn't doing it.

The undertone was that Joyce, the uncaring Irishman, was removed from the real world. He was poked and prodded – he was the villain.

For Joyce, this time was epitomised by one particular live TV appearance early on a warm February morning. He had walked the few hundred metres from his apartment in The Rocks to Observatory Hill, a small promontory, the highest point in the city, where the Sydney Observatory had stood since 1858. Overlooking Sydney Harbour, right next to the iconic bridge, there was a small bandstand, large enough to accommodate a few wind instruments. On this morning, the bandstand contained TV lights, cables and cameras for the breakfast show *Today*, with host Karl Stefanovic asking the hard questions.

As Joyce launched into the interview, out of the corner of his eye he noticed a man walking his dog through the park. The man spotted the familiar figure of the Qantas villain and shouted, loudly enough to be heard on the show, 'Hey, Joyce, you're a disgrace, sacking all those people!'

As a young Dubliner, Joyce had been a paperboy, and one of the eternal challenges of the job was avoiding unfriendly dogs. He knew from experience that it wasn't the big Irish wolfhounds that were the troublesome ones but the terriers.

As Joyce tells it, 'He let his dog off the leash and I had this little Jack Russell biting my ankles while I'm trying to do the interview. I thought, "This is a tough day at the office." As a paperboy, it was the little dogs, the little Jack Russells, that used to get me. They were a pain.'

His ankles survived the attack, but these were not good times.

To make things worse, Qantas staff had been working in the middle of a building site, with dust, crashing, banging, drilling and tradespeople everywhere. In some ways, the shambolic work environment was symbolic, as the shabby old collection of offices in connected buildings was being torn apart to create a new building that spoke of openness and a bright future.

If the Qantas operating model had a cancer, this was the period of surgery designed to allow it to re-emerge healthy and viable. But it wasn't as simple as that. As the name suggested, the airline was in desperate need of an *accelerated* transformation.

Beneath that simple term, there was a big human cost. Five thousand people were being sacked – not all at once, because that was logistically impossible, but it meant the threat of termination was hovering above the workforce like a plague.

It's easy to imagine that someone who can sack 5000 people does it dispassionately, even callously. That, certainly, is how many people saw Alan Joyce. There is no doubt he had made a 'bold' move, even a 'brave' one. It was designed to put Qantas onto a more stable financial platform, one that might survive in the long term, but could the changes have been made more gradually? And would that have been less painful? Was the CEO heartless?

Joyce had done the numbers, and what he saw was quite clear. Fuel prices were still nudging all-time highs. They had increased more than 50 per cent since he took over, and were Qantas's single biggest input cost. Given fuel represented around one-third of the airline's total expenses, it looked as if the business was going to have to be reshaped to account for this new cost profile.

Domestically, Virgin Australia – backed by powerful foreign interests, as Joyce saw it – was still refusing to accept that its market ceiling was below 35 per cent. Internationally, although the Emirates partnership was starting to gain traction, it was still early days, and the global economy remained sluggish. Business travel wasn't recovering as well as hoped. Joyce now felt that his 2011 transformation plan had not been bold enough.

Chairman Leigh Clifford publicly backed Joyce for another three years, giving him the space to shape his legacy. It was a vote of confidence, but it carried an implicit warning: carry through this transformation, or else.

In an opinion piece in early March 2014, just a few weeks after Joyce formally launched the Accelerated Transformation Plan, the chairman set out the tough conditions Qantas faced amid the perfect storm of foreign airline capacity, record jet fuel costs and weak economic conditions. These conditions, he said, demanded realistic, reform-focused leadership.

'Howling at management is the easy thing to do for the many commentators and others who fail to understand or choose to ignore the reality of global aviation, the particular circumstances of Australian aviation and the disadvantages created by government policy settings in this country,' Clifford wrote.

He also went into bat for his embattled CEO and the wider executive team:

For management itself, the task is to get on with the job. Alan Joyce is the right man to lead the change Qantas needs. As CEO he has already taken on many of the big challenges facing Qantas. This week he outlined a clear plan to address the challenges that remain. The priority now is to deliver that plan.[16]

In 2004, Joyce was appointed the inaugural head of Jetstar, achieving his goal of becoming an airline CEO by the age of forty. TOP: With his boss, Qantas CEO Geoff Dixon. BOTTOM: With Qantas ambassador John Travolta and *Kath and Kim*'s Magda Szubanski.

(Phil Weymouth/Bloomberg via Getty Images; William West/AFP via Getty Images)

The example of fellow Irishman Michael O'Leary, an aviation hero for taking the low-cost model to new heights in Europe, encouraged Joyce to pursue his own goals in the industry.
(Filippo Monteforte/AFP via Getty Images)

John Borghetti (right) left the Qantas executive team in 2010 to become CEO of Virgin Australia, working for readily identifiable part-owner Sir Richard Branson (below). Borghetti did not see eye to eye with the flamboyant knight.
(Scott Barbour/Getty Images;
Torsten Blackwood/AFP via Getty Images)

In November 2011, Joyce grounded the Qantas fleet while Prime Minister Julia Gillard was hosting the Commonwealth Heads of Government meeting in Perth. She was not amused. *(Paul Kane/Getty Images)*

Following the grounding, Joyce underwent a grilling by favourite enemy Senator Tony Sheldon at Senate hearings in 2012. He's flanked here by Jayne Hrdlicka, head of Jetstar, and Gareth Evans, chief financial officer. *(Brendon Thorne/Bloomberg via Getty Images)*

Joyce with his partner, Shane Lloyd. After strongly supporting the marriage equality movement, including the plebiscite in 2017, the two married in 2019. *(Cole Bennetts/Getty Images)*

A Qantas A320 in Indigenous livery in 2013, as part of the airline's Indigenous Flying Art series. Under Joyce's leadership, Qantas publicly supported the Yes campaign in the 2023 Voice referendum. *(James D Morgan/Getty Images)*

Qantas and Emirates A380s fly side by side over Sydney Harbour in 2013 to celebrate the highly valuable partnership between the two airlines. *(James D Morgan/Getty Images)*

The airline's leadership team in 2018: Andrew David, Gareth Evans, Joyce and Alison Webster (L–R). That year the airline posted a then record $1.6 billion profit.

(Brendon Thorne/Bloomberg via Getty Images)

Michael Caine, assistant secretary of the Transport Workers Union, at a Jetstar strike in February 2020. Jetstar had been problematic for the unions since its inception, as it paid lower salaries than Qantas. *(Brook Mitchell/Getty Images)*

In May 2020, during the COVID pandemic, Sydney Airport shut down its east–west runway in order to keep grounded Qantas planes in 'active storage'.

(James D Morgan/Getty Images)

Joyce reporting a $1.9 billion loss at the 2022 Qantas annual general meeting, one of the worst years in the airline's history, following its near death in 2020. *(James D Morgan/Getty Images)*

Linking Australia and the UK non-stop had been a pet project of Joyce's, seeking to overcome the 'end of the line' handicap that Qantas suffers. Here Joyce enjoys the first of these 'Project Sunrise' flights. *(James D Morgan/Getty Images)*

Qantas's announcement in May 2023 of its first woman CEO, Vanessa Hudson, to take over from its first openly gay CEO, both proudly representing the airline's diversity.

(Lisa Maree Williams/Bloomberg via Getty Images)

Joyce's term as CEO had coincided with one of the most turbulent periods in global aviation. Now, in 2014, the economy remained patchy and demand was affected by weak consumer confidence and tepid demand for air travel. The outlook remained uncertain, although the more optimistic watchers thought they saw a few 'green shoots'. But whatever happened next, there needed to be a revitalised and more efficient company to emerge into the new environment.

Shortly after unveiling the record interim loss, Joyce went into a meeting room with his top 100 managers.

'It was a terrible time,' he later recalled. 'The atmosphere was dreadful. Everybody's head was down. The press was giving us hell, but I said to the guys, "You could be part of the biggest turnaround in corporate Australia history. We're at a low, but we have the right strategy, the right approach, the right people, the most amazing brand and we could deliver on this."'

It was the irrepressible executive, as passionate as ever about getting the company on the right track. 'I believe my vision for Qantas is shared by many other Australians – a strong, iconic national carrier, here for the future,' he said. Joyce felt supported by Clifford, the board and key institutional shareholders, who remained impressed by Joyce's management of the company's cashflow and by how he'd held the balance sheet relatively steady despite the turmoil.

Joyce acknowledged that he was out of favour with a lot of people. Even if the public supported his vision, many disliked the methodology. But he was the one at the pointy end. 'It's not a popularity contest,' he said. 'And if you think doing the CEO job is a popularity contest, you shouldn't be doing it. I'm here to work for the board and for the shareholders and they're fully supporting me.'[17]

Joyce reckons he stared down more calls for his resignation in 2013 than any other CEO, or probably any other public figure.

But his own passion still burned brightly: his goal was to make sure the company survived and thrived into the future. 'And when that happens, that will be the time for me to go,' he said at the time. He liked to quote Irish poet Brendan Behan's line: 'The only bad publicity is your obituary.' Joyce wasn't ready for his to be written yet.

He saw his role as to defend Qantas against anything that threatened its wellbeing. 'When some of the union claims are going to put the company in financial distress and cause a lot of people to lose their jobs, I don't think that's fair,' he later told *The Weekend Australian*, 'and it's my job as CEO to stand up and fight.'[18]

PART IV
CLIMBING

The transformation of our business is a difficult process. Our employees have responded with great courage and good spirit to the challenges that we face, while maintaining the highest standards of performance.

—Alan Joyce

16

The Capacity Wars End

An uneasy truce was forming in the domestic market around Easter 2014. Joyce had softened his messaging about the 65 per cent market share target, referring more often to the primacy of network and frequency advantages. Qantas halted capacity increases in April, and in May announced a freeze in capacity for the July–September quarter. Virgin cut its domestic capacity in May and again in June. It was clear the three-year domestic market capacity war between Qantas and Virgin was finally over.

In almost two years of brutal expansion, the Qantas Group's combined share had edged slightly lower from 65.3 per cent in June 2011 to 63 per cent (taking into account Virgin's subsequent Tiger and Skywest acquisition), including an 80 per cent share of revenue from the corporate and government market. Virgin had boosted its share of revenues from corporate and government customers from 10 per cent to around 20 per cent, but this had failed to convert the overall domestic operation to profitability.

Joyce denied the capacity war was Qantas's fault. 'Qantas is certainly a very aggressive competitor in protecting its position,' he told the *Australian Financial Review*. 'We always have been and always will be. At the end of the day, I always had a good relationship with John when he worked at Qantas.

We don't have much to do with each other now. You wouldn't expect us to. [ACCC chairman] Rod Sims would be very worried if we did.'[1]

John Borghetti said there was 'a hell of a gap' between supply and demand in the domestic market, but insisted Virgin was in a much stronger position than Qantas, whose 'slash and burn' approach would impact service and impact the product.[2]

Virgin bore financial scars from the fare war too, and it was taking longer than expected for its chairman, Neil Chatfield, to figure out how to avoid any potential conflicts of interest arising from his high-flying incoming board directors from Etihad, Air New Zealand and Singapore Airlines. These board members were initially expected to be in place by April 2014, but that was pushed back to July. The big egos of Hogan and Luxon would require some deft management, while Singapore Airlines still hadn't announced its pick.

Qantas, meanwhile, was making some internal management moves. Experienced executive Andrew David joined in July 2014. He'd had stints at British Airways in the late 1980s and at Air New Zealand through a tumultuous period from 1990 to 2004, before becoming chief operating officer at Virgin Blue under Brett Godfrey.

After leaving Virgin, David took the role of CEO of Tiger after its grounding, spending eighteen months getting it back in the air. He then joined Jayne Hrdlicka at Jetstar, where he spent a year helping guide the development of fledgling carrier Jetstar Japan.

David says he initially hesitated to join Qantas. 'I knew that Alan was on a journey to change the culture, but I wasn't sure whether it was for me. I'd been at [carriers that were] new, whereas Qantas was, at that stage, nearly ninety years old, [with] all of those issues to deal with.'

According to David, Alan Joyce, like Brett Godfrey, possesses three key qualities.

'Look around the globe – it's people with those qualities that are the ones that exceed and excel,' David says. 'I've met plenty of people with high intelligence and high energy, but they don't necessarily have high integrity. Alan and Brett have all three in spades . . . I joined Qantas because I could see what Alan wanted to create. I was convinced that he was the right type of leader.'

The results of the capacity truce were almost immediate. As costs came out of Qantas under the Accelerated Transformation Plan, its position began to improve. The price of jet fuel was also starting to recede.

In August 2014, Qantas unveiled a record full-year statutory loss of $2.8 billion. It was driven by a horror underlying loss before tax of $646 million following the domestic capacity wars. (Virgin reported a full-year underlying loss of $211.7 million.) Qantas's record loss was also a result of ongoing international losses, as well as one-off costs associated with the transformation plan and a massive non-cash write-down of $2.6 billion to the value of the Qantas International fleet.

Qantas had decided to create a new holding company structure and establish a corporate entity for Qantas International. 'The government made the call [on the *Qantas Sale Act*] and that allowed us to restructure International and, as a consequence of that, we took the fleet write-down,' Joyce said.[3]

The move was designed to allow Qantas to seek further investment in the International business – for example, selling up to a 49 per cent stake in Qantas International. CFO Gareth Evans clarified that the airline was not actively looking for a new partner, but was structuring the business in a way that 'provides us the maximum level of optionality to be involved in partnerships, alliances or consolidations in the international business over the long term'.[4]

Joyce was clearing the decks. While the full-year numbers were 'confronting', he said, they represented the year that had passed and Qantas had now come through the worst.

But not everyone was convinced and there were yet more calls for Joyce to stand aside. The *Australian Financial Review* reported: 'Focus has intensified on Joyce's tenure as Qantas's performance has gone to hell in a handbasket during his six-year tenure. Questions about succession planning are expected to be raised at the company's annual general meeting.'[5]

As the weeks went on, passenger load factors rose across the board and yields at Qantas International continued to trend upward. The Aussie dollar had also retreated back to near its 'sweet spot', to the low 80 US cents.

By October 2014, Joyce could see clear evidence that Qantas was on track with its plans. The ALAEA had just agreed to a new four-year deal that included a pay freeze for the first eighteen months. Similar deals were struck with the TWU and other union groups. Employees accepted the eighteen-month pay freeze without much of a fight, to the surprise and satisfaction of management and the board. Leigh Clifford later recalled that the Qantas employees were extremely responsive to the need for change in early 2014, despite some 'debate over whether we were fudging the books'.

The Qantas Group revealed an underlying profit before tax for the first quarter of the 2015 financial year and was on track to deliver an underlying profit for the first half of the financial year of between $300 million and $350 million.

The Accelerated Transformation Plan, coupled with a more benign operating environment, was delivering results, and the voices calling for Joyce's head were silenced. Warnings of an investor revolt over Joyce's pay at the annual general meeting in late October were unfounded: his remuneration for the 2014 financial year was approved. While he did not receive any bonuses, investors signed off on a long-term incentive plan with high achievement hurdles.

Joyce said the airline could not ease off in the process of change and would continue to show the same rigour and discipline as it had through the transformation process. It was music to shareholders' ears. After over three years languishing below $2, the share price finally cracked through this barrier in late November 2014.

As another tumultuous year drew to a close, Joyce was ready for a break. In early December, he bought a luxury five-bedroom, five-bathroom home in Palm Beach, north of Sydney, for $5.25 million. He acquired the residence – which boasted a swimming pool on a clifftop block overlooking Whale Beach – on a rapid two-week settlement in order to secure the residence in time for the summer holidays.

Joyce also received an early Christmas gift from his chairman. In an extended interview with the *Australian Financial Review*, Clifford noted that while his CEO had been subject to some unfair and unjustified criticism, Joyce had shown 'amazing resilience'. 'I'm pretty proud of the way he has handled that,' Clifford said. He added that the job cuts announced by Qantas would 'understandably cause some controversy; the perceived solution in some cases was if you could just get rid of Alan, and probably me, things would be hunky-dory'. But Joyce was ready for the big decisions and was a strategic thinker. 'Alan is a guy you can bounce things off and he can bounce things off you; he is a very capable individual and a very intelligent individual.' Neither he nor Joyce was going anywhere, concluded Clifford.[6]

It was time, therefore, for some potential aspirants to Joyce's job, Simon Hickey and Lyell Strambi, to head for the exit. This prompted Joyce to announce a further shakeup to his executive leadership team in early 2015. John Gissing's role would expand to Group Executive of Associated Airlines & Services, reporting directly to Joyce. Andrew David took on Strambi's role as CEO of Qantas Domestic. Joyce said the changes would result in a 'flatter' management structure. Under the theme of transformation, the roles of deputy chief financial officer, QantasLink chief executive officer and Qantas chief operating officer were not being replaced.

Big changes were also coming to the finance portfolio. Group CFO Gareth Evans shifted over to become CEO of Qantas International and Freight, and was replaced by his long-time deputy, Tino La Spina. The new man would spearhead the establishment of the Qantas Group's financial framework, to guide the airline's thinking on shareholder value creation, its optimal capital structure and capital allocation.

The 'Three Pillars of the Financial Framework' would go on to feature in every Qantas annual report from 2015 onwards, as Qantas joined the ranks of other leading 'ROIC-star' airlines – those obsessed with 'return on invested capital'.

The Qantas board was also going through a quiet revolution. Qantas strengthened its marketing clout with the appointment of Todd Sampson as a non-executive director from 25 February 2015. Sampson had a diverse range of expertise in marketing communication, new media and digital transformation, and was at the time the national CEO of the Leo Burnett Group.

The *Australian Financial Review* described Sampson as an 'unshaven, T-shirt-wearing leftie who grew up on a hippy commune in Canada but went on to establish Earth Hour and name his kids after Care Bears – what could possibly go wrong?!'[7] Sampson had been put forward earlier in 2014, when names were being assembled for a potential standalone board for Qantas Frequent Flyer.

As it happened, Qantas's transformation was being aided by some clever marketing. In late 2014, the airline unveiled its new brand campaign, titled 'Feels Like Home'. The ad series told the stories of five Qantas passengers and their journeys home to Australia, culminating in their being welcomed at the airport by loved ones. Filmed in London, Santiago, Los Angeles, Hong Kong, the Pilbara and Sydney, the series features Qantas employees as well as customers. There was a renewed buzz about the brand, and many customers and employees were in tears when they watched the ads for the first time – the visuals and the music captured what Qantas meant to them. The campaign was an excellent success online, with over 1.6 million people watching the ads through social media within the first month.

In an outrageous twist, just prior to Qantas's new campaign, Virgin rolled out its own, featuring an actress peering out of the window of a high-rise Sydney apartment, then emerging from a lift and walking through the building's lobby. Sharp-eyed spotters quickly realised it was the Cove building in The Rocks – the building Alan Joyce called home. Brilliant. Joyce was away on business at the time, but his partner, Shane Lloyd, was home during the filming.

There are numerous traits that underpin the value of a brand. For an airline, the most fundamental of these is safety, an area in which Qantas enjoys global renown. And from this, many other key elements flow.

After taking over at Qantas, Joyce held the airline's Air Operator's Certificate. Being the accountable manager for the AOC was and remains vitally important to Qantas. As John Gissing explains, the holder has 'a direct relationship under the Civil Aviation Act with the chief pilot and the chief engineer – and you're on the hook for safety outcomes. It's the best way to learn, as you get to know them in their areas of expertise, and understand the safety culture, the layers of protection, how assurance systems work, why we audit so intensively and where and so on.

'Alan was smart enough to recognise almost immediately that if you get all of that right for safety, it all applies across the balanced scorecard. The safety imperative is the most important thing for us, always has been . . . Safe organisations are typically good across the balanced scorecard because they've got the right culture and reporting sense of continuous improvement. They're deeply curious. They want to learn. They see [that] when things go wrong elsewhere, the best thing to do is go and find out how, why, what can we learn? If people make mistakes, the worst thing you can do is blame. It's best to be blame-free and open.

And why wouldn't you have that same culture in finance, in commercial, in customer service?'

According to Rob Gurney, Joyce would never challenge anything with a safety-related dimension. 'On a question about an aircraft type requiring inspections, he could have said, "Look, are you sure you're not overreacting to it – are you sure you need to ground the whole fleet?" There were none of those conversations. He would just say, "If you feel that that's the right thing to do, you're responsible for it. I'll back you and support your decision."'

When it comes to building and maintaining brand status, commercial success is the *sine qua non*. Without it, there is no airline. Establishing vital partnerships is more difficult without it. The quality of the product is impossible to maintain unless the funds are there. And, on the personal front, the CEO's residency is likely to be short without it.

It took a while for Joyce to gain a full understanding of the complex workings of the giant beast that was Qantas, and to recognise where it should head. His analytical mind needed to comprehend it fully. While not naturally unsure of himself, he also needed to develop the managerial confidence to make sweeping changes.

Like a surgeon assessing an injured patient, he had to work out his priorities: the problems that were life-threatening, the ones that needed to be fixed with urgency, while at the same time keeping a close eye on damage that could be attended to later.

In his tumultuous early years in the most conspicuous corporate role in Australia, Joyce came to know the media landscape well. 'I take everything I read in the press with a pinch of salt,' he remarked in 2014.[8]

Joyce had been the most written about, watched and listened to business person in Australia for three years in a row. He only lost top spot in 2014 because casino boss James Packer had a fistfight outside his Bondi home with Nine Network CEO David Gyngell in May.

'The focus on this iconic brand is huge,' Joyce said. 'Qantas gets what we call the "Himalayas of coverage" as a consequence of this. So when it's bad, it's very bad and there's a lot of attention.'[9]

Being so conspicuous made Joyce an easy target. If your car breaks down, you don't blame the CEO of Ford. But if your Qantas (or Jetstar) flight was late or cancelled, there was only one person to blame (and the brand was in the gutter again).

At what other Australian company, Joyce later recalled, would the CEO have to go on morning TV and respond to a poll that said 90 per cent of people said you should resign?

'I answered, "I'm not a politician. I don't have to listen to polls. I'm doing a job. I'm determined to do the right thing by Qantas and its people. I'm making sure that the company is successful now and into the future,"' Joyce says. 'And at the end of the day, it's my shareholders and my board that matter. They're the opinions that matter, not the general public opinion.'

His media skills evolved and improved. From his initial awkward and nervous public communications, he became a consummate professional who largely controlled the narrative (despite showing the occasional tin ear). He believed a CEO should never hide: a leader who pushed other executives into the spotlight around key issues was dodging their responsibility.

When tough decisions need to be made, the CEO needs to 'front them', he says. 'But then we go back to business as normal, and the plan now would be for a company spokesperson to take on responsibility going forward. And that's the right balance, because if the CEO is dragged out for everything, it makes everything a big story potentially, when you don't want it to be.'

The flipside of the massive media coverage, Joyce points out, is that when it's good, 'Qantas gets a huge amount of coverage that other airlines can't get, which helps you in marketing and in presence. It also allows me, because of the high public profile, to make a stand on social issues that I find important, and it allows the company to portray its position on our social issues, which is also important.'

17

The Best of Times?

By the first quarter of 2015, Qantas was flying strongly again. The turnaround program delivered $900 million in benefits in the first half of the 2015 financial year, which pulled Qantas out of a loss-making position. In the international business, which had undergone such painful reorganisation, Qantas had by 2014 successfully taken its cost base down by 20 per cent. The company now had a strong foundation for sustainable growth, Joyce said, and the outlook was positive for a profitable full-year result.

By mid-May 2015, Qantas stock soared to its highest point in seven years on news the company was on track to reduce its debt by a billion dollars for the financial year. There were undeniably some tailwinds – fuel prices had dropped and the Aussie dollar returned to its long-term average – but the message was clear: the ship was turning around. Joyce insisted he wasn't focused on the share price, but Qantas was winning the popularity contest among analysts.

Again and again, Joyce stressed that the key was having the right strategy and making sure the team was working together. 'It's that capable group of individuals, which I think is one of the best management teams on the globe,' he said.[1] That may have been the case, but Joyce's continued encouragement made sure his team bathed in the glow of the success.

Joyce was also encouraged by the continuing support from the airline's chairman, Leigh Clifford. He would later say he felt it was up to the leadership of the company to give strong direction and a compelling vision of a high target. 'But I never thought – and I don't think anybody in that downbeat room in February 2014 thought – that we could do the turnaround as fast as we did,' he later recalled. 'The one thing the managers remembered was not the bad numbers that we had, but that comment – "We could be part of Australia's biggest turnaround" – which probably now had become the world's largest aviation turnaround as well.

'Three dramatic actions changed everything for International,' Joyce says. 'One was the partnerships and the joint ventures, particularly the Emirates partnership, which was a game changer. It changed Europe from a big loss-maker into a profit centre, which was phenomenal. The second was that technology was becoming our friend. And we could see that we could do things like Perth–London and that technology eventually would change the whole dynamic on International. And the third one is that we did that restructure in 2013–14, and subsequently reduced our cost base dramatically.'

Qantas had discovered in its research the importance of International to both the Loyalty and Domestic businesses, as Joyce explains: 'You look at this as a network proposition: we're going to make an 18 per cent margin on Domestic. You'd ask, "Are we less attractive if you haven't got an international arm?" Absolutely. And what is the number one driver for loyalty? It's International. You absolutely must have it.'

Reputationally too, Joyce had engineered a remarkable turnaround. He'd set the bar high for himself, and cleared it.

The second anniversary of Qantas's partnership with Emirates followed in April 2015, by which time over 2 million codeshare customers had travelled on both carriers. Qantas passengers were able to access more than seventy Emirates destinations in Europe, the Middle East and North Africa with one-stop service over Dubai.

The airline unveiled a bumper underlying profit before tax of $975 million for the financial year ended 30 June 2015 – a $1.6 billion turnaround from the previous year. Joyce said $1.1 billion of cumulative transformation benefits had been realised, including $894 million of benefits unlocked in the 2015 financial year alone. Virgin's $49 million full-year underlying loss looked very ugly by comparison.

For Qantas, this was payback time, an exercise in rejoicing, as it signalled at least partial victory. Management pay freezes that had lasted three years now ended. For over 10,000 employ-ees under enterprise bargaining agreements who had agreed to the eighteen-month pay freeze, the reward was a $90 million one-off bonus. Long-suffering shareholders were rewarded with a $500 million capital return.

'We do need to give our shareholders appropriate returns,' Joyce had told the *Australian Financial Review* in late 2014. They had not had a dividend since 2009. 'We need to, at the appropri-ate time, when we have a stable environment, have stable cash flows coming in and we have a strong balance sheet.'[2]

That time had finally come.

As the turmoil faded, a musical endeavour within Qantas started to emerge. Gissing had a budding bass player in his team, Nick Tyral, who first floated the idea of putting together an in-house blues/rock band. Gissing, who played guitar and harmonica, was a big Neil Young fan. He approached the Head of Global Sales & Commercial Planning, David Orszáczky, about the idea. Orszáczky, a gun guitarist himself (and distant relative of Hungarian-Australian jazz and blues legend Jackie Orszáczky), quickly jumped at the chance to help knock a setlist into shape.

Word got around, and electric guitarist Gareth Evans – by day the CEO of Qantas International and Freight – was duly recruited, along with a talented line-up of singers and a fine rhythm section from various parts of the company, including cabin crew and engineers. Chief Pilot, Captain Dick Tobiano – a handy guitarist with his own covers band outside of work – also joined. Qantas soon had its very own in-house rock band, The Captains of Industry. 'The Captains' started rehearsing ahead of their first gig in August 2015, a party at Qantas HQ to raise money for the charity Royal Institute for Deaf and Blind Children, long a favourite cause of the Qantas cabin crew community.

Meanwhile, the refurbishments of the Qantas headquarters had been completed and a shiny new campus emerged that mirrored the rebuilding of the airline that Joyce was undertaking. Out of the construction site arose a soaring, glazed four-storey steelwork atrium structure, with cantilevered balconies and office pods, as well as the Qantas boardroom, extending into the atrium space, above a communal undercover zone dubbed 'The Street'. The award-winning project was designed to allow for maximum flexibility and staff connectivity. A signage system connected each of the three previously unconnected buildings with street addresses and precincts along The Street, including a reception lounge, theatre, bistro, café and bar.

'I always remember when The Captains did their first gig on a Friday night with the bar open,' says Joyce. 'I said to the guys, "If you're really bad, it's going to be terrible for the charity, and I don't trust you guys – I think you are going to be really bad.'

But The Captains were a hit and Joyce's scepticism was unfounded. 'We made some money for the Royal Deaf and Blind, and we didn't sound too bad either,' recalls Gissing. 'But it was an important thing at the time, The Street was new and it was about getting that real sense of community.'

'A lot of people have said to me that that was a bit of a cultural turning point for the airline, a really positive jolt,' adds Orszáczky.

*

With the balance sheet looking better, new aircraft were back on the agenda. Eight new Boeing 787-9s were ordered, to join the Qantas International fleet from 2017, progressively replacing five ageing 747s. Four 787-9s would arrive in the 2018 financial year, and another four more in 2019.

The state-of-the-art 787-9 brought much greater efficiency, with big reductions in fuel burn and reduced heavy maintenance requirements. Its range also opened up new destination possibilities around the globe. As Olivia Wirth explains, committing to the 787-9s was an important moment for Qantas culturally. 'It was about reinvestment and it was about a new aircraft type,' she says. 'Having gone through those difficult times, [ordering] the 787 . . . saw the resurgence of Qantas International to the rightful place that it plays for us in the Group.'

The 2015 results also signalled a big payday for Joyce and other senior executives. They had foregone pay rises for three years, with no short-term bonuses since 2013 and no long-term bonuses since 2009. Joyce's pay had fallen from $3.3 million in the 2013 financial year to $2 million in 2014, dropping below Borghetti's $2.78 million in salary and bonuses at Virgin. In fact, Joyce's remuneration between 2011 and 2014 was in the bottom twenty-fifth percentile of CEO pay in Australia. But he wouldn't stay in that lowly band for long. In 2015, Joyce's pay packet soared to $11.9 million, including a base salary of $2 million, plus almost $1 million in short-term share-based bonuses and $6.9 million in shares, as part of long-term incentives.

Leigh Clifford was at pains to point out that the size of Qantas's payments to its executives reflected the strong turnaround of the company, driven by the market value of Qantas itself, which had ballooned from $2 billion to around $8 billion between 2011 and 2014.

Throughout 2015, there was concern about a slowdown in the resources sector, as it shifted from construction to the production phase, and what that meant for the broader economy. Qantas had seen a steady drop in passenger demand in and out of parts of Western Australia and Queensland, and had adjusted its capacity accordingly.

But as the mining boom faded and the dollar returned to more typical levels, Australia once again became more attractive to foreign tourists, thanks to their renewed buying power. Tourism to Australia was growing strongly, rising 6.5 per cent in the twelve months to August 2015. Travel from China was soaring, up 21 per cent. This influx of tourists was a distinct positive for Qantas's domestic operations.

Other sectors of the Australian economy were strengthening too, including financial services, professional services, education, construction and infrastructure. Joyce commented at the annual general meeting in October 2015 that a rejuvenated Qantas International was reaping the rewards of its transformation and growing into markets where there was solid demand, such as Sydney–Hong Kong, Melbourne–Hong Kong, Brisbane–Tokyo Narita, Sydney–Tokyo Haneda and Sydney–San Francisco. The growth was achieved in a cost-efficient manner, using the existing fleet. Two Boeing 747-400 aircraft originally slated for retirement by June 2016 were retained to help meet the strong international demand.

Interestingly, both the Jetstar and Qantas international operations were beginning to see the role a lower Australian dollar was playing in global traffic flows, according to Joyce. At the price-sensitive end of the market, the Qantas Group was seeing greater demand for holidays in the Asia-Pacific region or at home in markets such as Queensland. At the premium end, business demand was robust and there was a noticeable uptick in inbound tourism as Australia became a more attractive holiday destination.

Joyce later commented that the lower dollar seemed to be having more of a positive effect on demand into Australia than a dampening effect on travel demand out of the country. Australians tend to compensate when their currency is weaker by spending less when they are away, rather than by changing their destination altogether, he said.

All this added up to bigger profits for Qantas, facilitated by the power of the dual-brand strategy and the reforms to the international arm of the business.

Another profit upgrade in December 2015 propelled the share price back above the $4 mark, which it had broken earlier that year. Joyce closed the year on a high, saying the anticipated first-half result reflected strong performances from each of Qantas's core businesses, including a record half-year result from Qantas Loyalty. Shareholders were again rewarded with a $500 million share buyback, thanks to the strong balance sheet.

Qantas International achieved a four-fold improvement on the prior year. This was underpinned by its three cornerstone partnerships – with American Airlines, China Eastern and Emirates – as well as by its ongoing cost controls. Considering the position Qantas International was in just a few years before, the turnaround was remarkable.

By now, the Group was in rich form. The profits were enabling investments in technology and product improvements to build customer satisfaction and loyalty. The carrier announced it would introduce an onboard wi-fi service across its domestic fleet, with trials from late 2016. More flights were announced to South-East Asia, including Bali, Singapore and the Philippines, as well as to New Zealand. The flights used Boeing 737s that had been freed up by reductions in domestic capacity, particularly in some regional resources markets.

Jetstar was also proving its worth to the Group, making a strong contribution to earnings. The losses in the offshore ventures had eased, helped by a reduction in unit costs and a drop in fuel prices.

Globally, the airline industry made a breakthrough in 2015. It was the first time the world's airlines, combined, achieved a return on their cost of capital, as more favourable economic conditions and the lower fuel price drove profits. 'There's not many industries that would regard that as a proud moment, but we do,' Joyce said. 'And in 2016, it looks like it'll be the second year in our history that we'll achieve it. The North American carriers are performing exceptionally well, because they've gone through Chapter 11, they've managed capacity and their profits account for over half the world's profitability.'[3]

Qantas regained its coveted investment-grade credit rating from Standard & Poor's in the week of its ninety-fifth birthday, in November. The return from junk-bond purgatory was welcomed by staff, to Joyce's surprise and delight. 'I didn't think that many people would pay attention to that, but with our staff, that was a big indication of the health of the business and it turning the corner,' he says. The rehabilitation was complete in early 2016, when Moody's Investors Service also upgraded Qantas's credit rating.

Over the fence, Virgin was in strife. The carrier tapped its four major shareholders for a twelve-month $425 million unsecured loan, to help fix its balance sheet amid ongoing losses and sky-high capital expenditure. Borghetti was still trying to deliver his corporate-focused strategy. Air New Zealand's Christopher Luxon soon after resigned from the Virgin board and put the airline's 26 per cent stake up for sale. He had been agitating for Virgin to rein in its spending – and for Borghetti to step down.

No such problems for Qantas. Another earnings announcement saw another record profit. For the twelve months to 30 June 2016, Qantas reported a 60 per cent lift in underlying profit before tax to $1.53 billion, eclipsing the previous high-water mark, under Geoff Dixon. It was the best annual result in Qantas's history.

For Joyce, it was a time for healing some old wounds. As in 2015, he splashed some of the spoils on 25,000 of the company's staff and shareholders. Full-time employees each received a $3000 bonus, and part-timers $2500. Shareholders received another

$500 million return in the form of a fully franked final ordinary dividend of 7 cents per share and an on-market share buyback of up to $366 million.

A buoyant Joyce was now sporting a new smile and new hair-style. He could certainly afford the expensive dental work and new look – his remuneration had risen just over $1 million in the financial year to $12.96 million, aided mainly by a jump in the Qantas share price, which boosted his long-term and short-term bonuses.

In August 2016, Joyce was interviewed at an industry confer-ence by CNN's Richard Quest, who put it to him that he'd 'got lucky' as a result of the friendlier fuel price.

'The results for 2015 were a record result,' the CEO replied. 'If it was just fuel, then every other airline in the world would be seeing a similar improvement. And if you take our most com-petitive airlines in the region – and the stat I use to explain the difference between us, that's Air New Zealand, Singapore and Virgin Australia – if you take their entire profitability last year in 2015 and add it together, Qantas, for the first time in its history, had a bigger profit. So there's more than fuel going on here.'[4]

Joyce was right. He had steered Qantas towards a much brighter future and kept the accelerator down on his Transformation Plan, which ended up delivering $2.1 billion in cost and revenue improvements – $100 million more than expected.

The Captains of Industry rocked The Street at Qantas HQ once more in 2016, and this time Joyce let his hair down. 'He'd had quite a few chardies – Alan doesn't mind a chardonnay,' recalls Orszáczky. 'And to see him wheeling around the dance floor, heckling the band, shouting out requests – that was pretty great. Alan was obviously feeling far more relaxed at that point – he was probably thinking, "We've done it, we've come through the bad times. Look at this, we have a bar, we have a campus, we're a smarter company, we're doing well." And it just felt like we were part of a really good time at Qantas.'

The Captains played a few gigs at Qantas HQ, and one externally – a memorable CAPA gala dinner. They had the audience up on the dance floor with a tight version of 'What I Like About You' by the Romantics, with Gissing tearing it up on harmonica, and delivered an electrifying rendition of Bruno Mars's 'Locked Out of Heaven'.

One wag who attended that gig wondered if 'heaven' was a euphemism for 'Qantas'. But the days of the union lockout were long gone. For Joyce, it was time to bulletproof the airline.

PART V

CRUISING

'We are the oldest continuously operating airline in the world, and we've always reinvented ourselves and disrupted ourselves before somebody else has. And I think we're always on edge.'

—Alan Joyce

18

Bulletproofing the Icon

As the various parts of the transformation plan steadily moved into place and Joyce could see some light at the end of the tunnel, it was time to make sure that the whole complex operation would endure for his transition – and his legacy. The Net Promoter Score was back up at peak levels, implying high customer satisfaction. He switched gear to focus on what he called 'bulletproofing' the airline. This would include developing non-flying revenue sources and leveraging the power of the group's brands.

The Qantas brand was rock-solid again. Despite regular announcements during Joyce's tenure that the brand was tarnished and beyond redemption, somehow it had persisted, defying gravity. In 2015, it was the only Australian entry on the *Forbes* 100 list of the world's most reputable brands.

It wasn't just the popular impression that counted – although that is important in attracting passengers, even where price is king. (Qantas's unique combination of brand-driven factors allows it, for example, to charge three times the price of the competition for a Perth–Sydney business-class flight. It's almost witchcraft.)

Being perceived as reputable made it easier for Qantas to attract the interest of other, similarly powerful brands. This opened up many partnership opportunities, both with other airlines and with non-aviation companies.

The Group was back in profit and all the signs were pointing in the right direction.

This book has focused mainly on the big-jet side of the Qantas Group: Qantas International, Domestic and Jetstar. They are the most conspicuous and best-known entities. In good times they are the biggest earners, so it is crucial to ensure they are positioned sustainably, because they are the most susceptible to external risk.

There could be no clearer example of how profitable but risky a business it is to fly big jets as Qantas going through COVID, then recovering. In the record 2023 financial year, Qantas's domestic operations generated earnings before taxes of $1.27 billion; Jetstar made a further $404 million profit. This was the market Joyce had once described as the 'billion dollar market' (although Jetstar included its international operations too). In the previous year, damaged by COVID, Qantas had lost $765 million and Jetstar shed another $796 million.

The Qantas International results include freight, a less fragile and recently solid performer, while Qantas Domestic includes the regional and fly-in-fly-out (FIFO) mining and resources operations, which have also tended to be more reliable than their big brothers.

But it is the non-flying arm that is the most reliable. Qantas's Loyalty program offers the best example of the power of the pull of the brand. Together with the airline operations, there is a delightful virtuous circle: the strong airline brand attracts leading retailers and credit card companies, which pay for the privilege of association, and then the growing aggregation of quality brands in turn makes others keen to buy in. The Loyalty business is also largely shockproof. Remarkably, even during the pandemic, when all around it was crumbling, it was able to generate strong revenue. Its profitability scarcely dipped, rebounding still more strongly in the 2023 financial year to a very healthy $451 million. Since 2019, membership has risen by more than two million, to over 15 million.

Joyce had focused on building the Jetstar brand into another valuable asset, both at home and in Asia, and aligning it to work with other long-haul airlines to strengthen the Qantas operation.

The core Qantas brand would also get a cosmetic refresh at the start of 2017, a new look for a new era. For only the fifth time in nearly a century, the flying kangaroo – the image that had featured on every aircraft since World War II – was rejuvenated.

Predictably, the rebrand was criticised both on the grounds that it was hardly different, and that it was a travesty of the original flying kangaroo. But it was all part of the rejuvenation on the road to enduring sustainability.

Alan Joyce once described Qantas Loyalty as the glue binding the Qantas Group together – a big asset that would only get better. Its success, he said, reflected the strength of the Group's customer proposition across Qantas Domestic, International and Jetstar.

Qantas Frequent Flyer was launched in 1987 as the Captain's Club, with 50,000 members. Its proposition was mostly around earning and redeeming points on Qantas flights. At first, the program relied heavily on non-flight reward options, including fine china and glassware, exercise equipment, and even a ride-on lawn mower. In the early days, it was often joked that the Club was only good for buying a toaster.

It grew fast. In 2001, tiered flying recognition levels (Bronze, Silver, Gold and Platinum) were introduced. By the time Joyce was installed as CEO of Qantas in late 2008, he inherited a frequent-flyer program boasting some 5 million members. In his first partial financial year as CEO, the program generated over $1.1 billion in revenue.

Through the early months of Joyce's reign, although the airline struggled, the frequent-flyer business became an even bigger jewel in the crown. A Woolworths supermarket partnership was introduced in 2009, marking the steady drift away from the traditional frequent-flyer model towards one with a large coalition of corporate partners. By 2012, the generic branding of 'Loyalty' was introduced, incorporating the frequent-flyer program with its other marketing services.

The coalition model typically offers lower profit margins, but all its profit is generated from partners external to the Group, making it the purest example of diversification away from the flying business. In other words, the loyalty business offered a handy source of cashflow from something other than flying big lumps of metal around the planet. Because of this, the program was one of the key focuses of Joyce's tenure as CEO. In the early 2010s, it was adding around 2000 new members every day, so expectations were constantly growing for members to gain value from the program.

In December 2013, Joyce announced his comprehensive structural review of the Qantas Group. The review did consider the partial sale of Qantas Loyalty, but after careful consideration it concluded that the program still offered major profitable growth opportunities, and there was insufficient justification for a partial sale.

It wasn't the first time a sell-down was mooted. In 2009, the airline had ruled out an initial public offering of the business. Instead, Joyce and his team decided to invest in the area. Qantas acquired Accumulate Loyalty Services in Melbourne for an undisclosed sum in 2011, and set up media analytics company Red Planet later in 2014 to analyse the information and data the program collected. The following year, as the 'big data' potential became apparent, Qantas took a controlling stake in analytics and actuarial business Taylor Fry, to beef up the airline's analytics capability.

There was a cultural aspect to it as well. Airlines by nature are focused on safety and operational performance, so they tend to be risk-averse. Wirth explains that a real shift in ambition for Qantas Loyalty occurred during Joyce's tenure, giving its leadership the freedom to be aspirational with it.

'Loyalty . . . was evolving into taking calculated risks and being bolder and braver too,' she says. 'You need to constantly be exploring what's the next opportunity and frontier and partner. And you have to be constantly evolving in order to remain relevant, but also to continue to bring revenue through the door.'

Years later, Joyce reflects that Qantas would never move away from the flying business. All the other parts of the business were dependent on that. 'One of the biggest reasons people are part of the [frequent-flyer] program is access to flights, and in particular Qantas International,' he said. 'So that was why it was important that we fixed Qantas International back in 2013.'[1]

Wirth agrees. 'The dream of using points on an international flight in first class drives consumer behaviour, because that's what they ultimately want,' she explains. 'They work towards it by earning points. So International is our halo product, but it's not just about our own metal [aircraft], it's also about our partners, so that's where the oneworld partnership, the Emirates partnership and bilateral partnerships with other airline partnerships are important for points redemption.'

Most points are still burned on domestic routes, but having access to upgrades and seats on international flights remains important. Qantas worked hard to protect that.

Considering the circumstances, the performance of Qantas Loyalty through the pandemic years was remarkable, and justified the effort of prior years to diversify and develop the non-flying business areas. Profitability was maintained in Loyalty and margins held relatively steady at levels the flying business could only dream of.

In Joyce's fifteen years at the helm, some 10 million frequent flyers were added to the program – one in every two households in Australia is a member of Loyalty. But total member numbers are somewhat of a vanity number. As membership numbers soared, top-line revenues from the loyalty program did not keep pace. Revenue per member fell from $181 in the 2009 financial year to $144 in the 2023 financial year, while profit per member slid from $39 to $30.

There is a known tipping point in the industry after which new members will produce materially less revenue, especially in a coalition program model like Qantas Loyalty. Early adopters generally offer the highest level of activity – and growing the program beyond those members requires increasing efforts to produce similar results. Later joiners typically produce lower levels of activity.

Overall, though, Qantas has done a remarkable job with Qantas Loyalty, and it is seen as a global benchmark. Its valuation has risen to over US$4 billion, according to On Point Loyalty, an analyst of frequent-flyer programs. The Qantas program ranks thirteenth on the list of the most valuable programs in the world. It's a highly creditable result, given the much larger population bases enjoyed by programs in the United States, Europe and Asia – and given Australia's more stringent financial regulations.

Qantas Loyalty has pushed the boundaries of the partner model, including new lines of business such as insurance. A remarkable 35 per cent of all Australian credit card spend accrues Qantas Loyalty points.

But by far the biggest positive has been the program's consistent profit contribution to the Qantas Group. It is on a path to generate $500–600 million in the 2024 financial year. 'We're not hitting the ceiling,' Wirth says. 'We are a large program, but we are by no means topped out, because it's all ultimately about engagement. How do you get the members to participate? We have ambition to grow and double the business again by 2030.'

The carrier has never been able to fully realise the value of Qantas Loyalty in its share price and market capitalisation – but perhaps that's the price it has to pay to keep the Group strong.

*

The role of Jetstar in Australia for the Group had evolved over time, to the point where it has become a major operator in its own right, by 2023 flying nearly 80 aircraft.

When the business started domestically, there were certain routes that it would operate for Qantas. The dual-brand strategy had, by 2015, become central to the success of the Group, especially domestically. It gave Qantas access to a broader range of customers and created flexibility in how it managed routes. Those that were becoming unprofitable for Qantas might be manageable for Jetstar, with its lower cost base.

The internal competition sparked by Joyce and Borghetti continued when both moved into other roles. It became first Buchanan versus Strambi, and then Hrdlicka versus David. 'You do want the person running Jetstar to say, "How am I going to run the best low-cost carrier?"' Joyce says.

From the start, Jetstar was a solid financial contributor, posting profits in every year after Joyce became CEO of Qantas prior to COVID, with the exception of 2014. But Jetstar's strong domestic results often masked troubles at the international and offshore Jetstar ventures, particularly in the early 2010s. For example, in 2014, the Jetstar Group posted a loss of $116 million, despite the domestic part of the group finishing the year in the black. That year, Qantas decided that no new Jetstar ventures would be established while the Group focused on its Accelerated Transformation Plan. Growth was slashed at Singapore's Jetstar Asia, while Vietnam's Jetstar Pacific was also forced to slash unit costs and needed to be recapitalised.

Qantas eventually headed for the exit in Vietnam. It had first bought a shareholding in Pacific Airlines from the Vietnamese government in 2007, and the carrier became known as Jetstar Pacific from May 2008. Growth plans saw the airline operating up to thirty A320s by 2020, but it reached only seventeen A320s by mid-2020. Intense domestic competition and persistent losses led Qantas to sell off its stake to Vietnam Airlines, and the carrier reverted to its original name.

'On paper Vietnam has all the hallmarks of a great place to be running an airline,' said Jetstar Group CEO Gareth Evans. 'But domestically Vietnam is an incredibly competitive market. There is 35 per cent capacity growth going on.'[2]

Qantas retains its Jetstar Asia venture in Singapore, which remains a key hub for the carrier into Asia, as well as connecting with Qantas services there.

A domestic Qantas and Jetstar executive team now meets every six weeks to go through the domestic market and to work out where to grow or reduce the red or orange tails, and to sharpen both carriers' network strategy. 'It's done in a harmonious way now – it wasn't always like that,' says Andrew David. 'It's taken a long time to mature, but that's a real strength that we've got there and the way we go about it. And it's done with the thought that ultimately there's one share price and one business here. There's two brands, but it's one business. And so you make those decisions cognisant of the Group first.'

Olivia Wirth believes the Qantas Group has become more sophisticated about how it thinks about core passenger segments. 'The reality is, they may choose to travel with Qantas for work or if they're going away for a weekend with their husband or wife. But when they're going on a family holiday, they're travelling with Jetstar,' she points out. 'So if you have a true level of sophistication at a customer level, you need to be able to make sure that the program can work across both brands.'

Partnerships have long been priceless for Qantas, given its position 'at the end of the line'. By 2013, it had solid partnerships covering most regions of the world.

But with Chinese tourism to Australia taking off, Qantas was missing out in a big way. The Chinese airlines were powering into Australia, led by China Southern. In 2015–16, visitor arrivals from China soared 23 per cent to 1.1 million.

Despite this, China was a very difficult market to service. A simple operation flying into Beijing or Shanghai could not possibly tap the potential of the vast population, which was spread right across the country.

Qantas was uncompetitive in China for two reasons: the ticket sales process greatly favoured the home airlines, who dominated marketing and sales outlets across the country, but the Chinese airlines also had lower costs and fares that were uneconomical for Qantas. Added to that, Chinese tourists increasingly used intermediate airlines, such as AirAsia, Singapore Airlines and Cathay Pacific. Qantas's full-service model relies heavily on carrying business travel, and there was simply not enough higher-fare traffic to be profitable.

Meanwhile, Virgin Australia was improving its access to the Chinese market. From 2012, Singapore Airlines held 19.9 per cent of Virgin's equity. So Virgin began codesharing on Singapore's extensive network into China, over the Singapore hub. It wasn't just the end-to-end travellers, but also the onward internal travel once tourists arrived in Australia. Qantas picked up many of these, but now Virgin could have its brand imprint all the way through.

With its Jetstar Hong Kong venture stuck in regulatory limbo, Joyce now reframed the discussions with China Eastern's chairman, Liu Shaoyong, around Qantas mainline. In November 2014, the airlines announced a five-year joint venture to commence in mid-2015, alongside the signing of the China–Australia Free Trade Agreement.

Joyce told *The Australian*'s *The Deal* magazine that the China Eastern relationship had built up over time. 'The Chinese take a much longer-term view of things,' he said. 'That relationship also has a social aspect to it. The Chinese like to have a few drinks. We have had occasions where you have the formal sit-down approach and then, in the Chinese context, a lot of the business is done over dinner. You get a sense of what they are after, their concerns. There are a lot of similarities between Australians and Chinese. People like to celebrate.'[3]

The China Eastern pact built on a codeshare arrangement the airlines had reached in 2008. It was ultimately aimed at opening up new routes between Australia and mainland China, such as between Brisbane or Perth and Shanghai. It started small, with the co-location of both carriers' operations in Terminal 1 at Shanghai Pudong International Airport.

The ACCC signed off on the agreement in August 2015. It was ultimately a way for Qantas to tap into the vast Chinese market without the high levels of financial risk that went with flying its own expensive large pieces of metal.

The deal didn't involve equity, but it did open up new markets and destinations for both airlines, including Qantas codeshare services operated by China Eastern to eighteen cities in China, and new destinations such as Changchun, Jinan and Wuhan. Access to the broader China market was estimated to deliver more than $80 million to Qantas in annualised net benefits.

Qantas's framework of partnerships in key markets was taking shape. The China Eastern deal complemented the extensive Qantas–Emirates partnership for Europe, the Middle East and North Africa, and the Qantas–American Airlines partnership for the United States.

For Latin America, Qantas switched its focus from Buenos Aires, Argentina, to Santiago, Chile, the home of its oneworld partner LATAM, in March 2012. Passengers could connect onto LATAM services to almost every country in Latin America. The initial three-times-weekly 747-400 flight increased to four times a week in 2014, and Qantas deployed 787-9s to Santiago when it phased out its 747-400 fleet.

Qantas continually looked to firm up international partnerships, including with deeper joint-venture arrangements that often bumped up against competition barriers. The ACCC had to be convinced that the interests of consumers and the wider public were served whenever there was a risk of reduced competition.

Much later, in December 2020, Qantas and Japan Airlines would seek ACCC approval to establish a joint business on routes between Australia, New Zealand and Japan. But with far less competition on the nonstop Japan route than there was on the Kangaroo Route to Europe, the Pacific route to the United States or between Australia and China, the ACCC blocked the Qantas–Japan Airlines venture.

Qantas's alliance with American Airlines also faced regulatory barriers both in the United States and Australia, which would diminish the full benefits both carriers were seeking. It's a seasonal leisure market, but a strong one, and has typically remained profitable when other international markets haven't. Qantas and American had been partners for three decades.

Both were founding members of the oneworld alliance, but from December 2015 they sought to shift their joint venture to a more detailed revenue-sharing agreement, as Qantas unveiled plans to return to the Sydney–San Francisco market. It took many months and much work to win approval from the US Department of Transportation. The US market has always been a vital one for Qantas, so pushing the regulatory barriers to their limits was worthwhile.

Qantas's westbound partnership was far less problematic. In 2018, the ACCC approved the extension of its comprehensive partnership with Emirates for a further five years. The revised Emirates deal was also adapted to add Singapore and Perth to the Dubai transit point for reaching Europe. As part of the changes, Qantas rerouted its daily QF1 Sydney–London A380 service through Singapore (rather than Dubai) from March 2018, and upgraded its existing daily Melbourne–Singapore flight from an A330 to the larger A380.

There were strategic synergies between Qantas and Jetstar Asia in Singapore, as both used Changi Airport to connect passengers between Asia and Australia – mimicking Singapore Airlines, but on a smaller scale. 'It's not just the standalone financial performance of Jetstar Asia that is important to the group,'

Evans explained to *Forbes*. 'With the re-hubbing of Qantas International into Singapore, we are undertaking and operating a dual-brand strategy within that market.'[4]

(India will one day become Australia's biggest market, but is difficult for Qantas to service. Unlike China, where non-stop flights are easy, connecting Australia's east coast with India requires very long sectors and the 'end of the line' handicap means Singapore Airlines can penetrate the Australia–India market more readily. An April 2022 codeshare agreement with India's largest airline, IndiGo – which has just shy of 1000 planes on order – will add to the Qantas Group's route palette.)

Qantas also established the historic 14,500-kilometre Perth–London journey in March 2018 using the new 787-9 Dreamliner, a pet project of Joyce's designed to restore the airline's key role on the Kangaroo Route. A seventeen-hour flight, this was the first nonstop air link between the antipodean countries.

In October 2021, Qantas and Emirates announced plans to extend their alliance for a further five years, from March 2023 through to 2028. The ACCC delayed authorising the extension until August 2023, but meanwhile permitted it to continue under interim authority.

Joyce said the Emirates move marked the continuation of one of the most significant bilateral partnerships ever seen in aviation. 'We called it "seismic" when it launched in 2013,' he observed. Back in December 2008, Joyce had spelled out the ingredients needed for a potential equity or merger partner: the right partner with a good brand fit, the right network reach, and attractive scale and economies. At the time, he was obliquely referring to the mooted merger with British Airways initiated by his predecessor.

What he didn't mention was the human side: the vital chemistry that had to be present at the highest levels. And with Emirates he'd found it in spades.

'I've come to really respect and like Tim [Clark],' Joyce says. 'I think he's one of the best CEOs of aviation. What he's done [at Emirates] has just been unbelievable. Over the years, if ever the teams had a disagreement, I'd just pick up the phone to Tim and we'd get it resolved because the chemistry worked.'

As Joyce sees it, the key to the Emirates success was continuous communication and having like-minded people working together. The management teams regularly caught up. 'When we did Perth–London and Emirates did Dubai–Auckland, that could have strained the relationship. But it didn't. Each airline needed to have its own freedom, while being respectful of and working with the other,' he says.

Any established airline's biggest capital expenditure is the billions of dollars invested in planes. Qantas had always been keen to fly suitably iconic aircraft, from the Super Constellation of the 1950s to Boeing's 707 and 747 (before its merger with Australian Airlines, it had been the only airline in the world to operate an all-747 fleet). But the days of flying romance were long gone by the time Joyce arrived. Government subsidies were no more and economics was the game. Competition grew by the hour. He inherited the fleet decisions of the late 1990s, the four-engined Airbus A380, which offered passengers a new level of space and comfort, and then the twin-engined 787 Dreamliner, which boosted efficiency and lowered fuel burn.

The inheritance of these fleet decisions meant Joyce had to find efficient replacements for the workhorse A330s used on Asian regional and trunk domestic routes. Today their average age is over sixteen years. (At his final results day in August 2023, Joyce announced firm orders for twelve A350s and twelve 787 Dreamliners to fulfill this role – but the first won't start to arrive until 2027, when the A330s will average twenty-one years of age.) His quest for aircraft for the rest of Qantas's domestic and regional routes was dubbed 'Project Winton'. And there was also Joyce's pet project, the ultra-long-range 'Project Sunrise' missions.

Joyce's first major legacy fleet decision came in early 2018, when the airline updated its Qantas Group A320 family order to include eighteen A321LR aircraft bound for Jetstar, to arrive between mid-2020 and mid-2022. They would operate on a mix of domestic and international routes.

Engine and airframe technology was improving fast, and ordering needed to as well. In June 2019, the original order was updated when Qantas secured up to thirty-six of the game-changing Airbus A321XLR (extra-long-range) aircraft, to enter the fleet from the 2024 financial year. The rest of the order comprised a further ten A321LRs and forty-five A320neos.

These planes, all twin-engined and single-aisle, are game-changing because of their greatly improved per-seat flying costs – as much as 40 per cent below that of their predecessors – and because of their long-range potential. Where the 737s and A320 single-aisle aircraft currently in operation in Australia are happiest flying routes up to about 2000 kilometres, the fuel-efficient XLR can fly commercially up to almost 9000 kilometres, possibly even putting sectors like Melbourne–Tokyo within reach.

Airline network planners love them because they are also at home flying much shorter sectors, making them very flexible. This means extensive network options for the several different airlines in the Qantas Group. The new aircraft could be used to open up new destinations or replace less-efficient widebody air-craft on existing routes. Depending on cabin configuration, the XLR can carry up to 244 passengers, with its much lower fuel burn per seat.

Joyce's next major fleet decision came during the COVID-19 pandemic, when Qantas selected the Airbus A320neo and the highly versatile Airbus A220 families for its domestic fleet renewal program. The carrier committed to 134 orders, including twenty more A321XLRs and twenty A220 aircraft, plus ninety-four purchase right options over ten-plus years with deliveries from the 2024 financial year onwards, to phase out its Boeing 737-800s and 717s.

Through the two deals, the Qantas Group could draw down on a total of 299 deliveries across both the A320 and A220 families as needed over the next decade and beyond, making this the largest aircraft order in Australian history.

The A220 became popular with airline customers in the United States and Europe because it has the capability to fly longer sectors between capital cities, as well as smaller regional routes. The regional market was a crucial one for Qantas – and another area where Joyce was focused on building resilience.

Andrew David says the board deserves 'huge credit' for the re-fleeting decision. 'That was a monumental day with the board to get that signed off,' he reflects. 'And those decisions are going to prove their weight in gold, because it's going to set us up.'

One of the lower risk elements of the Group's flying operations is regional domestic. Qantas started as a regional operation in far western Queensland. Its roots were in the bush, and freight (mail) featured right from the start. It made complete sense that Joyce would strive to strengthen these two vital, if sometimes overlooked, parts of the Qantas franchise.

As part of the bulletproofing across the Group, in February 2019 Qantas acquired a 19.9 per cent shareholding of Australia-based charter operator Alliance Airlines. This was a significant and profitable service provider to the resources sector, which continued to stimulate solid travel demand in Western Australia and Queensland, in particular. Alliance had also been a long-term provider to the Qantas Group, and flew regional services on behalf of the national carrier.

After Qantas announced its planned acquisition of Alliance, Regional Express (Rex) announced its acquisition of charter operator National Jet Express from Cobham Aviation, while Virgin Australia had been steadily expanding its resources flying operation.

Joyce had a longer-term plan to take a majority position in Alliance – to better serve the charter market and unlock synergies – but that ambition, and the initial shareholding, once again thrust Qantas before the competition regulators. It would be another exhausting experience, with the ACCC thrice delaying a determination on the matter.

Qantas upped the ante in May 2022, reaching an agreement to acquire Alliance in full, which by then had a fleet of seventy jet aircraft seating up to 100 passengers each. Alliance accounted for around 2 per cent of the total domestic market, and Qantas was Alliance's biggest single customer. It had entered a long-term agreement that saw Alliance operate up to eighteen newly acquired E190 jets for QantasLink.

But the ACCC blocked the move in April 2023, saying 'Combining such an important player with Australia's largest airline, Qantas, would be likely to substantially lessen competition.' It was a rare blow to Qantas and Joyce, who vowed to seek more information from the competition body about its decision. Nonetheless, Qantas's strength in the regional market remains as powerful as any competition body is likely to permit.

Better success was to be had in the domestic freight market. With the international and domestic transformation largely complete, the focus had switched to freight, which had been until then a quiet but positive contributor to the Qantas Group's fortunes.

What happens below the floor in an aircraft can be as vital as what happens in the cabin. The belly-hold of an aircraft can be an economic engine room. Joyce knew that, and he and his team set about improving Qantas's belly.

Qantas and Australia Post had a history of working together right back to when the national carrier first started flying airmail in 1922. In 2015, the entities signed a five-year contract for Qantas to transport Australia Post's domestic mail, parcels and Express Post until mid-2020. The deal, with a value in excess of $500 million, was embellished a year later when the two companies announced a dedicated domestic air-freighter network to be used exclusively by Australia Post and StarTrack customers.

The dedicated network would consist of six freighter aircraft featuring StarTrack livery, as well as priority access to cargo space in the Qantas Group's passenger fleet. Five of the dedicated StarTrack freighters were to come from Qantas Freight's existing fleet, with a sixth larger aircraft, a Boeing 737-400, soon to join the fleet.

Joyce said Qantas's Transformation Plan had sharpened the efficiency and flexibility of its freight business, and the agreement would help its biggest customer better coordinate their supply chain.

In 2019, Qantas expanded its domestic and international air freight agreement to support the growing demand for parcels under a seven-year partnership worth $1 billion. The deal aimed to benefit online shoppers and businesses across Australia by providing Australia Post customers with access to Qantas Freight's dedicated aircraft, and priority access to the cargo space on up to 1500 Qantas and Jetstar passenger flights to over 110 destinations each day, in addition to space on partner airlines globally.

It was a prescient deal, given the COVID lockdowns would soon induce a boom in parcel deliveries. The Qantas Group earned net freight revenue of over $1.3 billion in the 2021 financial year, accounting for some 22 per cent of all revenue that year. Typically, freight contributes around 6 per cent of Group revenue.

Then there was the supplier cost side, another area always under scrutiny. Confrontation had been commonplace in the travel agency distribution arena. Dominated by a handful of big global distribution systems (GDS) players – Sabre, Amadeus and Travelport – wielding complex tech-speak and myriad three-letter acronyms (or TLAs), air ticket distribution was a perennial flashpoint for airlines, particularly when times were tough. The GDSs would typically charge upwards of US$4 for every segment (one-way trip) sold through their system, often remitting a large part of that to encourage travel agents to book through the GDS. It was a major expense for airlines.

The global financial crisis had put the spotlight on GDS technology, service and pricing practices. Qantas was keeping a close eye on developments, especially the IATA's push for industry-standard new distribution capability (NDC).

In 2015, the IATA published the first official NDC standard: a travel industry–supported program launched by the industry body for the development and market adoption of a new, XML-based data transmission standard. Frustrated by the 1960s-era technology still powering the GDSs, the NDC standard aimed to enhance communications between airlines and travel agents, so as to provide more airline product features for agents to share with the travelling public.

For airlines, the new standards meant they could build sophisticated new technology platforms and bypass the GDSs completely – or at least be in a stronger position to negotiate with them. In early 2018, Qantas announced its new Qantas Distribution Platform (QDP), as part of the airline's plans to enhance the airline retailing, booking and servicing to deliver a more personalised experience for customers.

Qantas, with its large corporate footprint, took the bold step of evolving its indirect agent booking channel. It signed a deal with Corporate Travel Management (CTM) in November 2018 to allow select corporate customers to book via the new QDP.

Building off the QDP announcement in 2018, the airline unveiled the Qantas Channel in August 2019. This was a new offering that allowed agents who signed up to show their customers a wider range of fares and new, 'richer' content that wasn't available through traditional booking systems.

The majority of Qantas's key agency partners agreed to participate. Those that didn't would incur a 'channel fee', in addition to no longer being able to access content via the QDP. For the agents, it was a case of 'use it or lose it'.

Qantas also partnered with the GDSs to make the Qantas Channel available to agents globally. The digital environment had changed the way it needed to work with its trade partners. In this more cost-effective way, the airline also gained better control of its customers' data, while improving the service delivery.

By 2022, Qantas's next-generation distribution platform had been rolled out for international travel agents in the United Kingdom, the United States and South Africa, and more markets were being added.

It was a textbook example of Joyce's focus on costs, and on investing in solutions and technology to drive change. External suppliers and providers were ripe to challenge, but Qantas's own loyalty and customer data offered a juicy internal opportunity that was becoming irresistible.

The Qantas Group had all its bases covered – indeed, it had great strengths across its entire network, spanning international, domestic and regional passenger and freight markets. The Qantas and Jetstar dual-brand strategy meant Qantas was uniquely positioned in both the leisure and the premium sectors of the market, its international partnerships were in place, and it was all held together by a world-leading loyalty program.

The Group had come to perform as a much more coherent entity, with inherent synergies and the prospect of genuine sustainability. Joyce had instilled a new can-do culture in the Group, and customer satisfaction was riding high. If not quite bulletproof, it was as close to it as an airline group with its particular domestic and international profile could be.

19

Walking the World Stage

For a young CEO from an Australian airline based in Sydney, far from the centre of decision-making and daily dealings, establishing high-level relationships is not easy.

Europe's airline leaders bump into each other frequently, figuratively and physically, as they progress up the corporate ladder and deal with organisations such as the European Commission. American CEOs and their teams are also constantly eyeing their competitors – although, for fear of running foul of US anti-trust laws, they rarely talk directly with them.

The contacts Alan Joyce made in his early days as a CEO would prove valuable. His connection with Tim Clark, Emirates' CEO, would mature into one of Qantas's watershed deals, although at first the two were fierce, even bitter, rivals. It was only later – when Joyce was chair of the IATA board in 2012–13, and Qantas's share price was dipping below $1 – that they laid the foundations for the most important partnership the airline was ever to have.

The annual IATA gathering provides the perfect forum for airline leaders to build relationships, which can lead to powerful commercial tie-ups. The 300 or so CEOs often turn up to the association's annual general meeting with their international affairs and alliances heads in tow, hoping to hammer out bilateral deals and talk to the bosses of the global airline alliances, SkyTeam, Star Alliance and oneworld. Those groupings often make major announcements of new partner airlines joining the fold.

The annual general meeting also brings together the heads of the supply chain – the aircraft and engine manufacturers are all there. But unlike inside the flashy pavilions of the Paris or Farnborough air shows, the IATA meeting is a far more nuanced affair. Heads of the aircraft leasing companies invite the airline bosses to their hotel suites, hoping to negotiate fleet leasing and capacity deals.

Leasing companies own over half of all the world's aircraft, so they are important players. Airbus and Boeing, the major airframe manufacturers, alternate offering showy dinners for airlines and other invitation-only guests alike, with expensive entertainment and plenty of spruiking. The drinks flow freely. Each get-together is a heady cocktail of networking and deal-making, receptions and speeches.

Amid it all, the IATA holds its annual general meeting, a mostly stuffy and procedural affair at which the industry group lays out its strategic agenda for the year, whether it's carping about airports, high fuel prices, economic conditions, intermediaries or the latest health crisis. In the airline industry, there is always plenty to moan about.

The association members also formalise plans to address safety issues, standardise practices and address central challenges like reducing aviation carbon emissions. The airline industry was the first to identify and make plans to address that problem some three decades ago.

'IATA got the whole industry together and said, "What is the airline industry going to do about its impact on the climate?"' Joyce says. 'The outcome was phenomenal because we got the whole industry to agree to it – that we would, as a group, reduce our emissions by 1.5 per cent every year. We would then focus on sustainable fuels so we could get ourselves into a position where we are taking substantial amounts of emissions out and moving progressively to new technology that would help us do it.'

Joyce was in his element when the IATA caravan rolled into Dublin in 2016. He says it was probably the best IATA conference he'd attended. 'The IATA AGM is an amazing get-together of world aviation leaders,' he enthuses. 'Number one, it's very informative in terms of what's happening in trends in the industry. Secondly, it's a great policy and debating forum of the issues we face as an industry and how the industry's going to handle them. But even better still, it gives us a great opportunity to meet with partners, to meet with other airlines and to conduct a huge amount of business in a short space of time.'

In Cancún, Mexico, for the 2017 IATA meeting, with Qantas's transformation complete, Joyce was riding a wave of confidence. He proudly announced that Sydney would be the host venue for the 2018 gathering of the world's airline CEOs and other delegates.

Sydney's International Convention Centre was duly booked and preparations began. It would be the third IATA annual general meeting to be held in Sydney, after the 2000 and 1961 editions. As host, Joyce would act as chair.

As the CEOs gathered in Sydney in 2018, the headlines started flowing. 'Boys' club on parade as women struggle for top airline positions,' wrote one newspaper.[1] 'Fuel and fury dominate IATA boys' club gathering in rainy Sydney,' said another.[2] The official photo of the IATA's board of governors on the eve of the gathering told the story: of the twenty-six airline bosses, twenty-five were men. Christine Ourmières-Widener, CEO of Flybe Group, a small regional UK carrier, was the sole woman standing among the sea of suits and ties.

Qatar Airways boss Akbar Al Baker was among the suits. Always controversial, he managed to create more headlines the next morning by denying there was any gender inequity at his airline. Of his own position, Al Baker added, 'Of course it has to be led by a man, because it is a very challenging position.'

As groans and boos rang out, Joyce, who was seated next to Al Baker, went to the Qatar Airways CEO's aid. 'Akbar said he was going to stop saying controversial things – he lasted ten minutes. Ten minutes!' Joyce said jovially. 'Is that all we're going to get out of him? Ten minutes?'

Al Baker back-pedalled. 'I have to put out some fireworks to motivate people to ask more questions,' he said, before adding that he would keep quiet.

Joyce immediately adopted a more serious tone. 'For a lot of airlines and businesses, if you're not tapping into diversity and inclusion, you're going to be at a disadvantage. We're all looking for the best talent out there, and if airlines and some companies are only looking for males, they're not going to do well,' he said.

Joyce added that Qantas's senior management team was 40 per cent female, including the heads of the International and Loyalty businesses. He attributed the dramatic turnaround at Qantas to the fact the airline had embraced diversity so strongly. 'It's the right business thing to do and it's the right moral thing to do,' Joyce said.[3]

Al Baker later issued a statement saying he had only been joking, and that he was known for his 'lightheartedness at press conferences'.[4]

The international CEO circuit consists of more than attending large conferences. Those might provide unique opportunities for doing deals and forging partnerships, but the need to fuel the financial machinery means meeting investors face-to-face.

The company needs to attract large investors, like superannuation funds or managed funds, to become equity holders in the business. This is where its investment-grade rating is so important. Because most such investors are risk-averse, the competition between airlines chasing a piece of this pie is intense.

That's why airline CEOs and their chief financial officers dedicate a lot of time on investor 'roadshows' around the world.

Making face-to-face contact is invaluable in building up trust and investor confidence.

For Qantas, living in a small financial marketplace puts it at a significant disadvantage to the North American and European airlines. There just isn't enough capital available in Australia to support the financial needs of high-risk companies such as airlines.

On the plus side, Qantas does have the advantage of ready access to the corridors of power in Canberra. It is probably in the 'too-big-to-fail' category of Australian businesses, even if this would be vigorously disputed. It's also the dominant member of a so-far perpetual duopoly. Even so, it makes little sense, given the financial impediments Qantas faces, to cap its foreign investment at 49 per cent.

For the Qantas CEO, spruiking the company's numbers is one thing – and a critical one – but analysts and investors want to test out the senior management team to get a feeling both for their competence and their ability to implement the strategies they're selling.

As a new CEO back in 2008, Joyce had his work cut out persuading investors. This was only made more difficult when the share price languished in the doldrums and the world ran into the brick wall that was the global financial crisis. More recently, however, when Joyce climbs out of his first-class Qantas seat 1A in Europe or the United States, having performed his anti-jetlag exercises, his reputation precedes him into the next meeting. That is a priceless asset, and has delivered tangible returns.

Back-to-back meetings with investors and lenders requires a high level of candid disclosure. Over the years, trust develops – or does not – as the other party tracks each outcome to see if the assertions the CEO made have borne fruit. After fifteen years in the role, it has become second nature for Joyce. He is known globally, and his personal connections are immaculate and longstanding. In that respect, among airline CEOs he is a rare species.

This part of the job attracts very little attention, outside that of the very private analyst and investor world, but it underpins an airline's success or failure.

Spruiking the brand around the world also has its glamorous side, and during his time as CEO of Qantas Joyce rubbed shoulders with Hollywood celebrities, sporting champions and fashion models. It was clever strategic marketing, with an eye on generating goodwill and PR for the Qantas brand.

Possibly the most high-profile relationship was with Qantas's 'ambassador-at-large', actor John Travolta. He assumed that role in June 2002, when the Geoff Dixon–led Qantas joined him to launch the 'Spirit of Friendship' tour, which aimed to foster goodwill and encourage people to travel after the events of 11 September 2001. It started a massive, multi-decade PR coup.

Aviation-tragic Travolta had learned to fly light aircraft at age fifteen, and began to buy aircraft in his twenties. He was fascinated by the mystique of Qantas and purchased a Boeing 707 painted in its original 1960s Qantas branding and livery, keeping it at his Florida mansion, which boasted its own runway.

'Aviation has always rescued me from anything in my mind that is blue,' Travolta once said, adding that he could just look at an airline schedule or brochure and be encouraged. He shared Joyce's passion for collecting and reading aircraft schedules, so the pair hit it off immediately.

Travolta flew in for the Melbourne Formula 1 Grand Prix in 2010, linking with another Qantas ambassador, the F1 driver Mark Webber. Travolta then flew his 707 to Johannesburg just prior to the kick off of the 2010 FIFA World Cup in support of the Qantas Socceroos. The world tour next took him to Buenos Aires. Travolta showed up again in November 2010 to help kick off Qantas's ninetieth anniversary celebrations, piloting his 707 to Brisbane, Melbourne and Sydney.

In that same year, Qantas teamed up with Travolta to bring US television star Oprah Winfrey and her entire studio audience to Australia for an event at the Sydney Opera House. Oprah had a massive worldwide audience, and the resulting publicity was credited with sparking a surge in Americans' interest in holiday-ing in Australia. That success spawned a follow-up with *The Ellen DeGeneres Show* in March 2013, which resulted in another spike in inbound ticket sales from the United States.

Qantas was a regular participant in the annual 'G'Day USA' event, which promotes travel to Australia and celebrates Australian success in the United States. Signing model Miranda Kerr in 2012 as a Qantas ambassador helped draw more star power to the events.

Adam Goodes, an AFL star and prominent Indigenous Australian, became a Qantas ambassador in October 2013 – and, in fortuitous timing for the airline, was named Australian of the Year in January 2014. Joyce announced that, with Goodes's help, Qantas would increase its engagement with its employees and customers on Indigenous issues. 'His involvement is a key part of our strategy to create positive change through sports, as well as through education, employment and the performing arts,' the CEO said.[5]

Aussie golfer Greg Norman joined the airline's ambassador network in 2015, the same year as actor Hugh Jackman. Olympic gold medallist and 1998 Australian of the Year Cathy Freeman is another former ambassador, as are F1 driver Daniel Ricciardo, Socceroos goalkeeper Mark Schwarzer and rugby union great John Eales. This promotion of the brand by association with prominent popular figures, most famously John Travolta, works enormously effectively. By transferring their positive image onto Qantas, the airline's brand is enhanced, as well as generating valuable publicity.

In Qantas's case, the brand is elevated further by blur-ring it – to their mutual benefit – with promoting Australia. Thus the Peter Allen song 'I Still Call Australia Home' becomes indistinguishable from the Australia brand in its marketing impact. The song was recently revived in a new commercial to coincide with the reopening of the country after the worst of COVID. Featuring iconic Aussies Kylie Minogue, tennis star Ash Barty and actor Hugh Jackman, Joyce spoke of relaunching it as 'the national carrier's anthem' in the same breath as showing how 'Australia's stunning natural beauty and unique culture while celebrating the incredible resilience . . . has really shone through recently'.[6] (The commercial also fulfils other agendas by including children from Qantas's birthplace, Longreach, Adam Goodes, members of Bangarra Dance Theatre, swimmers Bronte Campbell and Ellie Cole, and Aboriginal Elder Rene Kulitja.)

Portraying Qantas in this light achieves the marketing goal of appealing to expatriate Australians but also underpins the hard detail of the international marketing road trips (financial results, fleet renewals, sustainability credentials, etc.). These strategies are by no means unique to Joyce, but he has used them effectively, as well as introducing his own elements.

20

Redefining the Airline Leader

Steve Jobs was a genius as an entrepreneur, and touched billions of people's lives. Yet some of his dealings were morally questionable and he was frequently brutal in his relationships, with competitors, partners and staff alike. Similarly, in a later era, another entrepreneur, Elon Musk, has shifted the world on its axis with Tesla, SpaceX and others to come. But is he a great CEO – a model for others to follow? Hardly.

In developing their consumer products, both men have displayed highly creative thinking, well beyond the capabilities of most mere mortals. They can be admired for this, but does their leadership stand as an example for the CEO of a large, established company to follow?

Although successful, Michael O'Leary, CEO of Ryanair, is publicly abrasive. He's renowned for comments such as 'What part of "no refund" don't you understand?' and 'The airline business is mostly run by a bunch of spineless nincompoops who actually don't want to stand up to the environmentalists and call them the lying wankers that they are'.

The originator of the LCC model, Southwest Airlines' Herb Kelleher, was at the other end of the spectrum. Widely considered the best airline CEO of all time, Kelleher was inspirational, innovative and established a remarkably human-centred culture. In an industry whose leaders are frequently lacking in all of those characteristics, he was a giant.

A key purpose of leadership, Alan Joyce maintains, is to ensure you inspire people to feel engaged with the direction you have mapped out, especially when reform is needed. 'This lies in carefully considering a path of action, front-footing the tough decisions, and ensuring you are doing your very best to explain your course of action as you go,' he says. 'I think people will come with you if they have faith that your actions are considered, and that they match your words. They may not necessarily understand or agree with your whole plan. But constant explanation is critical.'

Joyce was always careful to surround himself with talented individuals he could trust to deliver his direction. 'You always select the best people that you can for the roles that are out there,' he says, 'and the best thing you can do is give them the framework of what they should be doing within their job. Give them support, and give them advice, give them coaching when it's needed, but you don't try and do the job for them.'

Success in the role is most simply measured in terms of commercial effectiveness. If the company isn't profitable and sustainable, there's no business to lead, no employees to provide for, no customers to please. So that has to be the starting point – but the journey is almost as important as the destination. Today's CEO has to aspire to achieving a much more complex array of goals.

Although it's not widely recognised in the heat of day-to-day pressures, if a legacy airline such as Qantas is to survive and succeed in the twenty-first century, it needs to be a vastly different company from what it was twenty years ago. And Joyce has been in the hot seat for most of that time.

As Alfred Kahn, the godfather of airline deregulation in the United States, said forty-five years ago, you can't make an omelette without breaking eggs. In that case, it was about moving away from a heavily regulated industry to one driven by competition, where efficiency ruled and the consumer benefited. It meant lower fares, improved service – at least in variety and frequency of routes – and, as a result, more competition.

Even if an omelette is clearly needed, that doesn't mean the eggs are going to be pleased. And in Joyce's tenure, there have been many unhappy eggs. As always, the unhappiest shout the loudest. He navigated through an extraordinarily difficult period, and has left Qantas in a position where it is strategically sound and has the potential to be sustainably profitable.

There are two clear periods of his leadership at Qantas. For the early years, up until around 2013, he had little choice about what to focus on. The airline was endangered, as competition overwhelmed it. Survival was everything, and there were few clear paths Joyce could take. But, as the years following 2013 showed, there's more to leadership of a large organisation. Once the economic wobble was more or less righted, and as the Transformation Plan started to bear fruit, there was space for other priorities to come to the fore.

Traditionally, CEOs focused their public commentary mainly on economic, trade and industrial relations issues. Joyce was no different in this and made regular forceful contributions. As the business turnaround in the mid-2010s gained momentum, and with Joyce's longer-term future looking more secure as a result, he began to share his views on other issues, including societal reforms. He also became increasingly vocal about a range of challenges and opportunities confronting the national economy more broadly.

In an address to the National Press Club in late 2015, Joyce lobbied for diversification of the economy, and the need to build resilience through investment in tourism development, customs and immigration processes, and infrastructure. This was a time when the nation was being impacted by structural changes in the mining industry as China's economy came off the boil.

Joyce was also pushing for macroeconomic reforms to the tax system and industrial relations system through his role on the board of the Business Council of Australia.

'Reform should be geared towards making us a more prosperous nation overall,' he told the gathered media. 'Reform is about finding a workable middle ground, to get you from where you stand to where you need to be.'

Cultural issues were also on his radar – in particular the 'tall poppy syndrome', the idea that Australians like to criticise those in society who have been successful. 'I think we need a culture in this country where we encourage businesses to take risks by celebrating entrepreneurialism and not circling when there is a whiff of failure,' Joyce said.

Unsurprisingly, he expressed support for free trade and competition – but not to the detriment of the national interest. Here Joyce's idealism was tempered by his company's best interests. 'The government must always be conscious of ensuring Australian companies are operating on a level playing field. Opportunity must be reciprocal,' he insisted.

At the time, the federal government was flirting with the idea of opening up some northern Australian areas to foreign airlines. Australian carriers were not providing adequate service across the Top End, and regional communities were suffering.

'For instance,' he continued, 'it would be misguided to allow foreign carriers to fly in from overseas and operate as de facto domestic airlines in Northern Australia . . . In other words, to let AirAsia fly a route like [Kuala Lumpur] to Darwin, and then pick up domestic passengers on route from Darwin to Cairns, would allow foreign carriers to operate as de facto domestic airlines. This is an opportunity that would never be extended to Australian airlines in other countries in exchange.'

Keeping foreign airlines off domestic routes is hardly a revolutionary policy: almost no country permits that sort of operation.

And allowing AirAsia to run a Darwin–Cairns service would be seen as the thin end of the wedge. But Joyce's opposition highlighted the conflict between national and regional interests and those of the airlines, where the interests of the airline are assumed to be paramount.

Even today, almost a decade later, there is no daily nonstop return service between Darwin and Cairns, and you'd be lucky to find a round-trip fare below $1000, even on Jetstar. It could be argued that there is insufficient demand to support a higher level of service, but the reverse could be argued too. Meanwhile, a return fare for Sydney–Perth comes in at half the price for twice the amount of flying time.

Reform is always more painful if it threatens someone's interests; when people's jobs are at stake, the pain is magnified.

Joyce also took his activism in new directions. His cancer experience had focused him on the issue of men's health. 'Men's health is not something that's talked about a lot, because men don't like to talk about it,' he said. 'Just as many men are dying of prostate cancer [in this country] as breast cancer in females, and yet only one in ten men go and get the tests every year – and I was one of them.'[1]

News of Joyce's May 2011 cancer scare had eventually surfaced two months later, when Qantas announced it would fly nurses from cities and towns across the country to undertake training to become Australia's first specialist prostate cancer nurses, under a partnership with the Prostate Cancer Foundation of Australia. Qantas also undertook to help to build awareness of prostate cancer with passengers through advertising, inflight announcements and onboard messaging.

Joyce announced the partnership by unveiling a specially painted Qantas Boeing 737 aircraft featuring the foundation's distinctive blue ribbon. Qantas also supported the 'Movember' campaign to promote men's health issues, adding a well-sculpted moustache to another of its Boeing 737s.

*

From the start, Joyce had been clear with his people – and with the Australian government – about the need for reform at Qantas, explaining why change was needed, how the company would do it, and above all the risks of doing nothing. After all, he had led the charge with Jetstar; it had been the reform that was essential to combat the rise and rise of Virgin Blue. At the time, it was revolutionary.

Then there was the broader picture. It wasn't just reform of costs and expenditure.

Joyce now began to engage actively in important social debates around diversity and inclusion in the Qantas workplace. He believed that the more 'pro-diversity' a workplace was, the more likely it was to attract a wide range of talent, and that it would benefit from a plurality of views. So he participated in the Male Champions of Change Coalition, the aim of which was to help achieve gender equality in senior leadership roles. Formed in 2010 following a meeting between a handful of CEOs and the then Sex Discrimination Commissioner, Elizabeth Broderick, today the coalition includes over 250 industry leaders.

Airlines are a remarkably boysy business. At the end of 2023, Australia boasts three female airline CEOs – at each of Qantas, Jetstar and Virgin Australia (former Jetstar boss Jayne Hrdlicka). Beyond Australia, there are, incredibly, only eight more: three in Europe (one of them at Aer Lingus), two in Africa, two in Asia, one in Canada, and none in the United States.

That means Alan Joyce has his direct imprint on more than a quarter of the world's female airline CEO complement. This is no coincidence. In his advocacy of diversity across a range of areas, the Aussie from Ireland has had a colossal and very visible impact.

His approach extended externally as well. Joyce made it known that if a Qantas executive was to speak at a conference, it would be on condition that the panel discussion had a gender balance. This was particularly challenging for event organisers in an industry with few female executives, but it helped drive a shift away from the 'male, pale and stale' panels that had become so prevalent. Without doubt, it sparked debate about diversity in industry.

Qantas had a reputation of being socially active in the 1990s, and its status as the national carrier made the company even more focused on social issues. The airline was one of the first sponsors of the Sydney Gay and Lesbian Mardi Gras, well before Joyce arrived in the company. The move arguably was not entirely altruistic, as research showed that the gay sector was a highly valuable, big-spending market. Nonetheless, Qantas was an early and consistent supporter.

In the mid-1990s, the airline had its aircraft painted in Indigenous artwork as part of its reconciliation action plan, and it gained worldwide recognition as a result. An affirmative-action policy of hiring Indigenous employees also existed well before Joyce arrived.

'When we have solid foundations like that, I feel it's my job as a custodian of this amazing brand to build on that and to make sure that the company is at the forefront of it,' Joyce says.

The issue of marriage equality was becoming more and more prominent as the 2010s progressed and several attempts were made to legislate it. The Greens had pushed for a marriage equality act, putting legislation before the federal parliament in 2010, but it had failed to pass. The ACT had passed legislation in 2012 allowing gay marriage, but it was struck down by the High Court as being inconsistent with the 2004 *Marriage Act*, in which marriage was explicitly defined as a union between a man and a woman.

Initially the Coalition government intended to hold a plebiscite or referendum on the issue, but ultimately it decided upon a non-binding voluntary postal survey, to be held between September and November 2017. There was little controversy among the Qantas management team when they discussed the issue and how the airline would respond.

'We thought there was a clear role for the company to play in it,' Joyce says. 'As a gay CEO, I thought there was a need for me to be active in it.'

21

The Long Road to Marriage Equality

Alan Joyce's stance on diversity and inclusion reaped rewards within Qantas during the difficult transformation years. When asked what lessons he took away from what happened during the Qantas turnaround, he says: 'You develop a plan and you get as much diversity and collaboration together. But it's diversity of thinking in many different forms. And I think we are very passionate about all forms of diversity.'

This attitude began to spread. Internal success encouraged Joyce to take his message outside the company. He first publicly expressed support for marriage equality in May 2011, in a speech at the National Press Club, where he highlighted the importance of diversity and inclusivity in society and called for marriage equality as a matter of human rights.

Joyce's advocacy on social issues, namely LGBTIQ+ rights and marriage equality, took on a bigger public face from late 2014. Apple chief executive Tim Cook came out in November 2014 and Joyce saw Cook as a key role model for other people struggling with the issue.

In an article in *AFR Weekend* at the end of 2014, Joyce said it was great that there were a number of openly gay CEOs in Australia. 'I've been to loads of functions with Shane and nobody has ever had an issue. We should be proud of where we live,' he said. But Joyce added that Australia was 'a bit behind' on the global marriage equality debate; it was important that we caught up.

Joyce also noted the casual racism that was endemic in Australian corporate and social life, with his Irish heritage derided or his thick brogue ridiculed. 'In some cases, it is unfortunate we classify race in terms of people's colour . . . but calling somebody a leprechaun or using abusive language about my Irish heritage is just as bad,' he said. 'That form of racism seems to be in some way acceptable, but it is not acceptable.'[1]

Ireland, meanwhile, was undergoing massive societal change. Its constitution, adopted in 1937, included a ban on divorce. Garret FitzGerald's Fine Gael-Labour Party bill in 1986 sought to amend the constitution to allow divorce. 'The constitution had essentially been written by a very strong Catholic,' Joyce says. 'The opinion polls [in 1986] were leaning towards a "yes" vote. Then the Catholic Church one weekend told everybody to vote "no". So we lost that one.' The referendum was defeated 63.5 per cent to 36.5 per cent.

'Then the second referendum [on divorce] came up [in November 1995], and the Catholic Church did the same thing. But the Irish population had changed, and divorce got through [narrowly, by 50.3 per cent to 49.7 per cent]. Then contraception and abortion got through. It was a big change from where it was. Irish society had become more secular than probably most places in Western Europe.'

Scandals that had arisen in the Catholic Church had a big impact, Joyce says. 'The paedophile priests scandal, the Mary Magdalene schools, the terrible treatment of unmarried women, and the deaths of all of those kids out of marriage, those horrendous stories in Ireland moved the dial quite a bit.'

In May 2015, Ireland held a referendum on marriage equality, and 60 per cent of the Irish people voted, with some 62 per cent in favour. It became the first country in the world to do so.

'I was in tears when that result came through,' Joyce says. 'This country that I left, when homosexuality had recently been illegal, had turned in twenty years to embrace the LGBTIQ community. What an amazing change.

'Back in 1996, if you told me that Ireland would become the first country in the world to legalise same-sex marriage through a popular vote, and to elect an openly gay prime minister [Leo Varadkar] twice, I probably would have laughed at you.'

Meanwhile, Joyce's globetrotting shareholder roadshow trips convinced him that the investor community would back his stance on the social issue. 'I had one big shareholder in Boston reading all the clippings on what we were doing. "You are not doing enough," he said, "you're not putting enough behind this, because that's why we invest in companies like you."' This investor believed that companies with strong environmental, social and governance capabilities – known as ESG – outperform.

Joyce was also convinced there was a business case for it. 'We could see in the research, our customers were really behind it . . . Places like the Eastern Suburbs [in Sydney] at 78 per cent in favour of it – they're Qantas customers.' Qantas also had a very strong LGBTIQ+ staff community, who were also backing the company's stance.

Chairman Leigh Clifford was supportive of marriage reform, but did his own due diligence, polling Qantas shareholders and customers. He reported overwhelming support back to the board. The Qantas chairman then spoke with Joyce and said, 'Be arm-in-arm with the rest of your supporters in the business community on this issue.'

The CEOs of over 300 major Australian and foreign companies with a presence in Australia publicly supported same-sex marriage; one vocal supporter was the chairman of Wesfarmers, Richard Goyder, later to become Qantas chair. Goyder wrote: 'While Australia continues to exclude same-sex attracted people from this important and highly valued institution, it sends a message that discrimination on the grounds of sexual orientation remains acceptable.'[2]

But you could have been excused for thinking Joyce was alone. 'Well, of course Alan [was left] standing there when the rest stepped back,' says Leigh Clifford. 'Alan became the face of it, and quite often he was saying nothing, but there'd be people . . . virtually putting words in his mouth.'

Joyce was encouraged by the progress various countries had made on these issues, and was motivated to ensure the momentum for change was maintained. 'You can't take it for granted and we have to keep on pursuing the changes that have occurred everywhere,' he said at the time. 'I think everybody has to be vigilant that that doesn't happen and this is a very important topic for a lot of people.'[3]

By October 2015, Joyce's advocacy had gained global attention. That month, LGBTQ Inclusion Awards group OUTstanding and the *Financial Times* announced the publication of the 2015 power list of leading LGBTIQ+ professionals. Joyce made his first appearance in the Top 100 list, at number 2.

Being the CEO of the Qantas brand meant Joyce received vast attention in the media. It wasn't something he engineered, although Joyce did not shy away from the publicity. 'That [media attention] allows me to make a stand on social issues that I find important and allows the company to portray its position on our social issues, which is also important,' he acknowledged in an August 2016 interview with CNN news anchor Richard Quest, also an openly gay man. Joyce saw the cause of equal marriage as being entwined with diversity more broadly. Advocating for diversity was important in itself, he argued, but it also led to a more productive workforce.

He continued: 'So on marriage equality, we've been personally very outspoken because I think that's very important for our customers, our employees, and eventually our shareholders, the same on Indigenous recognition and gender equality. And we're very vocal and very out there on all of those issues, which I think I'm pretty proud of and I think our employees and our customers are. And having that attention allows you to leverage it, by promoting those causes.'

Of course, advocacy on these matters was also deeply personal for Joyce. 'There's a lot of gay young people out there,' he told Quest, 'and I've had some heartbreaking letters written to me about people that have struggled with their sexuality, have struggled with coming out of their families, have struggled with their careers. Having some role models out there shows you can have a successful career, there is a meritocracy in a lot of companies around the globe and you can thrive.'[4]

A couple of months before the Quest interview, the IATA annual general meeting had been held in early June in Dublin, which was invaded by over 1000 aviation visitors. For a whole week, the city was bathed in sunshine; the temperature even hit 25 degrees one day. In a few spare moments between the back-to-back meetings, Joyce took a stroll down to St Stephen's Green, an area he knew well from his early days.

Named after a thirteenth-century church on the site, the green had been a battleground during the 1916 Easter Monday Rising in the struggle for Irish independence, when the Irish Citizen Army attempted to overthrow the British. This bright, sunny day in the city brought many locals to the green, as Joyce related to Richard Quest.

'And this young man came over to me, and . . . he said, "I'm shocked to see you. Are you Alan Joyce?" I said, "Yes." He asked, "What you doing here?" I said, "I'm at a conference." And he then told a story of reading about me, of the Irish link, how he was struggling in university, how he was struggling coming out to his family, how he wasn't in a great mindset. And then the inspiration that that gave him made a big difference.'

The moment had a big impact on Joyce. 'And . . . he later sent a book to me, which had an inscription in it,' he continues. '"Alan, meeting your heroes sometimes can be said to be disappointing. I've really enjoyed meeting you. You've been a true inspiration and you've changed my life."

'Now, when you find out that the suicide rate of young gay people is seven times the national average for males here, making that type of difference and showing that you're a role model . . . So if you get some headlines that you're the gay CEO or you get some headlines that attack you for doing what you're doing, you live with that.

'Because if you're helping people get through their lives, they're coming out, helping people not commit suicide, then that to me is a huge benefit of the role that we're playing. I think you [Richard Quest] are playing that role too. I hope I'm playing that role and we can make a difference.'

By 2016, Australia was in the throes of deciding whether to hold its own equal marriage plebiscite, and at the political level there was much dog-whistling about the need or otherwise for it.

Polls were consistently showing support of between 60 and 70 per cent for change, but few whistled louder against extending the definition of marriage to include same-sex couples than the former prime minister Tony Abbott, who argued: 'This debate is about changing marriage, not extending it. And if you change marriage, you change society; because marriage is the basis of family; and family is the foundation of community.'

In October 2016, Joyce published an op-ed piece titled 'Do it without anti-gay vitriol', in which he addressed the concern that a debate on the issue would only generate division:

[A]s most gay people will tell you, get in an argument with the wrong person, and it's not long before they reach for an anti-gay slur. It's certainly happened to me.

And that, in a nutshell, is why a lot of people oppose a plebiscite on marriage equality. Because they know that when the debate starts, the slurs won't be far behind.

We've already had marriage equality advocates compared by conservative commentators to the Nazis and
ISIS because all three are apparently 'totalitarian' in their
approach. That's an extremely hurtful comparison when you
consider the murderous behaviour of these groups towards
homosexuals.[5]

It didn't stop the vitriol. *Daily Telegraph* columnist Miranda
Devine penned a column in late 2016 in which she said Joyce
had 'turned Australia's beloved national airline into a tool of
the same-sex marriage lobby' and that he 'blackmails everyone
who's anyone – including advocates of traditional marriage –
into silence with membership of Qantas's "elitist" Chairman's
Lounge, "the hottest ticket around"'.[6]

Joyce and Devine had engaged in a heated debate about
marriage equality at a function several months before. Devine
said Joyce 'accosted me at a party once to rant furiously [but]
I can handle myself just fine against angry leprechauns'.[7]

In March 2017, Australia's federal Immigration Minister,
Peter Dutton, raised the (slightly) wider concept of whether it
was appropriate for corporate leaders to campaign on social
issues at all, saying they should 'stick to their knitting'.

Singling out Joyce, he said: 'I think it's unfair to use the
brand of a publicly listed company, and indeed, in some cases,
the resources provided to that company by shareholders for
these issues which are completely outside the domain of these
companies.'[8]

Joyce promptly retorted that 'they absolutely should':

Qantas (and its CEO) is often called on to speak publicly on
issues like company tax, industrial relations and trade. And
we do. Because these are important issues that ultimately
shape what kind of society we live in (which is the point of
economics, right?). We're pleased to include marriage equality on the list.[9]

In the same piece, he argued:

> Qantas's identity is the Spirit of Australia, and one of the
> most fundamental values in this country is the notion of a
> fair go. That's why Qantas speaks up on gender equality.
> And recognising our Indigenous people. And for marriage
> equality. I have no doubt we'll add to this list as time
> goes on.

Outside the political arena, homophobia could be more explicit.

Two months later, in early May 2017, Joyce was on a business mission to Western Australia, speaking at a conference
before 500 business people at Perth's Hyatt Hotel. A Perth man,
67-year-old Tony Overheu, hid patiently behind a curtain and
screen at the rear of the stage, waiting for the right moment.

A former farmer, Overheu was incensed by 'corporate bullying' in the marriage equality debate, believing Qantas's public
stance had crossed a line. While Joyce was being interviewed on
stage, Overheu emerged and slammed a pie into his face.

Olivia Wirth was sitting in the audience and watched the
attack unfold as though it was in slow motion. 'When it happened, Alan didn't really know what to do,' she says. 'He started
to walk off to the side and I immediately went over. The media
was there as well, so I got his jacket, blocked the cameras and
took him off to the side so they weren't getting even more coverage – they had got enough footage as it was. I took him off to the
side, called security, did as much as I could.

'But in the first exchange I had with him – behind the curtains, still with pie on his face – he took off his glasses and he
said, "Oh, Liv, I think there's going to be a problem." "What,
Alan?" He took off his glasses and he was wiping the cream off of
his face and he said, "Liv, I swore!" I said, "Oh, mate, that's not
the story! What, do you think you're going to get in trouble with
your mum?" He wiped himself up, and in true Alan style, got
back on stage and continued the speech.

'It's my favourite story about Alan. I think it says a lot about Alan as a human being, because it occurred when an awful thing was happening to him.'

'I'm not a big pie eater,' Joyce told the audience when he resumed the interview. 'But I need a good dry cleaner before I leave Perth, so if you have one, please recommend it to me!'

As Joyce explains, it was a very angry, forceful pie to the face. 'It was very much a message of "I want you to stop talking about [how] you're a powerful gay man and I'm threatened by your commentary and your insistence on it." But my reaction to that, like all bullies, is that you stand up to them.'

On principle, Joyce pressed charges. 'No attempt at bullying us into suppressing our voice will work,' he said, 'and my intention is to send a message that this type of behaviour isn't acceptable.'

Overheu said he had planned his attack carefully but didn't mean to hurt anyone. 'It would appear that Alan Joyce is very much part of a network trying to subvert the federal parliamentary process around the issue of marriage equality,' he said.[10] Overheu was charged with common assault, trespass, damage and giving false evidence to the police. He pleaded guilty, avoiding jail and a criminal conviction, but had to pay $4057.50 in fines and costs. He also received a lifetime ban on flying with Qantas, Jetstar or any partner airline, such as Emirates.

The Perth incident only fuelled Joyce's resolve as the campaign on same-sex marriage entered its final stages. His long-term partner, Shane, was the merchandise manager director for the marriage equality campaign, while the partner of Qantas's then head of strategy worked as the videographer on the campaign. Qantas's head of government affairs was also on the board of the campaign. 'So we were very involved in it,' Joyce says.

At least someone approved of the job Joyce was doing, and the role he was playing in the campaign. The following month,

Joyce was included in the official list of recipients in the Queen's Birthday Honours List for an Order of Australia. He said he was 'truly honoured by the award', which 'also recognised the work of thousands of people who made Qantas an institution that Australians can rightly be proud of'.

Joyce had been lucky to spend all his professional life working in aviation, he said, as it was an industry that was a force for good because it's ultimately about connecting people. 'And that encourages a diversity of ideas that makes Australia the kind of place it is today. The notion of a "fair go" has to be one of the most important Australian values, and it's been a big driver behind my work promoting equality. We're lucky to live in a very accepting, open society and we need to keep championing the need for everyone to share in the same opportunities.'

The campaign was coming to a head.

On 15 November 2017, the results of the postal survey on same-sex marriage revealed that 61.6 per cent had voted yes, meaning Australia became the twenty-fourth country to embrace marriage equality. Remarkably, the result was very similar to Ireland's. Although it was not binding, the wide majority support would lead to same-sex marriage being legalised in Australia in December 2017. The ACTU had supported the cause and campaigned on its behalf, but the powerful TWU took no position.

The day the results were released, Joyce gave an emotional speech, having been named the *GQ* Business Leader of the Year. He couldn't hide his delight. 'What an amazing day,' he said. 'I always knew Australia is an amazing country. This is a country where an openly gay Irishman can become the leader of one of the most iconic brands in the world . . . A company which embraced an Irishman to become its leader because it's a meritocracy . . . Anybody that saw today would've been so proud of the people of Australia.'

Joyce noted that two key events – Peter Dutton's knitting comment and the Perth pie attack – 'brought us to the forefront of the campaign. Our politicians didn't get us there,' he added, 'the people did.'

No Qantas funds were spent on the campaign. Joyce and his New Zealander partner, Shane Lloyd, donated a million dollars to the campaign, 'because we were massively outmatched by the church, who supported the "no" campaign', he said. 'We were doing it all just with personal profile and the company's profile, but it showed you that the community, the shareholders and the employees got behind it.'

Andrew David remains impressed by Joyce's commitment. 'What he did with marriage equality and the way he stood up, it was clearly something that was very close to his heart,' he says. 'On so many things like gender equality and marriage equality . . . he will stand up and he will be counted.'

Joyce and Lloyd were among the first to celebrate the opportunity to marry, after nearly two decades together, in a ceremony at Sydney's Museum of Contemporary Art on 2 November 2019.

Qantas has at times been accused of being selective in the social causes it gets behind. Less than twelve months after the marriage equality result, a human rights organisation pressed Qantas to stop transporting refugees offshore on charter flights paid for by the Australian government. The Australasian Centre for Corporate Responsibility and a refugee legal service filed a shareholder resolution at the airline's 2017–18 annual general meeting calling on Qantas to 'stop deportations and removals to danger'.

Chairman Leigh Clifford said, 'We believe that these groups should take their concerns up with politicians directly rather than use airlines or other business as part of their campaign.' If the resolution had passed, Clifford argued, it would have put the airline in the role of 'third umpire' on individual immigration cases and 'undermine' the legal system.

Controversies of a sporting kind then cropped up, in the form of high-profile Qantas sponsorships of the Australian rugby union side, the Wallabies, and the Australian men's test cricket team.

In March 2018, Cricket Australia faced a massive global controversy when members of the men's test team were found to have tampered with the ball during a match in South Africa. Qantas issued a statement saying the saga was deeply disappointing and 'certainly not what anyone expects from our national cricket team'.

Joyce publicly urged Cricket Australia to resolve the matter urgently and 'make a statement to the rest of the world' over the scandal. Qantas hadn't threatened to drop its sponsorship of Cricket Australia and was nowhere near doing so, according to Joyce, but he wanted the organisation to 'do the right thing'. 'I came to Australia twenty-two years ago,' he said. 'Australia, they know the significance of a fair go, being sportsmen and sportsmanlike. The [ball-tampering scandal] has damaged our reputation worldwide.'[11]

Just over a year later, Joyce was confronting more sports sponsorship drama. On 10 April 2019, Wallabies player Israel Folau, an evangelical Christian, put up a post on social media that said 'drunks, homosexuals, adulterers, liars, fornicators, thieves, atheists and idolators' would go to hell unless they repented. It sent Rugby Australia into damage control.

Qantas issued a short statement noting its disappointment at Folau's actions, and that it was pleased that Rugby Australia had condemned the comments. Joyce and the airline stayed silent until, a month later, a three-member panel found that Folau had committed a high-level breach of the professional players' code of conduct and terminated his playing contract.

Joyce said he supported Rugby Australia's verdict and was quite happy with the organisation's response and process. 'We don't sponsor something to get involved in controversy,' he noted. 'That's not part of the deal. We expect our partners to take the appropriate action. It's their issue, they have to deal with it . . . and shame on you if it happens a second time.'[12]

The timing couldn't have been worse for Rugby Australia, as it was in the midst of contract renegotiations with Qantas. A sponsorship extension was eventually renewed later in 2019, at a lower rate than previously, according to reports in the *Australian Financial Review*.[13]

At the end of 2020, Qantas ended its thirty-year partnership with Rugby Australia and withdrew its cash sponsorships of cricket, soccer, the Olympics and Paralympics in Australia, as it axed $20 million in sports sponsorships across the board.

Joyce's confidence in using his position to promote social causes grew almost in step with the rising importance of environmental, social and governance (ESG) issues over recent years. Popular pressures intensified for businesses to perform responsibly on these issues, and many senior investors' requirements increasingly rank their investment behaviour according to the ESG performance of the companies in which they invest.

At the same time, studies (and opinions) on the impact of this form of social leadership by large corporations are mixed, often arguing that it can solidify opposition and create division. Alternatively, if leadership means what it says, some level of controversy will be inevitable – not an attitude of, to quote from the UK television show *Yes Minister*: 'I am their leader, I must follow them.'

Yet not every cause can be given support. Selecting where (and how actively) to lead and when to step back can often be a subjective decision. There are no clear guidelines.

From Joyce's 35,000-foot perspective, on issues like marriage equality, where a substantial proportion of Qantas' electorate was supportive, and there was little in the way of political divisiveness, publicly espousing support on the back of the Qantas brand was relatively uncontroversial.

It becomes more questionable when clear political lines are drawn, and the nation is divided on the merits of putting the weight of the national icon behind one side or the other. Such was the case with the 2023 referendum on the Voice to Parliament.

While it could be argued that supporting the Yes campaign was morally and historically appropriate, this was clearly a more contentious issue. According to media reports, even the Qantas board was divided on the merits of putting the brand behind support for the Voice – or to be more accurate, to do it so conspicuously.

The latter point is key. It places any Qantas/Joyce intervention in a very different place from other companies. The publicity given to relatively small 'Yes23' logos on the sides of four aircraft (out of a Group fleet of nearly 300) predictably brought howls of protest from some quarters, including the predictable 'I'll never fly Qantas again'. Yet almost every other major company in Australia also came out publicly in support of the Yes23 vote; no one suggested they would stop shopping at Woolworths or Bunnings due to their support.

Finally, the bottom line is the bottom line. If, as argued by Don Argus, former BHP Chairman, there could be financial consequences if the Voice referendum passes, directors have a fiduciary duty to ensure as far as possible that there will be no financial harm to shareholders' interests.[14]

Joyce has felt it necessary to stick his neck out on many social issues over the past decade. The level of intensity he has applied in leveraging his profile in support of causes is personal to the man. He is part showman, but predominantly driven by passion for the cause at hand. It will be interesting to see if his successor, Vanessa Hudson, is similarly active in using her position to press for change.

22

Before the Storm

Through the latter 2010s, Joyce was determined to see through his Transformation Plan. His systematic bulletproofing and value-exposing work of all parts of the Qantas Group had yielded spectacular results, including successive billion-dollar underlying profits before tax between the 2016 and 2019 financial years, despite rising jet fuel prices through the period.

Qantas had produced combined underlying profits before tax of $564 million between 2010 and 2014. The airline would then rack up over $6.7 billion in combined underlying profits before tax in the second half of the decade. Most observers wouldn't have believed this was possible.

Virgin, by contrast, only managed one year of profit in that timeframe, in the 2012 financial year, during the 'slow bake' and grounding of Qantas. John Borghetti unveiled the airline's fifth consecutive loss in 2017, of $3.7 million. His likely successor, John Thomas – the consultant credited with helping turn the US major airlines around – had left the company just ten months after joining. The head of Virgin's low-cost carrier, Tiger Airways, Rob Sharp, filled Thomas's role, while Borghetti would stay on longer than planned.

Joyce said in August 2017 that although the Transformation Plan had run its course, aviation was a competitive business and Qantas took nothing for granted. 'We have no intention of being complacent,' he said. 'That's why we're taking the energy and focus from the turnaround, and putting it into continuous improvement.' Joyce now unveiled a program to deliver $400 million in annual cost and revenue improvements. 'And it's already started,' he said.[1]

With the company on a stable footing, it was time to plan for the future. In November 2017, Joyce's executive team underwent its first reshuffle in over three years. He spoke of the need to drive the next phase of ongoing improvement and innovation. And the CEO himself was staying put. 'As long as I'm enjoying the job and the board and the shareholders want me to continue, which I hope is still the case, I'm going nowhere soon and that will continue,' he said.[2]

Even so, it was appropriate to prepare the ground for an eventual succession. Among the changes in Joyce's direct reports, Gareth Evans – who was firming as Joyce's replacement – moved from CEO of Qantas International to become CEO of the Jetstar Group; he was replaced by executive team newcomer Alison Webster.

Olivia Wirth, meanwhile, took on additional responsibilities for customer and digital strategy, in the new role of Chief Customer Officer.

Andrew David shifted from CEO of Qantas Domestic to assume responsibility for Qantas Freight, Catering and Airports, while Jon Scriven, the Group Executive of People and Culture, retired and made way for Lesley Grant, who in turn passed the role of CEO of Qantas Loyalty to Jayne Hrdlicka.

Hrdlicka had been the CEO of Jetstar Group for five years, but her stay as Loyalty boss would be short-lived. With Joyce's hands still firmly on the controls, Hrdlicka recognised that she would have had to wait several more years for a tilt at the CEO's role. She left the Qantas Group in March 2018 to become CEO of fast-growing milk company A2.

'Because I've known Jayne for a long time, it was disappointing,' Joyce says. 'I could see she wanted to run a publicly listed company and that was the right thing for her to do. But we wished her all the best and still do. Jayne is very capable, one of the best executives I've worked with,' he says. 'Within Jetstar, she focused a lot on the ancillary revenue component and brought a lot of value to that as well. Ryanair is probably the only airline that's ahead of Jetstar in ancillary revenues.'

Hrdlicka's departure prompted Joyce to switch Wirth again to the role of Loyalty CEO, from where she eventually featured in the succession race for Joyce's role. Vanessa Hudson was promoted to the role of Chief Customer Officer, joining the Group Management Committee and reporting to Joyce for the first time.

Hudson's career with Qantas started just after the merger with Australian Airlines and just prior to the float of Qantas in 1995. Then chief financial officer Gary Toomey had sacked the internal audit department and hired twenty-five chartered accountants to come in and find all the low-hanging fruit. Hudson was number one in the door.

She worked her way up to the role of Executive Manager of Commercial Planning, and in October 2013 she shipped off to Los Angeles to look after the jewel-in-the-crown US routes as Senior Executive Vice President of the Americas. Hudson returned to Sydney in July 2016, becoming Executive Manager of Sales and Distribution, before being elevated to the Chief Customer Officer role in February 2018. In June 2019, she was appointed Group Chief Financial Officer Designate, and officially took on the role five months later.

The changes meant the gender balance of Joyce's top executives remained constant, with five women on the eleven-member team. The CEO said there were a number of very high-calibre individuals in the Qantas executive team who had a deep understanding of the business, naming Wirth and Hudson as 'two standout examples'.[3]

Hrdlicka and Joyce wouldn't have known it at the time, but her departure set in motion a sequence of events that would eventually see Australia's three leading airlines headed by women. Hrdlicka would become CEO of Virgin Australia in November 2020, Stephanie Tully was appointed CEO of Jetstar in September 2022, while Hudson would see off Wirth as the candidate to replace Joyce in 2023.

Meanwhile, Leigh Clifford's role as chairman was entering its final phase. Richard Goyder joined the board as a non-executive director in October 2017 and commenced his duties as a director after stepping down as the CEO of Wesfarmers in November 2017, after more than twelve years at the helm.

Wesfarmers was one of Australia's largest and most diverse companies. On his appointment, Goyder said he admired the way that the management team led by Alan Joyce had repositioned the Qantas Group over the past few years, and that the airline had an exciting future. He was also the incoming chairman of Woodside Petroleum from April 2018.

In June 2018, Qantas announced that Clifford would resign at the carrier's annual general meeting that October, and that Goyder would assume the role of chairman. A new face was also added to the board. Brimming with aviation industry experience and with a history of working with Joyce, former Cathay Pacific CEO and IATA director-general Tony Tyler joined the Qantas board in August 2018.

Clifford's eleven-year tenure covered one of the most transformative periods in Qantas's long history, and at the annual general meeting in Brisbane, Joyce thanked him for guiding the carrier through some of its biggest challenges. Joyce and Clifford were in ebullient form, unwrapping a record profit and gifts for shareholders and staff.

Clifford was bowing out on a high. History would show that he and Joyce had been a very effective duo.

Clifford always believed that public remarks by a company's chair and CEO ought not to show any separation. 'I think you shouldn't have, what I call, competition for the microphone,' he explains. 'When you fight for the microphone, you know, differences arise.'

Clifford and Joyce spoke often, but Joyce maintained that Clifford was not a micro-manager. 'He trusts people to get on with the job,' he says. 'He's very supportive but he expects results, and that's the way it should be.' Joyce was particularly fond of Clifford's earthy sayings. 'When we were going through some granular detail one time, Leigh grumbled, "I think we're taking the fly shit out of the pepper now! Please let's not get into that level of detail." Leigh was famous for his sayings that gave you the exact image of what he wanted.'

'I'll be judged by how the community and the market views the capability and success of the CEO that I appointed – and I reckon I get a tick on that regard,' Clifford told the *Australian Financial Review* a week before he stepped down.[4]

The chairman's move paved the way for succession planning for the CEO's role. By then, Joyce was on annual contracts, but continuing to enjoy the role. At the top of his to-do list were lifting Qantas Loyalty's annual profits above the $500 million mark, completing long-term re-fleeting decisions for the domestic and international operations, and launching nonstop flights to Europe and the United States. Qantas's 100th anniversary, in November 2020, was also looming.

As Joyce energetically moved towards the Qantas centenary, Borghetti's time at Virgin was up. In June 2018, he had announced he would leave the airline before his contract expired in January 2020. He said it was the right time to go, having stayed on longer than he originally expected, in order to complete Virgin's transition into a true alternative to Qantas.

Virgin had been destabilised by its foreign ownership structure, with constant speculation about which investor might drop out of the unprofitable airline, following Air New Zealand's high-profile exit.

According to Joyce, Borghetti had done a great job with setting up and marketing Virgin's product. 'I just don't think the strategy was right,' he says. 'I think a strategy that moved Virgin up-market to try and compete against Qantas was doomed for failure.' And, in a reversal of his earlier thinking, 'At the end of the day, the better strategy was where [Brett] Godfrey was, in the middle of the market.'

And what of the rivalry between Joyce and Borghetti?

'For me, it was never personal with John,' the Qantas CEO says. 'I never get to a personal position on these things. I don't know what John would say, but for me, it never was personal. It was all about the business.'

Paul Scurrah became CEO of Virgin Australia in March 2019, and, after announcing Virgin's seventh consecutive annual loss, he revealed plans to cut 750 jobs, delay aircraft deliveries, scrap unprofitable routes and reorganise the senior management team. 'We have strong revenue growth and we have a problem at the cost level,' Scurrah said[5] – which was true enough for the whole of the Borghetti era.

Joyce, meanwhile, powered on. He had shown his true colours, made the big calls and built a team culture that would now have to face the ultimate test.

PART VI

TURBULENCE

'We know that, no matter how tough it is in the moment, we've always come back from a crisis stronger than before.'

—Alan Joyce

PART VI

TURBULENCE

23

Descent into Chaos

It was 7.30 am on an early autumn Sydney morning. The mood in the second-floor boardroom at Qantas HQ was ragged. Floor-to-ceiling windows looked down over The Street below, the wide indoor thoroughfare of coffee stands and restaurants. On any normal morning it was bustling, with bench tables for casual business meetings and visitors wearing lanyards being escorted around.

Today, however, although it was a working day, The Street was deserted. Despite its panoramic, brightly lit open area, right now it was a gloomy place to be.

On the second floor, at the end of the long wooden table, with his back to The Street, sat Alan Joyce. He was a man under enormous pressure.

Just days ago, although already it seemed like a world away, Qantas had been flying high, reporting strong profits, and the outlook had looked particularly positive. In the last days of 2019, the share price had hit an all-time high of $7.40. Now, in late March 2020, Qantas was running out of cash. The share price had slumped to a low of $2.14 on 19 March, meaning two-thirds of the company's capital value had vanished in the space of ten weeks. Qantas was just seventy-seven days from closing down.

The hurricane that was COVID-19 had struck with full force. Thousands of people were dying around the world, intensive-care wards were full, people were queued in ambulances outside hospitals and dying before they reached the entrance. In Sydney, the cruise ship *Ruby Princess* had released hundreds of infected people into the community.

The steep gradient of the infection and death curve was terrifying. There was seemingly no prospect of a vaccine. There was absolutely no idea when, or even if, the spread would stop. No one was certain how the virus was spread. But one thing was clear: airlines could not continue to fly, as they were spreading the disease like crop dusters. No industry was harder and more suddenly hit than the travel business.

Qantas had an annual wages bill of over $4 billion, or over $350 million per month. With salaries, debts to service and a fleet of very expensive aircraft sitting on the ground, the company was haemorrhaging money, with next to nothing coming in.

And now Joyce was being advised by his chief financial officer that there were just eleven weeks left before the airline would run out of cash. It would be just short of its 100th birthday. The executives were powerless to do anything about it. The world had stopped.

A large screen filled the wall opposite the CEO. On it were the familiar faces of board members and the senior management team from around Australia and overseas. The chairman was isolated in Perth – or 'North Korea', as Joyce would later call it. No one was smiling. All were looking at Alan Joyce. In fact, they were looking *to* Alan Joyce, as he was the man in the hot seat.

By this stage, the board was meeting remotely on a weekly basis, rather than the more normal monthly schedule. These days, there was no time to prepare board papers; presentations were done using PowerPoint as the situation changed on a daily basis.

With the novel coronavirus running rampant across the world, the first half of each meeting would be taken up by a presentation from the airline's director of medical services, Ian Hosegood. In contact with Australia's medical leaders and his international colleagues, he would provide a day-by-day update of what had been learned about the pandemic.

Qantas wasn't alone: almost every airline in the world was on the brink of bankruptcy. It's a capital-intensive industry that runs on cashflow, making it perfectly vulnerable to this mysterious, enigmatic disease that was killing people and closing borders.

People had simply stopped travelling, and, with national and state borders slamming shut, it was obvious there were no simple solutions to bring Qantas out of the gloom. No one had been through a period like this before. No one knew how much worse things would go, nor how long the crisis would last. But obviously something had to be done.

Joyce, with his mathematical background, liked to work out each issue methodically, yet in this case there was not enough data with which to make an ordered decision. He recognised, therefore, that the core methodology had to shift. He was fond of a saying often attributed to President Theodore Roosevelt: 'In any moment of decision, the best thing you can do is the right thing, the next best thing is the wrong thing, and the worst thing you can do is nothing.'

With Qantas staring at annihilation, Joyce knew he had to do *something*.

On 9 January 2020, Sydney was still cloaked in smoke from the worst bushfires in over two centuries. That day, the World Health Organization (WHO) noted a spate of pneumonia-like cases in Wuhan, in China's Hubei Province, that could have stemmed from a novel coronavirus.

Joyce saw a BBC news report on the outbreak. He rang Richard Goyder and said, '"We just need to keep an eye on this because this has the potential to be pretty bad for us." Since Richard was new to aviation, I said what we usually do, if [national] borders start closing or restrictions start coming in, is moderate capacity. That's the only lever that we can pull.'

Qantas was no stranger to the impact of health shocks and related disruptions. Just over a decade earlier, the 2009 H1N1 'swine flu' pandemic had delivered a $45 million hit to its 2009 earnings, while the severe acute respiratory syndrome (SARS) outbreak had wiped out its profitability in the second half of the 2003–04 financial year. There had also been the Asian financial crisis in the late 1990s, the bursting of the dotcom bubble in 2000, and the 9/11 terrorist attacks in September 2001, each of them punishing for the airline business.

Qantas had long maintained a risk register – a list of risks potentially affecting the carrier. A pandemic was on the register for decades, according to Joyce, because of what had happened in the past. Joyce later recalled that Geoff Dixon used to say airlines were subject to a 'constant shock syndrome', whether it be a geopolitical shock, an economic shock or a pandemic.

'You never know where they're going to come from,' says Joyce, 'but what's really important is your capability of dealing with whatever the shock is. It's like computer hardware and software . . . whatever the software, the crisis or risk, you put in, the hardware – that is your people and culture – can manage it. So it's all about getting the right people with the right can-do attitude, that take ownership. The second thing that's really important is to give people the autonomy to get on and get things done within that environment. Then, what you do is you practise all the time.'

Joyce and his executive team were about to get a lot of practice.

On 20 January 2020, novel coronavirus cases were reported in Thailand and Japan, prompting several countries to begin screening inbound flights from China. On 25 January, a man who had flown from Guangdong Province to Melbourne on 19 January tested positive for COVID-19 – Australia's first confirmed case of the new virus. He was followed by three men in New South

Wales later that same day. Two had travelled to Wuhan, and the third was a close contact of them.

On 21 January, with 200 infections and four confirmed deaths in China, a Chinese doctor named Zhong Nanshan confirmed that the novel coronavirus could be transmitted from person to person. Two days later, Chinese authorities took the unprecedented move of placing the entire city of Wuhan and its population of 11 million people into a strict lockdown. From that point on, almost everything that happened was 'unprecedented' – a word that would become common over the next three years.

On 29 January, the Australian government introduced a fourteen-day self-isolation period for travellers arriving from Hubei Province.

By 31 January, with global cases exponentially rising to 9800 and a worldwide death toll of more than 200, the WHO declared a public health emergency. Human-to-human transmission was quickly spreading, and the virus was found to be circulating in Germany, the United States, Japan, Vietnam and Taiwan. News reports were also coming in of more cases in Europe. Two Chinese tourists in Rome tested positive for the virus. An Italian man repatriated to Italy from Wuhan was hospitalised, and clusters of cases then emerged.

On 1 February, the Australian government mandate was upgraded to a ban on travel to mainland China and a fourteen-day self-isolation period for all travellers arriving from mainland China. Australia's focus was still on China, the biggest source of inbound tourists. The same day, Qantas announced it would suspend its Sydney–Beijing and Sydney–Shanghai services from 9 February. Hong Kong services continued intact. By 10 February, the novel coronavirus death toll in China had reached 900, surpassing the 774 deaths the country had experienced over the entire period of the SARS crisis of 2003–04.

In Australia, the virus still remained a vague threat. Many still had not heard of it, and life was continuing as normal – at least for those who weren't plagued by the bushfires.

In Sydney, Joyce fronted the media on 20 February for the routine announcement of the Qantas Group's interim results. These revealed a solid underlying profit before tax of $771 million for the six months ended 31 December 2019. But that was history, and a far cry from what was just around the corner.

By now, forward bookings were slowing. Joyce announced a 15 per cent cut in international capacity to Asia until at least the end of May, and the Group introduced an annual leave program to manage the employee impact of the slowdown. Qantas told the market it expected a 2020 financial year impact of $100 million to $150 million from the novel coronavirus, tempered by the rapidly falling price of jet fuel.

Looking ahead, Joyce announced some secondary impacts beyond China, with weaker demand showing up on routes to Hong Kong, Singapore and Japan. Traffic to the United States and the United Kingdom hadn't yet been impacted. This was similar to the SARS experience of seventeen years earlier. Joyce predicted demand into Asia would rebound, 'and we'll be ready to ramp back up when it does'.

Domestically, the news focus was still on south-eastern Australia, which was beginning to recover from the summer's devastating fires. These had burned over 8 million hectares across the south-east of the continent. Six per cent of New South Wales' landmass had burned, with more than 2000 homes destroyed. Tragically, twenty-five lives had been lost. One of two 'mega-fires' had been 380 kilometres long and alone covered 2.7 million hectares, making it one of the largest contiguous fires ever recorded globally.

Domestic demand weakness also emerged in February, attributed to the summer bushfires. Only 8 per cent of Qantas's bookings at the time were attached to an international trip, and Joyce pointed out that the percentage of those bookings from Asia was smaller again.

At this stage, the mood among the management team remained confident. The company had a well-honed risk assessment and management system. A few weeks into the crisis, Joyce asked one of the Qantas finance analysts to come up with a worst-case scenario. The analyst produced a slide of how events were likely to unfold, which included the domestic borders closing. The expected timeframe was six months.

John Gissing said he was surprised at the range of feelings at that time. 'Maybe I've been around too long, but I've seen my fair share of crises over the years,' he says. 'We had just come out of bushfires and I live on the South Coast – they were devastating. Things I've never seen before and horrific impacts on people. And I think that in those early days it was, "Oh, there's a pandemic, we've got a risk assessment for that – we've got some of the controls to manage it."

'There was a lot of optimism because history told us these things pass pretty quickly . . . [There were] others who were really a lot more concerned about where this could go, taking a worst-case scenario.'

Joyce remained cautious but untroubled about the potential impact of COVID-19. It was, after all, Qantas's centenary year and the carrier had seen its fair share of challenges in that time. 'Qantas is extremely well positioned,' Joyce concluded, 'a leading domestic business in a stable market with an international business carving out unique advantages in ultra-long-haul routes.'

Qantas was insulated – or so he thought.

As the days passed, COVID-19 spread further into Italy, Iran and other parts of Europe and North America. The worrying media coverage led to a sudden and significant drop in forward bookings. The speed of the pandemic's spread meant the scenarios around border closures – which Joyce thought would take months to play out – started to be realised in a few weeks.

On 1 March, the federal government introduced a ban on travel to and from Iran, and Australia reported its first home casualty from the outbreak: a 78-year-old man who had been a passenger on the *Diamond Princess* cruise ship. His wife was the second. Travel bans were introduced on travellers from Korea on 5 March, and soon after that on those from Italy, which was also being severely hit.

By 10 March, with the Qantas share price faltering to $4.45, the company announced further cuts to its overseas flying, bringing the total international capacity reduction for Qantas and Jetstar from 5 per cent to 23 per cent compared to 2019, and extended until mid-September 2020. Rather than exit the routes altogether, Qantas deployed smaller aircraft and grounded its A380 fleet for six months.

In response to strong customer demand for the nonstop Perth–London service, the existing Sydney–Singapore–London return service (QF1 and QF2) was temporarily rerouted to become a Sydney–Perth–London service from 20 April, and the much-anticipated Brisbane–Chicago route commencement was delayed from 15 April to mid-September. Jetstar made significant cuts to its international network, suspending flights to Bangkok and reducing flights to Vietnam and Japan by almost half.

Joyce was holding management team meetings on nearly a daily basis as he figured out how to react and what capacity to take out. 'We were always playing catch-up,' he says.

Olivia Wirth says the early weeks of COVID was a 'weird' time, because no one knew what was truly going on. 'We were dealing with a business issue – and we have lots of experience of dealing with business crises, particularly over the last decade – but this was actually a humanitarian crisis and a very personal one for our people. So we were dealing with multilayered things at once,' she says.

All the while, the company was responsible for making up-to-date disclosures to the ASX; its shareholders needed to know what was happening with their investment. Qantas scrapped its earlier impact warning and said it was no longer possible to provide meaningful guidance at this time. Worryingly for financial markets, the board decided to cancel an off-market share buyback that had been announced in February, in order to preserve $150 million in cash, although the interim dividend of 13.5 cents per share would proceed – for now.

As the weeks passed, the executive team recognised that this was a much more fundamental shock to the system. Joyce decided to forego his salary for the remainder of the 2020 financial year, the executive management team took a 30 per cent pay cut, and Goyder and the board decided to take no fees. Management bonuses were set at zero, and all non-essential recruitment and consultancy work was frozen. The Group asked all Qantas and Jetstar employees to take paid or unpaid leave in light of reduced flying activity.

The optics of these moves were good: timely and swift action was being taken. In an attempt to calm investors' nerves, Joyce said Qantas remained a strong business with a robust balance sheet and low debt levels, and reminded the market that most of its profit came from the domestic market. Qantas was therefore in a good position to ride this out, he said, especially with the bottom falling out of oil prices.

But Joyce was frank about the challenges ahead: 'I think this will be survival of the fittest and I think Qantas is one of the fittest and most dynamic airlines in the world. We know we can ride this out. Not all airlines around the world will.'[1]

On 11 March, the WHO belatedly declared the novel coronavirus a pandemic. The global share market rout gathered pace, led by airline and travel stocks. By now supply chains were being hit hard: it was becoming almost impossible to buy toilet paper, and brawls were breaking out in supermarkets where they were running low. The world was being turned on its head.

Damage to the travel industry accelerated quickly. On 11 March, US President Donald Trump announced a travel ban on non-Americans who had visited any of twenty-six European countries in the past fourteen days from entering the United

States, to take effect on 13 March. People travelling from the United Kingdom and Ireland were exempt. The move sent shudders down the spine of airline CEOs around the world.

Trump declared the novel coronavirus a national emergency on 13 March. Two days later, Qantas and Jetstar customers were offered the option of cancelling flights for travel up to 31 May and receiving a travel credit instead. The federal government introduced a universal precautionary fourteen-day self-isolation requirement on all international arrivals, and an arrival ban on cruise ships from foreign ports for thirty days.

Quarantine rules created the most challenging international operating environment ever seen for airlines, both commercially and operationally, and many airlines simply stopped flying to Australia.

On 14 March, a 500-person limit was brought in for all non-essential, organised public gatherings. Then, three days later, in response to massive falls in travel demand due to new government restrictions across multiple jurisdictions, including quarantine requirements and corporate travel bans, Qantas announced that international capacity across the Group would be slashed by 90 per cent until at least the end of May. Some 150 aircraft, including most of the Qantas Group's widebody fleet, were grounded.

The precipitous decline in demand and resulting cuts to flying had obvious repercussions. Qantas now had a significant labour surplus across its operations. With travel demand unlikely to rebound for weeks or possibly months, the carrier warned, the impact would be felt across the entire workforce of 30,000 people. Joyce didn't give specifics yet, and of course no one knew how long the problem would last, but he had to prepare the workforce for dramatic change.

'It's now fair to call this the single biggest shock that global aviation has ever experienced,' he wrote to staff. 'We can't shy away from the fact we have a very tough journey ahead of us. But we will get through.'

By now the markets were tumbling, house prices were slumping and small businesses were feeling the pain. On 17 March,
Qantas's share price closed sharply lower, at $2.86.

'We switched the business to very clearly come in with a plan to
reduce the cash burn,' Joyce says. 'There were a couple of things
we could do – one was obviously putting aircraft on the ground
and making a call about what goes into storage and what we
would maintain.

'There was, then, our people, where it's a big call. We were
the first company that used that provision in the *Fair Work Act*
to stand people down legally. And we implemented that because,
again, we just couldn't afford the salaries.'

Events were now cascading, and it was time now to pull out
all the stops.

On 18 March, public gatherings in indoor spaces were
limited to 100 people. That night, another COVID-carrying
cruise ship, the *Ruby Princess*, arrived in Sydney Harbour. The
Reserve Bank announced a $100-billion boost to the economy
and cut the cash rate to 0.25 per cent. Australia's borders were
slammed shut to non-citizens, while residents and Australians
were urged to return home as soon as possible. Australia was
now closed for business.

In an unprecedented move, Qantas unveiled a full suspension of
all Qantas and Jetstar international flights from late March. There
would also be a 60 per cent reduction to domestic flights. Two-
thirds of Qantas employees were temporarily stood down until at
least the end of May; they were allowed to draw down on their
annual and long-service leave, to preserve as many jobs as possible.

'That decision to stand down people was the hardest thing
I think we've ever had to do, and it was just heartbreaking,' says
Wirth. 'Alan cried when we made the decision to stand down the
workforce. He was not in a good way, because he was making
decisions that he just didn't want to, but he couldn't see any other

pathway through. It's those two big parts around what's right for the business, but then how do you not show compassion for the human being? Yeah, it was really tough. Bloody awful.'

Senior Group management executives and the board had their salary reductions increased from 30 per cent to 100 per cent until at least the end of the financial year. The interim shareholder dividend payment was also deferred until September 2020. More aircraft were grounded, taking the tally closer to 200. Rows of aircraft parked up at airports around Australia and the world would become enduring images of the time.

The only bright spots were Qantas's fleet of freighters, which continued to be fully utilised. Some domestic passenger aircraft were also being used for freight-only flights. Also, the mining industry, with its fly-in, fly-out workforce, was steaming along, and repatriation flights were being conducted on behalf of the federal government.

'Our people were doing some heroic things,' says Wirth. 'The volunteering, the amount of days that some of our people spent in isolation to continue to run those services was incredible. The personal sacrifice they made was extreme.'

On Sunday, 22 March, the National Cabinet decided all pubs, clubs, cafés and restaurants (excluding takeaway) would be required to close from 12 pm the next day. Gyms, indoor sporting venues, cinemas, casinos, nightclubs, places of worship and entertainment venues were also shuttered. Schools remained open, but were encouraged to provide access to online education. A rule was brought in limiting numbers at funerals to one person per square metre. Social-distancing rules were tightened two days later.

The next day, thousands of people were queueing at Centrelink for unemployment benefits – a scene that would repeat all week. Images of long queues, with all kinds of people, most of whom had never been inside a Centrelink office, led the evening news bulletins. The next day, the international travel warning was upgraded to a total travel ban.

Border closures and the cancellation of flights created another huge problem for airlines around the world: they were sitting on billions of dollars of unearned flight revenue. Their systems weren't set up to refund millions of cancelled bookings simultaneously, so they offered travel credits instead.

For Qantas, the Australian border closure triggered some $2 billion in flight credits. The fare conditions that determined which customers were entitled to a refund – and which were not – created confusion, and call centres were swamped with queries.

The contract between passenger and airline steeply favours the airline, allowing it considerable latitude. This imbalance is most noticeable when large numbers of people are affected, and it became a major issue during COVID, not just because of the money involved but because it was often combined with massive inconvenience to passengers.

In most cases, the non-delivery of the service was not the airline's fault, but the result of border closures – although, of course, in the minds of passengers, the airline had taken their money. But the last thing an airline or travel agent wants to do when they're staring bankruptcy in the face is to pay out money they haven't got.

Yet there was more to it than that. Suddenly there were hundreds of thousands of demands on Qantas's refunds system – and at a time when Qantas staff were among those who were falling ill. Moreover, many refunds are highly complex to get right at the best of times. 'When you have $2 billion of them, it was impossible for the call centres and the technology to manage it,' Joyce says. Call centre wait times blew out, and big volumes of calls were left unanswered. However good the reason, where money is concerned, people's tolerance is greatly diminished.

But for Qantas, cash was now the chief preoccupation. And with virtually nothing coming in, its reserves would soon run out.

24

Eleven Weeks Left

The Qantas analyst's six-month worst-case scenario played out in just six weeks.

The executive team quickly got an indication of how much cash the airline had left and how rapidly it was disappearing. 'We had a weekly burn rate, and that became very important,' Joyce says. 'We figured that we had eleven weeks left of cash before we'd go bankrupt. That meeting was probably one of the worst moments ever. My heart sank when I looked at the numbers and looked at the burn and looked at how big the problem was. So we had to take dramatic action.'

The revelation of how close to collapse the airline was shocked the company to the core. 'That was a galvanising moment for sure,' John Gissing says. 'To avoid that inevitability, we had to stop the cash outflow and it had to be fast.'

Events were moving rapidly. 'The biggest risk that we had at the time was liquidity, so we had to give the board comfort that we had a plan in place and we were getting on top of it,' Joyce says. 'Obviously, with eleven weeks left of cash, you had to make sure it was very clear that you're not trading while insolvent – which we weren't.' The last thing anybody wanted, on top of everything else that was going on, was to be exposed to criminal liability.

It wasn't just the board members who required comfort – there were thousands of dedicated people whose welfare hung in the balance.

'You just had to lift yourself up, because everyone was looking to the CEO for leadership,' Joyce recalls. 'And you had to show the confidence that we were going to get through it, that we had levers we could pull, and give people the confidence that there was going to be light at the end of the tunnel.'

There was concern at board level about managing the safety risks of COVID for the employees. Qantas had a couple of outbreaks, including a cluster in the Adelaide freight and ground handling workforce in late March. The board was keen to know the precautions that management were putting in place in order to keep those operations going. It examined the welfare of the employees, and what management was doing to support those who were being stood down.

The scale of the situation, Joyce says, meant the challenge was like trying to eat an elephant. 'It was one bite at a time to get through it,' he reflects. 'And that was the important part – breaking the problem down into manageable items that we could actually do.'

The management team worked on multiple streams of activity concurrently. One stream was focused on reducing the cash burn. Another stream studied the health and safety issues, such as the fly-in, fly-out activity, repatriation flights and freight operations.

A third stream looked at grounding and mothballing aircraft. 'It quickly became, "Where do you park all these airplanes?" The world is not built for a situation where most of the aircraft are on the ground,' Gissing says. '"Okay, let's start with the big planes, work our way down." We would create war rooms and information rooms. Engineering did that in the C building [at Mascot], where we just took over a whole space and said, "Right, this is the [aircraft] hibernation room. How do we do this? Who are the experts? What do we need to know? How do we get all the right players in the room to have this conversation?"'

Parking fleets of planes simultaneously required a big learning process – made even more challenging because just about every airline in the world was doing it too.

Another stream focused on restructuring the business for the longer term, and yet another on what Qantas would do to look after its people. 'A part of that,' Joyce says, 'was [that] I talked to the prime minister a couple of times about essentially what became JobKeeper.'

Excruciating as this period was, because it so adversely impacted thousands of people's lives, the executive team also felt the high energy and buzz that comes with a crisis. 'One of the best ways you can get through it is to just focus on what you can do – and that is very energising,' explains Gissing. 'I saw people who might have previously found it really hard to make decisions quickly suddenly find a way to do that.'

Not all of the Qantas Group was in the doldrums. Olivia Wirth was running the Loyalty business at a time when the rest of the operation, except for freight, was virtually non-existent. 'We were dealing with survivor's guilt, because we had 700 people who were still working when most of their other colleagues weren't,' she says. 'We were part of a lifeline, providing revenue that was going to help Qantas get back on its feet. This became a genuine rallying cry – it gave us a genuine sense of purpose.'

Gissing, who was responsible for regional operator QantasLink, also had a volatile mix. 'The resources industry was going nuts – I don't think we'd ever been so busy,' he says. 'The freight business was powering on, so we had revenue streams in those small parts of the organisation, but elsewhere [was] devastated.'

The executive team was running regular staff briefings, streaming them from the James Strong Auditorium at Mascot, usually reserved for media conferences. 'We had that set up for sometimes a daily town hall, telling our people exactly what we knew and what we were doing,' Joyce says. 'The Group Management Committee would be around the table, separated out, with hand sanitiser everywhere, wearing masks for periods of time.' Thousands of staff were tuning in remotely to the updates; on one occasion there were as many as 18,000 viewers.

Showing a human touch and caring for Qantas staff was crucial during that time because of how anxious people felt. Says one executive, 'The town halls were so important to fill the vacuum and show empathy, as everyone was going through their own personal issues.'

Staff were able to ask questions which were voted on, with the top ones answered by members of the committee. 'At the very start, there were a lot of technical questions about JobKeeper – when would their program be coming? What does that look like? How is it going to work?' says Joyce.

Wirth felt that, 'The worst thing was the way we had to communicate [bad news] in many cases. I'm always of the view that if you're delivering bad news, you do it in person, because you have to show empathy and compassion and give people time to process. These decisions weren't just impacting an individual. They were impacting households, they were impacting families, they were impacting multiple generations of people.

'And for many, Qantas isn't a job – it is how they identify with themselves. Qantas is part of who they are. If you're a pilot, if you're crew, if you're an engineer, these people, this is them. This is who they are. And so when you're making a decision that fundamentally changes that, it's just beyond words.'

Qantas sought temporary job placements for its staff and contacted 300 companies to help. 'Woolies was the big one,' says Joyce. 'We had 5000 people working at Woolies. I rang Brad Banducci [CEO of Woolworths] when we knew we were standing staff down. He needed people. We had too many people obviously with no work, so we found them places.'

'Some of the poignant moments were bumping into Qantas staff at Woolies, or other places of employment,' says Wirth. 'And they'd come up and talk to you about Qantas. There was such an element of sadness, but also of great joy to speak to them.

They said they couldn't wait to get back. So it was quite a moment to truly understand what the place means for our people.'

If Qantas was in trouble at this time, Virgin's problems were incomparable: it was facing the prospect of imminent collapse. Unions representing airline workers challenged moves by both Qantas and Virgin to shore up their businesses. They were mostly not at the table when decisions were being taken. When it came to the crunch, though, there were few realistic options available.

Joyce says Qantas communicated its plans and the reasons for its actions to the unions. The company's Treasury team (finance department), meanwhile, had drawn up plans to raise cash to plug the growing gap as ticket revenues dried up. The Group quickly completed a round of debt funding, secured by several of its wholly owned aircraft, raising $1.05 billion. It couldn't have been more timely, as Qantas had acted ahead of most other airlines.

This funding increased the Group's available cash balance to $2.95 billion. Qantas also had an additional $1 billion undrawn facility available, and a further $3.5 billion in unencumbered assets. This was a strong position, by global standards. The secured debt raising took the Group's net debt to $5.1 billion – still at the low end of its own long-term target range, with no major debt maturities until June 2021.

'Everything we're doing at the moment is focused on guaranteeing the long-term future of the national carrier,' Joyce said.[1]

Virgin Australia had gone into the crisis in a much weaker position. On 25 March, CEO Paul Scurrah announced that the airline would slash its domestic capacity by 90 per cent and temporarily stand down 8000 of its 10,000 employees. He announced the indefinite closure of Tigerair (formerly Tiger Airways), due to plummeting demand, but left the door open to its eventual revival. It was Scurrah's one-year anniversary as CEO of Virgin. It was not a happy one.

There was little comfort to be had from Canberra. In response to requests for funding support, Finance Minister Mathias Cormann confirmed that the government was committed to having two competitive domestic airlines. But, for now, that was just words.

Global COVID-19 infections had reached 422,000 and almost 19,000 people had died. From 28 March, all returning international travellers would have to complete fourteen days of quarantine in a hotel. The next day, gathering limits were drastically reduced to just two people.

At the end of March, the federal government announced its $130 billion wage subsidy package, JobKeeper, which was to last for six months. Eligible businesses would receive $1500 per employee per fortnight, to be paid in full directly to the employee.

And then there was silence. People living under flight paths enjoyed an unprecedented period that was virtually devoid of the rumble of jet planes overhead. Over 200 Qantas aircraft were grounded.

At the beginning of April, the seriously cash-strapped Virgin was in no position to emulate Qantas's debt raising. It approached the government for a $1.4 billion loan, then went into a trading halt on the stock market after the Morrison government turned down its request. Scurrah threatened the carrier would enter voluntary administration if it failed to secure government assistance within the month.

Virgin Australia's major shareholders – Singapore Airlines, Etihad Airways, China's Nanshan and HNA Group, and Richard Branson's Virgin Group – were each dealing with their own crises and unable to come to Virgin's aid. Joyce was actively lobbying to ensure Virgin didn't get preferential treatment, even if it was to save the airline. All government support, he insisted, should be industry-wide.

By mid-April, a deal had been thrashed out between the airlines and the federal government for the maintenance of minimum domestic and regional networks. The package kept essential travel open, as travel restrictions rendered most passenger flights unviable. It meant Qantas passenger flights would increase from 105 per week to 164 per week to all capital cities and thirty-six regional destinations. This was on top of a $715 million rebate package the federal government had announced for the aviation sector to provide fare reductions.

But it was not enough for Virgin. On 21 April, the company entered voluntary administration to recapitalise the business and help ensure it emerged in a stronger financial position on the other side of the COVID-19 crisis. It owed 10,000 creditors over $6.8 billion and had accumulated ten straight annual losses since turning a profit in the 2012 financial year.

There was not much sympathy to be had from its opponent. 'The one year they made money was the year we grounded Qantas and had the industrial relations actions,' Joyce says. 'I think that's the reality of where their strategy went.'

Virgin would continue to operate, with Scurrah as CEO, while the administrator, Deloitte, sought new investors. Early front-runners included Bain Capital, Oaktree Capital Management and Brookfield. Others in the race included US-based global LCC operators Indigo Partners, but the process was complex as due diligence and negotiations had to be conducted online.

In early September, US private equity firm Bain Capital was selected by Virgin's creditors to become the new owner of Virgin under a $3.5 billion deal. It would no longer operate as a full-service carrier and would instead operate a much smaller fleet of between thirty and sixty Boeing 737s. Some 3000 employees would lose their jobs – one-third of the workforce.

Rumours circulated that former Jetstar CEO Jayne Hrdlicka – much to the displeasure of some unions – would return to aviation to become the revived Virgin's new chief executive, following on from her advisory role to Bain during the bidding process. On 15 October, those rumours were confirmed when Scurrah resigned and Deloitte confirmed Hrdlicka would take over the role in November, when Bain took control.

*

In April 2020, Qantas introduced social distancing on its few remaining aircraft, and the domestic onboard service was scaled back, with cabin crew focused on inflight safety.

With vaccines under development and infection rates in Australia relatively low, it started to look as though 2021 would be a bonanza year for domestic travel. The Trump administration and pharmaceutical company AstraZeneca announced a collaboration to speed up the development of a vaccine, of which initial doses were expected to be available as early as October 2020.

Regional Express (Rex) took advantage of the turmoil at Virgin to announce it would invest $200 million to launch jet services between Sydney, Melbourne and Brisbane, taking the fight up to Qantas and Virgin. Rex was planning to lease up to ten former Virgin 737s, and would hire new pilots, crew and ground staff.

Qantas raised a further $550 million in debt financing against three of its wholly owned Boeing 787-9s as it extended its flight cancellations for June and July. This was opportunistic, as the future value of an aircraft, even a newish 787-9, was becoming doubtful. It looked as if a smaller industry would emerge from COVID, whenever that was to be. If that were the case, demand for aircraft would be diluted and prices would fall.

The timing was near perfect. The share price jumped and closed on the evening of 4 June at $4.49, meaning anyone who had been brave enough to buy shares in Qantas on 19 March had more than doubled their investment in just over six weeks. Qantas's rate of cash burn had slowed and would fall to $40 million per week by the end of June 2020, indicating it could now manage through the crisis and recovery.

Domestic travel restrictions started to ease across the country, prompting Qantas and Jetstar to announce an increase to the skeleton domestic and regional schedule. Group capacity increased from just 5 per cent of pre-COVID levels to 15 per cent by the end of June, and 40 per cent by the end of July. There was a lot of pent-up demand for air travel, which drove a big increase in bookings.

A couple of weeks later, Jetstar dropped a promotional sale, offering 10,000 fares for $19 apiece, which were quickly snapped up. But bigger plans were being drawn up at Qantas. Joyce and the management team were, at that stage, thinking this was 'the GFC and SARS on steroids', with a very slow and long recovery. 'We didn't know whether there was going to be a vaccine and we didn't know the impact it was going to have on demand,' he says.

Joyce reckoned Qantas had no choice but to take immediate action, to position the carrier for several years where revenues will be much lower. Plans for a restructure started to emerge. 'At the other end of this, we needed to be very different,' Joyce says. 'If we did nothing, we would've been gone. We just had to pull the levers, figure out what was working, [and] if it wasn't working, change it rapidly and go down a different path.'

Joyce and his team believed Qantas would emerge a lot smaller. 'We were unsure whether we'd bring back the A380s,' he admits. 'We knew we weren't going to bring back the 747s. We parked the A380s in the Mojave Desert so our engineers in Los Angeles could get to them and keep them maintained, to give ourselves the option on them.'

Qantas had multiple options in mind. 'There was one scenario where they could have taken five years to reactivate the A380s from when things opened up, because we thought that the demand would be very weak,' Joyce says. There were so many questions. The key one was how to restructure the business if it was a GFC-type loss of revenue for multiple years. 'How would the business be different on the other side of it, so it could come out surviving?'

Joyce argues that crises 'make us more open to doing things differently, as seen from the entrepreneurial spirit of so many businesses that had to quickly pivot in order to survive'. With the right decisions, this crisis could promote a solid survivor.

25

Turnaround – Again

Aviation is used to sudden shocks, but there had never been anything remotely on this scale. International aviation had completely stalled. Airlines around the world were implementing massive cutbacks, slashing 30 to 50 per cent of their workforces.

Joyce told the ABC's 7.30, 'A lot of these jobs . . . will not come back and the industry's going to be fairly radically different for some time. IATA has said airline travel will not get back to 2019 levels till 2023 or 2024. So we are trying to work on what's the best planning assumptions that we have.'[1]

Joyce and his team had spent weeks working out what the demand would look like through and beyond the pandemic. 'We did a lot of research, asking people about their propensity to travel . . . because people have gotten used to doing things differently, like video conferencing,' he told journalist Kerry O'Brien at a Griffith University thought leadership series. 'We've looked at what we think are the potential for substitutions, people wanting to travel domestically instead of internationally. And we've looked at our best plan over this period of time, of what that could mean.'

The research indicated that Qantas could get back to around 70 per cent of its domestic operations during the 2021 financial year, and back to 100 per cent in 2022. But the international arm had many question marks. 'Even if we find a vaccine, there'll be some time before that's active. A prudent assumption is some time in the middle of next year,' Joyce said.

As it turned out, it was far too early to be projecting a recovery. Nor was it to be a steady climb back up the mountain. Indeed, it would be a roller-coaster as the Delta and then Omicron variants of COVID-19 came through. The stop-start nature of the recovery was extraordinarily difficult to manage.

Even so, the assumptions provided a base for planning and a degree of certainty. At least the staff could have some sense of where management was heading, in black and white.

Joyce fronted the media on 25 June 2020 to announce yet another turnaround plan. This one was more far-reaching than even the 2011 International Transformation and the 2014 Accelerated Transformation agendas.

He unveiled a three-year plan to guide Qantas's recovery that contained three action areas: 'right-sizing' the workforce, fleet and capital spending, assuming a considerably smaller airline would emerge; restructuring to deliver ongoing savings; and recapitalising through an equity raising to strengthen the balance sheet. Some 6000 jobs would go. Many of the affected staff had spent decades at the airline. A further 15,000 workers would remain stood down. Around half of those stood down would be back flying domestically, Joyce estimated, by the end of the year. The remainder – mostly those supporting international flying – would return more slowly.

Around 100 aircraft were to be grounded for up to twelve months, and some – including the flagship A380 fleet – for longer. A321neo and 787-9 fleet deliveries were deferred, and the airline's six remaining 747s were retired immediately, six months ahead of schedule.

Of the Qantas Group's 29,000 people, around 8000 were expected to have returned to work by the end of July 2020, rising to around 15,000 by the end of 2020, in line with the opening up of domestic flying. That number would increase further during 2021 and 2022, as the international network returned, reaching 21,000 active employees by June 2022.

The job losses were right across the board. Half would be corporate roles (1450) and ground operations (1500), and the others flight crew and engineering. Despite the downsizing, Qantas believed it would shrink less than a lot of other airlines. 'Air Canada is forecasting a 50 per cent reduction in their size, Air New Zealand 30 per cent,' Joyce said. 'Airlines in Europe are all in the 30 to 40 per cent category. Given [our] Domestic operation, Loyalty and Jetstar, given some of the opportunities we think are here for us, we need to shrink by 20 per cent . . . We also figured that International is going to take a lot longer to recover. And that's where we came up with the 6000 [job losses].'[2]

Many of these rivals, some in full government ownership, were slashing their staff numbers, meaning a structural shift was occurring in the aviation cost-base landscape. In the cut-throat world of aviation, Joyce knew Qantas had to be among it, or risk being uncompetitive when the eventual upswing came.

Joyce denied the move contained an element of opportunism. 'I go back to 2013,' he told O'Brien. 'We had to make big changes to the airline. We took a lot of the fat out back then, because the airline needed to survive. And then over the next six, seven years, we recruited people. COVID knocked us for six and this is us coping with that environment. This is what's needed to survive.'

Joyce said the decision weighed heavily on him, but the collapse of billions of dollars in revenue left him little choice, if Qantas was going to save as many jobs as possible over the long term. 'What makes this even harder is that right before this crisis hit, we were actively recruiting. We were gearing up for Project Sunrise. We were getting ready to buy planes. Now we're facing a sudden reversal of fortune that is no one's fault – but is very hard to accept.'

But how would Qantas pay for all the redundancies?

'That's when we made the decision to raise fresh equity. A billion dollars of that was to do the restructuring to make what was ultimately 10,000 people redundant, which we didn't have the cash to do,' Joyce says.

As part of the turnaround plan, Joyce unveiled the airline's first equity raising in ten years, aiming for up to $1.9 billion in fresh capital, of which $1.36 billion in shares would be offered to institutional investors at $3.65 per share. The move sent the share price sharply lower – it closed on 26 June at $3.81, having been as high as $4.95 just a couple of weeks before – but the equity raising went through.

The main tenets of Joyce's post-COVID recovery plan were for a massive $15 billion in costs to be removed during the first three-year period of lower activity and $1 billion in ongoing cost savings per annum from the 2023 financial year. The twelve Airbus A380s were written down to their fair market value. They represented the majority of the massive $1.4 billion asset impairment charge in 2020, which reduced future depreciation expenses. The delayed interim dividend was now revoked, to keep another $200 million of cash on the balance sheet.

Whether a CEO and executive team with less experience would have navigated the situation this successfully is questionable. Much of this had echoes of Joyce's earlier years as CEO, although the hold was even deeper now.

'One slide that we [regularly] gave to the board had the cash burn per week, the cash we held and the number of weeks we had left to survive,' Joyce says. 'When that started ticking up, when we got more debt, we got the equity, when we got the cashflow down because we made all those actions, the number of weeks went from eleven to twenty-six, to fifty-two, to two years. And when we were at two years, we said, "We're okay. We can get through."'

As a condition of the equity raising, investors sought continuity of leadership. Goyder and the Qantas board asked Joyce to stay on to see the company through the post-COVID recovery period. It meant another three years at the helm. 'I felt I just couldn't walk out on Qantas in the worst time in its history, so I committed to at least that three years,' the CEO says.

Goyder said the Qantas Group had a track record of delivering the change needed to get it through tough times. 'A big part of that comes down to leadership,' he said, 'and Alan is without doubt one of the best airline executives in the world. He's steered the group through some extremely difficult chapters.'[3]

This is scarcely the image that Joyce enjoys among much of the world outside the airline business. There's plenty for everyone to dislike in him, one way or another. He casually sacks thousands of people. He shows no empathy when travellers are delayed or have flights cancelled; he destroys the revered brand; he's gay; he is – as Miranda Devine so delicately framed it – a 'leprechaun'; and he does it for the money. Essentially, according to this narrative, he was totally unsuited for the role. But the board and Qantas investors, at a time of massive stress for everyone, pressed him to extend for another three years.

Joyce had been preparing to exit the carrier in 2020 on a high. He said, 'I've been here for the global financial crises. I've been here when we had to ground the airline in 2011 with industrial action. I've been here in 2013 when we had to do the biggest transformation of our history. So I think that experience and that knowledge of the whole team helped, and it's the same team that went through these crises. The board really wanted to make sure that that was in place. And I was happy to commit to that.'[4]

Joyce wanted to get as many people back in jobs as possible – and he had a burning desire to see Project Sunrise up and running. For now, though, that was a distant dream. But at least Qantas's near-term survival looked assured.

By 7 July 2020, the United States had reported 3 million COVID-19 infections. Days later, the WHO announced that the virus could be transmitted through the air in crowded indoor spaces, and emphasised that infection could be spread by asymptomatic individuals. Remarkably, this was not yet common knowledge, and it created yet more concern for airlines and the travel industry, who had diligently been wiping all hard surfaces with sanitiser.

Shortly after this, the positive news broke that early trials of Moderna's vaccine showed it produced an encouraging immune response. The US government soon detailed plans for its vaccine rollout from January 2021. The number of worldwide deaths linked to COVID-19, meanwhile, had crossed the one-million mark.

July 2020 would also mark the last of the Qantas 747 fleet departing Sydney as flight number QF7474, bringing down the curtain on five decades of history.

As more state borders closed, Qantas's unused stock of business-class pyjamas, amenity kits and snacks were packaged up and delivered as care packs to people doing it tough in lockdown during the COVID-19 crisis. Sightseeing flights would follow, some across domestic borders, to keep the fleet flying.

The recovery would be far from a straight line. For airlines, the unpredictability of the virus – and government responses – created exponentially greater complexity, as fresh domestic border closures restricted their planned resumption of flying. Maintaining flexibility was key. But the subsequent open-close-open border policies of the states in the coming years was to prove far more costly and emotionally trying than anyone could have imagined.

JobKeeper was extended by a further six months to 28 March 2021, targeting businesses and not-for-profits that continued to be significantly impacted by the pandemic. But even that extended timeframe looked challenging for Qantas. The IATA now pushed back its global passenger traffic recovery projection until 2024, a whole year later than its earlier estimate.

Qantas had flown just 20 per cent of its pre-COVID domestic capacity levels in August after the setback of Victoria's border closure. Qantas's international operation was going nowhere.

On 20 August, Qantas announced it had limped to an underlying profit before tax of $124 million for the twelve months to 30 June. But this included the $771-million profit earned in the pre-pandemic first half (July–December 2019), indicating a steep second-half loss. Joyce acknowledged the quick response of the federal government. Qantas had received $515 million in government support in the reporting period, including funding for the maintenance of the minimum domestic network and repatriation flights, as well as $267 million in JobKeeper payments that were passed on to furloughed employees.

Given what now seemed likely to be an extended grounding of the international operation, Joyce moved to make more redundancies – including the CEO of Qantas International, Tino La Spina. Joyce had moved La Spina from the chief financial officer role to run Qantas International in 2019, when Alison Webster resigned, in order to keep the talented executive from being poached.

'The really tough part was then having to tell people that they would be made redundant,' Joyce says. 'Tino was doing a phenomenal job. We made redundancies on every level all the way through. That was tough. I had a number of people in tears. I was in tears, saying, "Unfortunately we're going to have to make you redundant. This is the restructure. This is how bad we think it's going to be in the recovery."

'And everybody knew it, but it was really hard. Just before COVID, we were making record profits, we were growing, we were looking at Project Sunrise – it was all looking really optimistic. And then the same people that were doing these jobs – doing a phenomenal job – you just had to tell them they were being made redundant. It wasn't their fault, it wasn't our fault, it wasn't the company's fault, but it was just something we had to do to get to the other side of.'

The CEO of Qantas Domestic, Andrew David, picked up responsibility for Qantas International. La Spina soon after became chief finance and strategy officer at Boral.

The airline also opportunistically announced a property review that might see its headquarters move interstate from Sydney, in what was an attempt to shave costs and attract support from state governments. No rock was left unturned in the search to reduce outgoings. (The review was concluded in May 2021 with no major changes to Qantas's presence in Sydney, Melbourne and Brisbane.)

By now, many workers across the global economy had made the shift to remote working and online meetings. Big question marks were being asked about how permanent this shift might be, and the ramifications for corporate travel globally, particularly in the professional services sector. In Australia at least, intra-state mining travel continued mostly unabated in COVID-free Western Australia and Queensland, but corporate travel volumes elsewhere had collapsed.

Qantas's first ever virtual annual general meeting took place on 23 October 2020, a month that saw South Australia, the Northern Territory and Tasmania opening their borders to most other states, and the lifting of some restrictions with New Zealand.

There was talk of the potential for 'travel bubbles' with parts of Asia, including South Korea, Taiwan and various islands in the Pacific, by early 2021. But the IATA again extended its prediction for the full recovery of global travel demand to up to four years.

Joyce took to the screen to say it had become crystal clear that, post-COVID, the Qantas Group had to be structurally different to how it had been. Consumer confidence and spending would be hit by the COVID recession, he said, affecting corporate travel, and the domestic aviation market would be extremely competitive. As the screens went blank at the end of the meeting, the share price jumped, closing the day at $4.55, having decisively moved back above the $4 mark earlier that month.

October and November saw more decisions around state borders that frustrated Qantas's resumption of flying and infuriated Joyce. He described it as a 'Rubik's cube approach', and said that while decisions around borders had initially been made on the basis of the health risk, increasingly they seemed to be driven by politics and populism.

It was against this backdrop that, on 16 November 2020, Qantas marked the 100-year anniversary of its founding. A deflated Joyce said distance had always defined Australia, between its cities and regional towns, and from the rest of the world. Before the interruption that was COVID-19, the airline was working on nonstop flights from the east coast of Australia to New York and London – the last frontier of global aviation.

But ironically, for most of its centenary year, it was the distance between Melbourne and Sydney (or any other Australian capitals) that had been the challenge. Joyce lamented the 'hard state borders that had been erected for the first time in, coincidentally enough, about 100 years'.

The timing of the anniversary could not have been worse, he acknowledged. While 2020 hadn't been the centenary year he'd planned, he still held the irrepressible optimism that marked his tenure as Qantas CEO, especially through adversity. 'I know the Flying Kangaroo will be back stronger than ever – and so will Australia,' he said.

Investors were also optimistic. The Qantas share price, having broken the $5 barrier just prior to the anniversary, closed at $5.19 on the airline's 100th birthday.

Stock markets more broadly were also cheered on 18 November, when Pfizer and BioNTech announced that broad-based trials of their vaccine showed it to be 95 per cent effective against severe disease. Hope was growing that there would be a way out of this crisis, thanks to advances in medical science, aided by billions in government aid.

Some green shoots were finally appearing in the domestic market, and Group domestic capacity rose to 68 per cent of pre-COVID levels by December 2021. Corporate travellers were back on the Sydney–Melbourne–Brisbane golden triangle again, and Qantas boasted of gaining corporate share, adding some twenty-five new large accounts over the year.

The rise in Qantas's domestic flying saw the number of full-time-equivalent roles back on the increase, from around 9000 in October to 11,500 in December. But approximately 13,500 staff remained stood down, collecting JobKeeper.

Joyce said the airline would be in a position to commence the slow process of balance sheet repair in the second half of the 2021 financial year, despite an $11 billion hole in the carrier's revenue. The COVID Recovery and Restructuring Program was on track to deliver at least $1 billion in annual savings from the 2023 financial year. As 2020 was drawing to a close, Qantas had shed over 5000 roles that it deemed were no longer needed at the airline.

Joyce said there had been a rush of domestic bookings as each border restriction was lifted, showing there was plenty of latent travel demand across both the leisure and business sectors. Investors were cheered, sending the carrier's share price to $5.49 by the close of trade on 3 December.

But significant uncertainties remained, particularly once broader government support was wound back. A vaccine hadn't yet been rolled out in Australia, and the risk of more outbreaks remained stark.

An irritated Joyce reiterated calls for the adoption of a national framework for border policy – a set of rules that reflected confidence in the testing and tracing systems that had been working well in New South Wales – to prevent more border closures.

The onset of winter in the Northern Hemisphere was driving a huge surge in COVID cases around the world. The United Kingdom confirmed that a highly infectious new strain was ripping through many communities, although it did not appear to lead to more severe disease.

As cases surged, the United Kingdom gave emergency authorisation for the AstraZeneca and Oxford COVID-19 vaccine, and Britain joined the United States in rolling out a mass vaccination program.

This offered a ray of hope. A vaccine was going to be the only way out of the deepest of holes, but it was to be many months before Australia received the volumes needed to move back towards normality. In the meantime, closure of the national border was providing shelter from the worst impact. For Joyce and Qantas, the source of frustration now was the way internal borders were being managed. In turn, this was to lead to a mountain of problems down the track, as flights had to be cancelled at short notice, leaving passengers stranded and out of pocket.

26

Twists and Turns

The start of 2021 brought more of the same. An outbreak in Sydney's Northern Beaches district over Christmas and New Year had a major impact on Qantas's profitability during the crucial holiday period.

Joyce describes that period as unbelievably disappointing for everybody. 'We had managed over a period of time to reduce the cash burn,' he says, referring to the stability in the intra–Western Australia, intra-Queensland and intra–New South Wales services. 'We were trying new routes, and then when the border started opening again it was phenomenal, because we then started Melbourne–Sydney again. The biggest route was starting to kick in, which allowed us to get the volumes going.'

Meanwhile, the general debate on the coronavirus had shifted from notions of achieving 'herd immunity' as the threshold for opening borders to the importance of the population being 'fully vaccinated'. This further delayed Australia's border reopening, as there was a lag in vaccination rates away from the virus epicentres, where there were low case numbers and few deaths.

By late February 2021, Qantas had trimmed its stood-down workforce from 13,500 full-time-equivalent roles to

11,000 – most of them associated with international flying. Those workers would remain on the sidelines for longer. Joyce announced that Qantas and Jetstar were pushing back the resumption of international flights from July to late October, as borders refused to open.

Some tentative trans-Tasman flying would eventually ramp up from July 2021, but the virus's continued spread abroad was a blow to the airline's international staff – and to Joyce, who was criticised by industry commentators for having been overly optimistic in his earlier assessments. Even so, the economy was stirring – and it soon began to rise as business activity lifted.

Around the same time, in February 2021, the governor of the Reserve Bank of Australia, Dr Philip Lowe, said he did not expect the conditions would be met – that is, for inflation to reach the 2–3 per cent target range – for interest rates to be raised until 2024. But the central bank would lift rates in May 2022, at least nineteen months earlier than expectations, when inflation reached a red-hot 7.8 per cent. Joyce wasn't alone in his misplaced optimism. Making predictions in these conditions was simply very difficult.

A month later, as optimism for a speedy recovery of international travel faded, the federal government unveiled an aviation support package, dubbed 'QantasKeeper' by some. The $1.2 billion industry-wide stimulus package was designed to help fast-track a recovery for domestic tourism, and subsidised an estimated 550,000 discounted Qantas and Jetstar fares to be offered in targeted markets.

It also provided direct support for around 7500 Qantas Group employees directly impacted by the continued international border closure to retain skills in the sector.

More unpredictable short-notice state-border lockdowns continued to throw schedules into chaos. By now, Qantas had a document for its airport managers and crew that listed hundreds of changes and updates about border settings. 'In most cases, the [state] premiers gave you a notice that a change would happen in the next couple of days and they would give their citizens time to get back,' Joyce says. Some of the updates to restrictions involved subtle changes that the airlines would have to account for, including changes to crew requirements.

Activating staff and aircraft were decisions airlines usually make over many months. Prior to COVID, airlines typically made scheduling decisions twice a year, reflecting the summer and winter periods. Now they were learning to cope with just twenty-four or forty-eight hours' notice before a change was implemented.

'Managing with that complexity was just something else,' Joyce says. 'You've just incurred a huge amount of cost because you've lost the person for a month. So you pay them the salary, and then you don't have any flying for them to do. The start-and-stop was just very detrimental at the time.'

Qantas and Jetstar had flatlined at about 60 per cent of their pre-COVID levels of domestic flying in the January–March 2021 period, but that was expected to increase to around 80 per cent in April–June, aided by the government's stimulus plan. Ultimately it reached 90 per cent, and Jetstar exceeded 100 per cent due to strong leisure demand. The budget airline even borrowed six A320s from Jetstar Japan to add capacity on leisure routes. The opening of a limited two-way travel bubble with New Zealand in mid-April also aided Qantas's recovery plan. Corporate travel, including the small business segment, had recovered to 65 per cent of pre-COVID levels.

Meanwhile, Rex was ramping up slowly, and Virgin had repositioned to refocus on serving the middle of the market and was boosting its flights. The carrier was operating some fifty-eight 737-800s, and in April 2021 announced plans to lease ten more and return more staff to work. Jayne Hrdlicka created some unfortunate headlines around this time, including 'Virgin CEO calls for open borders, even if "some people may die"' in the *Sydney Morning Herald*. Hrdlicka later conceded it wasn't her 'best couple of days', but her comments did help shift the narrative.[1]

Joyce wasn't convinced every carrier would survive the competitive domestic tussle. 'Rex and Virgin are positioned in the same territory,' he said. 'They're fighting in the middle of the market. They have the same aircraft and the same product on board. So it's the battle royale there and that will continue. Our position in the price-sensitive end of the market is very solid and has growth opportunities. Jetstar should become a lot bigger than it was going into COVID as we don't have Tiger in this space any longer. And Qantas at the premium end, we're very solid there. So we're obviously watching.

'I've never seen the domestic market supporting three carriers. Maybe it's different this time, but in the meantime it's going to be hugely competitive between all of the carriers in order to get there . . . Competition has always driven us to raise our game.'[2]

By mid-May, Joyce felt even more optimistic, and said Qantas and Jetstar expected to exceed their pre-COVID domestic capacity in the 2022 financial year, with all domestic aircraft back in service. In addition, travel demand between Australia and New Zealand was also steadily rebuilding, up to almost 60 per cent of pre-COVID levels.

All the redundancies associated with the job losses were on track to be completed by the end of the financial year and while international reopening languished, Qantas offered voluntary redundancy for Qantas International cabin crew, on top of the already announced cuts.

A two-year wage freeze was to apply to the next round of enterprise agreements across the Group, with 2 per cent annual increases after that, compared with 3 per cent pre-COVID. The airline also attacked travel agency commissions on international tickets when they resumed in July, to New Zealand initially, from 5 per cent to 1 per cent. Eight thousand employees remained stood down.

Australia's vaccine rollout was tardy, lagging those in the United States, the United Kingdom and elsewhere as the federal government fiddled, and this slowed Qantas's international reboot. Qantas's fundamental assumption remained the same: that once the national vaccine rollout was effectively complete, Australia could and should open up. Joyce argued that Australia risked being left behind when other countries were getting back to normal. 'Australia has to put the same intensity into the vaccine rollout as we've put on lockdowns and restrictions,' he said, 'because only then will we have the confidence to open up.'[3]

Strong domestic demand continued into June – but in June 2021 another huge setback emerged. Just as the skies brightened, the Delta variant of the coronavirus touched down in Australia and the cycle of state border lockdowns resumed. Domestic bookings cratered and Qantas was again thrust into crisis.

The carrier went from operating almost 100 per cent of its usual domestic capacity to less than 40 per cent in July. Joyce's executive management meetings again shifted online, and the Mascot headquarters became a ghost town. It was back to square one. On 3 August, the airline stood down 2500 operational crew for an estimated two months in response to the lockdowns.

There were just so many setbacks. The door would open and it felt so positive and then, 'Wow, "This really keeps giving, doesn't it?"' Gissing says. 'But as a leadership team, I think we had to keep a brave face on and stay positive. We were still doing the daily, weekly cadence. We were required to communicate more broadly to people and say, "It is what it is – there is no point worrying about things you can't do anything about."'

Financial numbers unveiled on 26 August were a sea of red ink, a record statutory loss before tax of over $2.3 billion. Some $16 billion in revenue had been foregone because of the pandemic, and this number was expected to reach $20 billion by the end of 2021. International borders had been closed, and over 330 days had experienced some type of domestic travel restriction.

The good news was that Australia's vaccine rollout had finally picked up pace. The nation was on track to have 80 per cent of its adult population vaccinated by December. Yet Joyce remained frustrated by the patchwork of rules and border changes, which came frequently and without warning. There was uncertainty about the international border reopening as well.

'Hopefully we get some consistency with National Cabinet pushing through to open up Australia, and for us to not be a hermit nation going forward,' Joyce said.[4]

The 80 per cent vaccine target triggered the resumption of international flying to Singapore, Japan, the United States, the United Kingdom and New Zealand, with flights to Bali, Jakarta, Manila and Johannesburg expected to resume from April 2022 at the earliest.

Joyce now announced that Qantas would bring five A380s back into service from mid-2022 – about a year earlier than planned – to fly the UK and US routes, and the other five by early 2024, depending on how quickly the market recovered. Qantas's remaining two A380s were to be retired. All the staff would also be called back in time for Christmas.

These were bold moves, and Joyce copped a lot of criticism at the time for being far too optimistic. 'Everybody thought we were crazy,' he recalls. 'We took actions that were brave at the time. In hindsight, they were absolutely the right things to do.'

Trading conditions had been diabolical, but there were some pointers to improvement.

'We did these sessions in the boardroom with our superb Director of Medical Services, Ian Hosegood, giving us a voice on the way this was likely to play out, with probabilities around different things,' says Joyce. 'When he saw the effectiveness of the vaccine and we saw the amount of people that were taking it, they were early indicators it was going to be a strong recovery. And that's when we started making the decisions to reactivate a lot of things faster and bigger than we were originally planning.'

The share price closed back above $5 on 26 August 2021 as the public vision of recovery improved. Things would surely get better from here!

At midnight on 31 October 2021, the Australian government finally reopened the national border. It had been closed for nearly 600 days.

When the international borders had begun to clang shut from March 2020 onwards, many of the hundreds of thousands of Australian passport holders living overseas were anxious to fly home.

Qantas's rival international carriers kept flying to Australia under significant duress, maintaining vital linkages for Australians to return home, albeit after lengthy hotel quarantine stays. A handful of foreign airlines transported the vast majority of departing and returning passengers and freight, including vital medical supplies, during this period.

That task became harder when, on 4 July 2020, for health and safety reasons the government capped the number of seats that could be sold on these flights, so that many 300-plus seat aircraft were carrying only a few dozen passengers. The foreign carriers stayed the course but the national carrier remained largely on the sidelines, except where the federal government underwrote charter flights. As a result, much of Australia's repatriation scheme relied on subsidies by foreign airlines and foreign governments.

There was anger online over Qantas's decision to cease its scheduled international flights. A Facebook page called 'Let's bring stranded Australians home' sprang up, providing useful tips for stranded passengers. The group had over 50,000 members at its peak, and there was plenty of vitriol reserved for the national carrier and its CEO. Posts praised foreign airlines for staying in the market and absorbing the losses. Many posters swore never to fly Qantas again.

Rightly or wrongly, though, Joyce was unswerving. He remained fixed on positioning the airline well for the inevitable recovery and not burning up the progress of the prior decade. The Australian government was happy to soak up the benefits of other nations 'subsidising' their carriers; it had other priorities.

Qantas operated hundreds of charter and repatriation flights on behalf of (and fully underwritten by) the Australian government to bring Australians home during the border closure, flying to thirty-one overseas destinations, including nineteen that were not part of the airline's regular network. Memorable efforts included some of the first repatriation flights out of Wuhan, in the early days of the pandemic, and a record-breaking repatriation flight of over 15,000 kilometres from Buenos Aires to Darwin that touched down on 7 October 2021 after seventeen hours and twenty-five minutes in the air. The flight crews rose to the challenge, glad to be in the air.

But it was a small group of foreign international airlines that operated the vast majority of the 10,000 commercial passenger flights into the major Australian capital city airports, delivering 350,000 arriving passengers, most of them returning Australians, during that period.

The actions of the airlines' teams in Australia and their flight crews, in the face of innumerable pressures, were nothing short of heroic. They worked tirelessly with health officials, government departments, airport partners and ground transport partners to overcome ever-changing rules and obstacles, including burdensome quarantine requirements. The stories of families reunited and loved ones returned will be etched into the memories of millions of people. And they were forged through the commitment of airlines that didn't give up on Australia.

A group of eight carriers – Air Niugini, Cathay Pacific, Etihad, Air New Zealand, United Airlines, Emirates, Singapore Airlines and Qatar Airways – together brought in the most inbound passengers to Australia, a quarter of a million travellers on some 8000 flights. The average passenger load factor was less than

15 per cent. Customers complained about the high fares, but these small passenger loads were nowhere near economic for the airlines, even if the flights were topped up by cargo. This was, on every estimation, a true and deep commitment to serve Australia and Australians.

Ironically, Qantas, which had fought tooth and nail to keep Qatar Airways out of the market prior to COVID-19, now largely surrendered the international market to foreign airlines as the pandemic struck. (That approach was not to persist beyond the COVID-restricted period.)

Almost a year earlier, on Qantas's centenary anniversary, Joyce said Qantas was probably best known around the world for its safety record, for its endurance flying and for a long list of aviation firsts. 'But for Australians,' he said, 'there's nothing quite like seeing the flying kangaroo at the airport, waiting to take you home.'[5] The almost complete lack of red tails around the world at the peak of the pandemic provoked severe responses from Australians stuck overseas.

For Qantas, it may have been the right decision. Red tails all around the world at this time would have meant even more red ink. But it certainly created discord with the public.

Joyce fronted shareholders at the carrier's 2021 annual general meeting – once again an online event – and said the airline's actions had been all about change, adaptation and defending its cash balance. Qantas had remained one of only seven airlines in the world to retain an investment-grade credit rating through the pandemic.

Over the year, Qantas had launched more new domestic routes than at any other time in its history, to make the most of travel between places that were open. Joyce said the airline's ability to adapt quickly meant that 95 per cent of the time its aircraft were in the air during the 2021 financial year, Qantas was generating cash, rather than burning it like many of its international rivals. He added that the difficult structural decisions – including the cutting of its workforce and the outsourcing of its remaining ground-handling functions – were particularly important as new competitors emerged. Those hard decisions would ultimately make the Qantas Group fit for the future. The share price closed at $5.62 on 5 November 2021.

All of Qantas's 22,000 employees would be returning to work by early December, but the workforce hadn't been this lean since the early 1990s, well before privatisation. Had Joyce slimmed back too far, especially in light of fast-recovering demand for air travel?

The carrier's first returning A380 re-entered Australian skies on 9 November, in preparation for the resumption of passenger services. Surging domestic bookings in the lead-up to Christmas 2021 meant Qantas was preparing to bump Group domestic capacity back up to 102 per cent of pre-COVID levels for January–March 2022, rising to 117 per cent in the April–June 2022 quarter.

Joyce said the Qantas Group had been able to accelerate the repair of its balance sheet and expected to finish the first half of the 2022 financial year with a materially better net debt position than it had prior to the start of the Delta variant lockdowns in June.

'The end of 2021 just looked like so much blue sky,' Gissing recalls. 'All the medical information coming through globally, infection rates and hospitalisations, was looking better. That December, we agreed to stand everybody back up and bring the aircraft back out of the desert. There was a lot of positivity and it felt like we were there.'

No sooner had Joyce and his team finished talking up the improvements and forward capacity plans than the Omicron variant touched down in Australia, putting another dent in consumer confidence just before Christmas.

To this point, Australia had been very effective at suppressing the virus, and when normal life resumed as borders reopened, the

highly contagious Omicron variants spread through the population quickly.

Joyce said in early 2022 that people who thought it was
possible to have planned accurately for the impact of COVID-19
were 'just kidding themselves'. 'You really just have to get all of
your systems capabilities up and running to be able to cope with
something as extreme as that,' he explains. 'You know you're
doing well when you get through to the other end, and think,
"Yeah, well, that worked." And if you control a one-in-100-
year problem like this, then you can deal with any other problem
that's going to potentially come up, whether it's left-field, whether
you've been taught it, or whether it's on your risk register or not.'

Another flashpoint emerged. In early February 2022, West
Australian premier Mark McGowan abandoned the plans to
reopen his state's border on 5 February and instead decided
to keep the borders shut indefinitely, as Omicron cases soared
in Australia's eastern states. The move led to hundreds of flight
cancellations.

Joyce was incensed. 'I think we should all be outraged by
that,' he said. 'The fact you can get to London, but you can't get
to Perth! There's not even a plan to open up. It's starting to look
like North Korea. It's going to be closed indefinitely at this stage
unless we have a plan to start living with COVID and opening up
the whole country.'

27

Another Whopping Loss

On 24 February 2022, Russia invaded Ukraine in an escalation of the Russo–Ukrainian War that had begun in 2014. Oil prices spiked and already stretched supply chains were thrown into further turmoil.

By late February, Qantas informed the market of another massive loss, this time for the six months ending 31 December 2021, a period blighted by the Delta and Omicron variant lockdowns in Australia. An underlying loss before tax of $1.28 billion and a statutory loss before tax of $622 million represented Qantas's fourth statutory half-year loss in a row, taking combined statutory losses since the start of the crisis to well over $6 billion and revenue losses to more than $22 billion.

'In all honesty, it's been a real roller-coaster,' Joyce said. 'It has been frustrating. But we kept focus and made a series of decisions that meant we finished the half in better shape than the circumstances would suggest.'[1]

One of those decisions was to sell surplus land in Mascot in 2021 to take advantage of the surging property market. The move raised over $800 million and was the main reason Qantas had kept within its target debt range. The airline also announced it would issue 1000 share rights to non-executive employees – worth around $4500 per employee at the time of the announcement – as part of an employee recovery and retention program. These shares vested in August 2023, by which time they had added nearly 50 per cent in value.

The outlook for demand was improving, and newly re-adjusted flying expectations pegged Group domestic capacity at 68 per cent of pre-COVID levels in January–March 2022, rising to 90 to 100 per cent in April–June as corporations began returning to their offices. Meanwhile, Group international capacity was expected to rise from 22 per cent of pre-COVID levels in January–March to 44 per cent in April–June.

Having seen the earlier response when borders reopened, Joyce was convinced that there was still huge pent-up demand, and that it was about to be unleashed. 'We wanted to put as much capacity in and get as many of our people back as we could. I think the intent was good and the intent was right.'

Joyce warned in early March 2022 that airfares would rise due to the surging global oil price as a result of the war in Ukraine, which was adding to inflation pressures around the world.

Supply-chain bottlenecks were also hampering airline operations internationally. Airbus and Boeing were experiencing difficulties with their lower-level suppliers for spare parts and other items in production lines. Qantas was one of hundreds of carriers impacted.

'Engine-maker GE told us of a small company of a father and two sons that produced the thermostat on their engine. The father died during COVID and the sons left the business to join a different industry,' Joyce recalls. 'When GE started trying to produce the engines again, they were missing the thermostat – they had this big pile of tens of millions of dollars' worth of engines and this little thing's missing.' There were similar problems right across the industry.

Qantas also had issues sourcing windscreens for the 787. 'We usually have spares and usually they're on callout and you get them very fast,' Joyce says. 'So the 787 would be typically grounded for twenty-four hours if that had happened. During COVID, we had one Jetstar aircraft that was out for five days because we couldn't get a windscreen. There was a worldwide shortage of them. These things really knocked us.'

By now, most Australians were starting to adjust to living alongside COVID-19, and they wanted to get on with their lives. Easter was looming and Aussies were itching to travel again, whether to visit long-missed relatives or just to have a holiday. Qantas was gearing up: Jetstar would be at 120 per cent of pre-COVID levels and Qantas at over 110 per cent for Easter.

As travel went from a standing start to full speed almost overnight, cracks soon appeared. Air traffic controllers were in short supply, and airports rushed to train security and other operational staff. Queues started developing at airports as increasing numbers of workers called in sick.

Qantas eased back on the capacity throttle for Easter, pegging Qantas at around 93 per cent of pre-COVID flying and Jetstar at 100 per cent. But still the queues grew. Flights were delayed and cancelled. And bags started going missing. So did staff, as Omicron surged through the workforce.

As the complaints mounted, television news bulletins and social media were full of stories of delays, long waits and cancellations. The airports and Qantas copped the brunt of the anger, which was fed by the disaffected unions, who blamed the delays on Qantas's cutbacks. It was no comfort that the exact same problems were occurring worldwide.

Joyce made matters worse when he misjudged the mood of travellers in early April 2022, suggesting they were partly to blame for the omnipresent delays. His analytical mind had isolated the various slow points in the boarding system, and passengers showing up late at their gates was contributing to some of the delayed departures.

'I think our customers are not match fit,' he said with a grin. 'I went through the airport on Wednesday, and people forget they need to take out their laptops; they have to take out their aerosols. And the amount of delays that are actually happening because of that.'[2]

While he was probably correct that some travellers were a little rusty, the comments kicked up a furore. It was a PR nightmare. Joyce hastened to redirect some of the blame to close-contact COVID rules, which had led to some 18 per cent of staff being absent at short notice. 'At the Easter school holidays, we had another wave of COVID and our sick leave went through the roof,' he acknowledges. 'So the combination of all those logjams resulted in just a terrible operation.'

The unions seized on the comments, saying Joyce's move to outsource ground handlers was to blame.

'Qantas sacked 1700 ground staff workers . . . and the catering has been outsourced as well to dnata,' said Flight Attendants Association of Australia (FAAA) federal secretary Teri O'Toole. 'So Qantas deliberately made these changes. And now to have the CEO come on and say it's the passengers' fault because they're not taking deodorant out of their bags at screening . . . It's just ludicrous.'[3]

For Qantas staff, difficult times were made more gruelling as passengers took out their frustrations on frontline staff. John Gissing notes that it was hard for exhausted teams to keep going. 'But we did, and it then rolled through to Easter and all the challenges we had right across the industry,' he says, 'and then the brand and customer impacts that were pretty unbearable for all of us because we care so much about it.

'You can't invalidate how people feel. It's real. We just have to keep bringing our people back to, "It is what it is. I know it's hard, but we've just got to keep doing what we do." And for some that have just come into the industry during that hiring that was going on, it was like, "I didn't sign up for this!"'

In early May 2022, Qantas announced that domestic travel was tracking ahead of expectations, and there was strong demand for international travel. After numerous false starts, Joyce was convinced that a sustained recovery in travel demand was underway.

Leisure demand was strong over the Easter peak, and business traffic was recovering more rapidly than expected as mask mandates were removed and people went back to the office.

Domestic corporate travel had reached 85 per cent of pre-COVID levels and more than 100 per cent for small businesses. Companies were clearly getting their people out and travelling again.

Qantas's international flying was slower to recover, as many markets remained closed or heavily restricted, but key routes like London, Los Angeles and Johannesburg were performing above pre-COVID levels, while routes to India, Europe and Korea were positive.

Around this time, Joyce and husband Shane Lloyd settled on a Mosman federation mansion they'd bought in March for $19 million. Photos of the fifteen-room luxury residence were splashed across news sites. The 'very private' property's six bedrooms, formal and informal living areas, a home cinema, wine cellar, netted harbour pool, jetty and private berth was suddenly very public.

The timing, cost and conspicuous nature of the acquisition, amid rising flight delays and baggage problems, was seen by some as 'tone deaf' and 'poor optics' for the Qantas boss. But Joyce was impervious to such criticism – it was as if he had a set of noise-cancelling headphones when it came to what was reported about him in the media.

'Why is it relevant what I do in my private life? I'm not a public figure,' he later told *The Weekend Australian*. 'People regard the CEO of Qantas as like a politician and it definitely shouldn't be. It's a business figure. It's been well reported over the years how much I get paid, so I do have the money because Qantas went to record profits and had a record share price.'[4]

This was accurate in all but one respect: however much Joyce might wish it not to be, the chief executive officer of Qantas is very much a public figure.

*

Qantas service standards were continuing to struggle. The strength of the rebound in demand had caught Joyce unprepared, even though he'd been criticised for his earlier optimism. Mishandled bags and flight cancellations were on the rise, queues at airports were growing, and on-time performance was deteriorating. Qantas needed to recruit again, and fast. Joyce announced that Qantas had 2500 roles to fill over the next twelve months.

Restarting an airline after a two-year grounding is complex. Add to that a tight labour market, and it was even trickier to achieve.

The strength of the recovery, coupled with high levels of sick leave – due to flu, COVID and isolation requirements – caught Qantas's slimmed-down workforce short, and the airline badly botched the restart. This was a common experience among airlines and their passengers all around the world, but for Qantas's loyal passengers, the troubles were still hard to stomach.

'Hindsight's a great thing,' Joyce says. 'You could say, "Well, should we have been expecting that?" But I don't think anybody knew the supply-chain issues or anybody foresaw the sick leave issues. We didn't forecast them. I don't think any airline did, such were the logjams in the system that we didn't know of.'

Publicly, Joyce kept insisting that airlines and airports in Europe, the United States and the United Kingdom were dealing with far more severe impacts. 'Look over there!' was a common refrain from the Australian carrier at the time. 'In an unprecedented move, Heathrow Airport has capped the number of passengers travelling through the airport and asked airlines to stop selling seats over the European summer because of a mountain of lost bags they're picking through,' Joyce argued, with cause.[5]

As a result of the strains, the Qantas share price dropped sharply in mid-June. Joyce sought to reassure travellers (and shareholders) that additional resources for the school holiday peak in July were in place to avoid the disruptions and service failures that were plaguing the airline.

Qantas's mishandled bag rate had reached eleven in every 1000 in July – about double the usual rate – and flight cancellations spiked to 7.5 per cent, compared to 2.4 per cent pre-COVID. On-time performance was just 52 per cent, way below pre-COVID levels of 80 per cent or higher.

On social media, a new piece of Australian slang entered the vernacular. When you were severely inconvenienced at an airport by luggage delays or flight problems, you had been 'Joyced'. One member of the public decided to take out their frustration on the CEO directly: a hooded figure was captured on security cameras outside Joyce's Mosman mansion at 2 am on 12 July hurling eggs and toilet paper onto the roof of the property.

Unbeknown to the egger, Joyce hadn't even moved in yet – nor was he in the country at the time. He was finally taking a break, holidaying in Italy and later visiting his elderly mother in Dublin. Andrew David was acting as CEO. But the point was made.

Calls for Joyce to step down were growing. 'Many Australians are of the opinion that Alan Joyce should move on – the reputational damage is enormous,' said Natalie McKenna, a lecturer in strategic communication at La Trobe University in Melbourne, talking with Bloomberg.[6]

Former TWU head Tony Sheldon – now a federal senator representing New South Wales – said Qantas's performance had become a drag on the economy. 'Things have to change and someone has to be held to account. Qantas's reputation has been Joyced,' he said.[7]

The ACCC, meanwhile, reported that Qantas-related complaints had soared 68 per cent in the 2022 financial year to 1700 as a result of its customer service issues and long call wait times. 'As Australia's largest airline, and an airline that generally charges a premium to fly, consumers expect a better service,' the agency said.[8] It had a point.

Several weeks into his break, Joyce phoned Andrew David and asked if he should come back. 'Every other time when I've been acting for Alan, if he asked me that question, I had said, "No, no, you don't need to come back – enjoy your holiday,"' David says. 'But I had been fronting media every day for a week – it was unrelenting! You have to be strategic and you've got to have a big dose of resilience. Everybody's got an opinion. Everybody's got an experience that they like to share with you, good, bad and indifferent. So I said to Alan, "Yeah, please come back – this is the time I need you back here."'

Joyce cut his trip short and returned to the fray. Leaders taking holidays during national emergencies had created headlines in recent years. Most notoriously, Prime Minister Scott Morrison's judgement was called into question when he holidayed with his family in Hawaii during the devastating 2019 bushfires.

Joyce confronted the criticism head-on. 'I have an 82-year-old mother [in Ireland] who is not very well and I shouldn't have to justify to anybody that I see her. I think it's completely unfair,' he told *The Weekend Australian*.[9]

Qantas had by now recruited an extra 1000 people, but the tight labour market was hampering its efforts to find more. And with the onset of winter, rising COVID infections were compounding staff shortages. It rostered more staff on standby, flights were consolidated onto bigger aircraft, and it doubled the number of customer support team members based at its airports and in its clogged call centres. Joyce developed a multi-million-dollar program to soothe disgruntled customers and asked managers and executives to help load bags – a move that only angered the unions.

'I never thought it would be harder to restart the airline than it was to ground it,' David says. 'It was so hard because the demand was there. If we didn't get the capacity in the sky, we were going to get accused of price gouging. So we had to get capacity back while also managing labour shortages, supply-chain issues, and ongoing sickness from COVID.

'We were disappointed because we weren't delivering what people expect of Qantas. As the national carrier, people have expectations of us. They either don't see or don't want to see what's happening in the rest of the globe.'

But the message from the public was getting through. Joyce acknowledged that if your flight to the Gold Coast got cancelled, it didn't make you feel any better that the delays were worse in Amsterdam.

'We plan new aircraft at least ten years ahead,' Joyce said. 'Our flights go on sale twelve months in advance. Training new people can take months. And it all has to come together to deliver on-time performance, measured in minutes. The pandemic has tested everyone . . . and aviation has been sorely tested. We're the first to admit we haven't gotten everything right lately.'[10]

On 21 August, Joyce issued a formal apology to the airline's customers in the form of an email and video message to millions of frequent flyers, offering them each a $50 voucher towards a return flight from Australia or New Zealand and a twelve-month membership status extension, as part of a $400-million customer package.

Despite a strong comeback in the last three months of the 2022 financial year, Joyce announced another stark set of numbers: an underlying loss before tax of almost $1.9 billion, and a statutory loss before tax of just under $1.2 billion. It took Qantas's total losses since the start of the pandemic to more than $7 billion – equivalent to the combined profits of the five bumper years in the lead-up to COVID – and lost revenue to more than $25 billion.

It had taken a while, but Joyce had admitted the airline's errors and set about fixing them. 'What we've always done, and what we've always tried to do, is front it,' he said. 'We don't hold back. We've apologised for the mistakes that we've made for not delivering for what the customers expect from us.

'I love Qantas. I think it's an amazing brand. I'm passionate about it. The board asked me to continue in this job to get it through this crisis. We will get it through the current problems that we have. And I think at the other end of this, Qantas will be stronger than it was before it went in.'

Joyce wasn't perturbed by the chorus of voices baying for his blood. He'd been through torrents of resignation demands over the years. Now the underlying message was upbeat, despite the terrible headline numbers. 'We can't bring aircraft out of storage fast enough,' Joyce said, as a strong recovery took hold.

Forward bookings were extremely strong, reflecting a resurgent economy primed by government stimulus and low interest rates. But the price of jet fuel was marching ever higher on the back of growing economies and the war in Ukraine. Accordingly, and along with measures to avoid more operational chaos, Qantas trimmed its capacity growth plans by around 10 percentage points.

Qantas now pegged Group domestic capacity at 95 per cent of pre-COVID levels in July–December 2022, and at 106 per cent of pre-COVID levels in January–June 2023. Group international capacity was set to increase as more A380s and 787-9s were added and as borders continued to reopen, with targets of 65 per cent of pre-COVID levels set for July–December 2022 and 84 per cent of pre-COVID levels for January–June 2023.

'We took twenty-five aircraft out of the system and we doubled our reserves of aircraft on the ground,' Joyce says about pulling back on Qantas's recovery aspirations. 'It meant we had all the costs of aircraft that could have been flying, getting people to see family and friends or to holidays, to get reliable operations back. But it worked, we got the operation back to normal.'

Qantas also announced its first share buyback since 2019, worth up to $400 million, to repay shareholders for their support, especially institutional investors who had come to the carrier's aid with the equity raising in the early days of the pandemic.

Shareholders were happy.

*

As Qantas's prospects improved, the recriminations increased in proportion. Sections of the media were keen to jump on any negatives, which both reflected and stimulated a lot of bad feelings towards the national carrier.

A scathing report by the ABC's *Four Corners* in early September took aim at Qantas for its strategic responses to the crisis, and focused on the service failures and higher fares that occurred during the restart.

Supportah TV News released a video in mid-August that included an interview with investigative journalist Michael West, who took up a popular thread at the time about government support for the airline industry in general, and Qantas in particular.

'No single corporation in Australian history has had as many handouts in public money as has Qantas: more than $2 billion,' said West. 'And it is a very poor taxpayer. What was given in return? What did the government demand in return for this two billion, this 2000-million-dollar subsidy, handout? Nothing. There was not one thing asked in return.'[11]

In a later interview with CNBC, Joyce said Qantas had received 'very little' funding from the government directly. 'When you break down that $2 billion, $1 billion of that was to rent our aircraft as freighters to keep the agricultural sector, the fishery sector alive,' he explained. 'So that was a service that the government paid us for. We didn't make very much money out of that. The second component of it was JobKeeper . . . so that [workers] could get through this, and that was essential to them. That was not money to Qantas. That was money that Qantas passed off to its employees.'[12]

Four Corners' reporter Stephen Long interviewed Steve Purvinas, the federal secretary of the ALAEA, who said lower staffing numbers, fatigue and distractions could lead to 'problems on planes'.

Steve Purvinas: When any given engineer goes into work today, they're loaded up with more work than they would've been pre-COVID. About two or three months into COVID, Qantas came out and said, 'We want to make 20 per cent of the engineers redundant.' They were oversubscribed. They ultimately let go near on 35 per cent of the engineers. And we were telling them all along that, 'You cannot do this. You won't have enough people employed by the airline to maintain the aircraft when things rebound.'

Stephen Long: It's hard to believe that Qantas, which has staked its reputation on its enviable safety record, would cut numbers so severely that it would impact on safety.

Purvinas: It's sort of like Qantas have had this long-term safety record, and they're now trying to cash in on it. That is, 'We'll let slip on some of these safeguards that were put in place over many years. We'll let some of the experience go. We'll push the guys further than they've ever been pushed before and hope that things don't fall apart.'[13]

Qantas challenged these claims that it had compromised on safety:

Unions . . . often use phrases like 'race to the bottom' when we make changes to our business and imply safety is at risk. In reality, aviation is one of the most closely scrutinised industries in Australia and Qantas would never, ever, compromise on safety. It's worth noting that *Four Corners* did not contact the Civil Aviation Safety Authority regarding any claims made in the program. CASA has since reiterated that it has confidence that Qantas is operating safely.[14]

It was not one of the ABC's finest hours in terms of balanced reporting.

Meanwhile, a spat over Joyce was developing between the *Australian Financial Review* and *The Australian*. The *AFR* ran a feature titled 'The ugly truth about Alan Joyce', in which senior correspondent Aaron Patrick claimed that, for about half a decade, Qantas had 'benefited one man above everyone else, including customers, staff and even shareholders: chief executive Alan Joyce'.

> Joyce has adroitly played the high game and the low game. He markets Qantas as the moral embodiment of Australian nationalism, while driving an influence-peddling scheme known as the Chairman's Lounge. He hires and promotes young, talented managers, but doesn't groom an obvious successor. His most egregious decision may have been [the 2019 decision] to buy Qantas shares using cash that could have been spent on newer planes and keeping good staff.[15]

The *Herald Sun*'s business commentator, Terry McCrann, shot back, firstly comparing the *Four Corners* exposé on Qantas to a double episode of *Seinfeld*: 'an extended show about big fat nothing'. At the other extreme, McCrann wrote:

> The *Fin*'s article showed a yawning lack of understanding about financial dynamics, criticising Qantas's extensive use of share buybacks. There is a very simple, utterly anodyne reason for the buybacks. They've been used as quasi dividends because Qantas had massive accumulated tax losses and so could not deliver franking credits. The buybacks served two purposes: to return cash to (mainly institutional) holders, and to manage capital efficiently.
>
> To say, as the *Fin* did, that this starved Qantas of cash that could have been spent on planes and staff, was just ludicrous and indeed embarrassingly ignorant. To say, as the *Fin* did, this was done to place 'Joyce's interests' above that of customers and staff was outrightly and indeed viciously offensive.[16]

Qantas chairman Richard Goyder stepped forward with a show of support for his embattled CEO. In an op-ed in mid-September 2022, Goyder said that judging Qantas's recent performance by pre-COVID standards and finding Joyce lacking as a result was like saying the pandemic never happened. 'Anyone who understands the industry thinks Alan and his team have done exceptionally well to steer the airline through a crisis that sent other airlines (and their creditors) packing,' he wrote. 'People who think Qantas couldn't have failed or was enriched by government handouts are simply wrong.'[17]

In September 2022, Virgin CEO Jayne Hrdlicka announced a partnership with Qatar Airways, an extensive codeshare tie-up covering 140 destinations worldwide, reciprocal lounge access and frequent-flyer program links.

The move fuelled speculation that the acquisitive Qataris might become a strategic investor in Virgin's initial public offering when Bain Capital exited after the turnaround. The only other Middle East option was Etihad, whose former investment in Virgin collapsed when it entered administration in 2020; it seemed unlikely to go around again.

Qatar Airways hosted the 2022 IATA annual general meeting in Doha. Akbar Al Baker and Hrdlicka took to the stage to celebrate the new partnership. Al Baker said, 'I don't know if Alan [Joyce] is here, but we tried to do work with [Qantas] for a very long time.' He added that Hrdlicka was 'new' to Virgin, but 'I'm sure she's very experienced in aviation'.[18]

Joyce wasn't in the room at the time, but he knew Qatar was upset. 'When the Emirates deal came up for renewal, Akbar thought [we would go with them] because we're [part of] oneworld,' he explains. 'But we are big into relationships and because our relationship with Emirates is so good, we were always going to renew it.'

It would have been a major upheaval for both Qantas and

Emirates if such a close relationship over a ten-year period were to be untangled.

Competition is sure to intensify with the new-look Virgin. Hrdlicka has moved the airline back to the 'sensible centre' of the market. She's had the great advantage in working for both Qantas and Virgin, so she knows their respective market strategies inside out.

'It's always going to be competitive,' Joyce says, 'and we're in a very competitive industry so I feel competitive against Jayne even if Jayne's a friend. And that's always going to be the case – as it was, I think, with John [Borghetti].'

Hrdlicka concurs. She told *The Australian*, 'I've got a long-standing relationship with Alan. We've worked together, we're good friends but we're fierce competitors and that's the essence of it. There is no scenario where anybody in our business or any other airline would do anything other than strictly adhere to competition law and competition boundaries and you can't argue if you look at what's happening in the country today.'[19]

PART VII

CONTRAILS

'Aviation years are really like dog years.
You age so rapidly running an airline.'

—Alan Joyce

28

The Gorilla Hoarding the Bananas

The market recovery powered on and, by mid-October 2022, Qantas had issued guidance of a massive underlying profit before tax of between $1.2 billion and $1.3 billion for the six months ending 31 December. Operational performance was also much better. Qantas had learned the hard way that maintaining pre-COVID service levels required a much bigger operational buffer. Spikes in sick leave and supply-chain delays meant having more crew and more aircraft on standby.

This created a dilemma. Demand was strong – people wanted to fly – but capacity had to be reduced so that Qantas could actually deliver its schedules. With the memory of July's operational meltdown and August's apology fresh in his mind, Alan Joyce kept a tight lid on capacity planning. To deliver the promised performance meant reducing seat numbers by a few percentage points across all parts of the Qantas Group.

Capacity restraint across the industry helped underpin strong pricing levels, which more than offset the higher fuel prices. It was opportunistic, but coming off the back of two years of big losses, Joyce must have felt it was time to recoup, while travellers were flush with funds. Nor was Virgin Australia in any mood to be discounting at this stage. Its private-equity owners had their eyes firmly set on an initial public share offering in 2023 or 2024, and they needed a set of solid results to take to the market.

The restraint put a rocket under profits at Qantas, and Joyce announced plans to buy back $400 million of shares on-market, to return surplus capital to investors now that strong future earnings were evident. It was a divisive move, welcomed by investors, who had foregone dividends, but derided by unions and some commentators and analysts. The share price surged, closing above the $6 mark on 19 October for the first time since late February 2020. Earnings guidance for the full year was upgraded soon after by $150 million. In other words, the business was earning $3 million per day more than management had expected just six weeks earlier.

But it had been an energy-sapping two and a half years, and more executive changes were happening around Joyce – not all of his choosing. Gareth Evans, the longstanding Jetstar CEO (and former CFO and CEO of Qantas International), decided to head for the exit at the end of 2022. Stephanie Tully was named as his successor, and Markus Svensson was promoted into Tully's chief customer officer role, reporting to Joyce.

Along with the board, the CEO had been carefully planning for his own departure too, moving top executives across different parts of the Group to give them wide experience. Evans was easily the best qualified, but the extreme pressures of the COVID period had changed his mind about his life–work balance and his ambitions at Qantas. 'I just don't want it,' he told Joyce around this time. As Joyce recalls it, Evans 'said he just wanted a sea change, something different. The stress was too much and he didn't want to go through that again. You had to respect that,' the CEO says.

Joyce tried his best to persuade Evans to stay. 'I think he's a fantastic executive, a fantastic guy. But unfortunately we couldn't keep him. It was painful – there were going to be three candidates to replace me. Gareth had an advantage over the other candidates because he'd run International, Jetstar and he'd been CFO. I thought he was going to go past my time.'

Andrew David and John Gissing – who had also been looking to retire around the time COVID struck – were also now
planning belated exits. Joyce was relieved that these experienced
campaigners had stayed the course through the challenge of
a lifetime.

A disruption-free Christmas and New Year followed and,
by late February 2023, Joyce was eager to unwrap the interim
result. In the six months to 31 December 2022, Qantas delivered
a record underlying profit before tax of just over $1.4 billion – a
massive contrast to the $1.3 billion loss in the same period the
year before.

Qantas had hit the trifecta of strong travel demand, higher
yields as industry capacity levels remained down, and benefits
flowing from its restructuring program, which by then were
estimated to be worth $1 billion. Shareholders would bene-
fit through a $500 million on-market share buyback. Staff were
also rewarded, with up to $11,500 in cash and shares and a
$500 travel credit.

COVID shutdown travel credits were gradually being whittled down. Qantas launched 'Find My Credits' in mid-2023 to
allow passengers to use their travel credits and refunds. By this
time, the number of COVID credits held by Qantas customers in
Australia had dropped to $400 million, of which $150 million
were sales with travel agents, and some 80 per cent of them were
still entitled to refunds. 'Our intent is trying to get it down to zero
by the end of the year,' Joyce says.

Airline technology is very antiquated. The airlines were early
adopters more than thirty years ago, but now that legacy was
proving hard to escape – a global problem for the industry. The
challenges present on many fronts in this complex industry, from
flying operations, through baggage tracking, selling tickets, data
analytics – and responding to customer complaints.

'Before COVID, we'd spent a lot of money on a new distribution capability, which we rolled out, which does make things a
lot easier,' Joyce explains. 'And with artificial intelligence on top

of that, it's going to be even more easy to do. It'll be a lot easier with NDC [new distribution capability] because the technology will be a lot more responsive and we're going to get people to be able to do a lot more in the Qantas app. But some of these technology things I've never managed to resolve.'

This would be an issue for future leaders to fix. For now, Joyce could finally breathe more easily. Qantas had come through the other side of the pandemic a structurally different company. 'Our domestic market share is higher and the demand for nonstop direct international flights is even stronger than it was before COVID,' Joyce said. 'This is the recovery our people, our shareholders – and, in many respects, our customers – have been waiting for. Because this result isn't just about a single number. Ultimately, it's about getting back to our best by reinvesting in the national carrier.'[1]

After three years of gigantic losses, the red tail was back in the black, and Joyce was tickled pink. In his remaining time in the CEO's chair, Joyce could finally frame his legacy around the future size and shape of Qantas, Project Sunrise and environmental sustainability.

The pandemic had forced airlines around the world to take a deeper look at their costs, and given them the chance to reassess their workforce and seek to reduce the influence of unions. In this, Qantas sought to follow the example of its global peers, but the reaction was fierce.

When Joyce took over at Qantas, the memory of Ansett Australia was still very fresh in the industry memory. It had offered the best airline product in Australia's domestic market for decades. Before Qantas was privatised, and while it was solely an international airline, it had partnered with Ansett in the domestic market, in preference to the government-owned Australian Airlines. Ansett had been a fixture in the skies, with some 16,000 employees.

Some Ansett staff had worked there all their lives; many families had more than one generation employed. It was 'a great family airline', Executive Chairman Rod Eddington famously said. 'But,' he continued, 'it's a lousy business.' Overburdened by costs and inefficiency, it abruptly collapsed just months after low-cost competition arrived in 2000, unable to adjust to the new world.

Joyce, who of course had cut his teeth leading one of the new-generation airlines, inherited from his predecessor Geoff Dixon the imperative to deal effectively with the airline's often militant unions. Joyce was no stranger to these issues, having been challenged at almost every step in establishing the Jetstar model. At Qantas, his goal was to ensure the airline could compete in this new environment, domestically and internationally.

In his final year as CEO, Dixon had become frustrated with several of the unions, which he felt were oblivious to the dangers rampant in the industry. He declared war on 'detrimental' claims by the unions, making industrial relations a key battleground. In a May 2008 interview with the *Australian Financial Review*, Dixon said: 'The management of this company has contributed far more to its well being and success than any bloody union has ... It is very important for unions to understand that it's more than just representing your people for a couple of per cent – it is really the long-term future of the industry.'[2]

Joyce wasn't ideologically opposed to unions. In an interview with the *Australian Financial Review* just after becoming CEO, he said, 'I come from a working-class background. Unions have a big role to play [and they] have done a lot of good things.' Joyce said he respected the right of Qantas employees to be represented by a union, 'but we also believe that it's important to have a productive and collaborative relationship with our workforce'.

The new CEO was keen to assert his authority, having been appointed by the board, to run the company for the benefit of shareholders. Joyce wanted to limit the influence of the powerful unions on everyday affairs, and to have a more active voice and a more visible presence, together with his management team, in the affairs of the business. Unions had been driving the bus of staff engagement at Qantas, Joyce thought, and he was keen to be the one behind the wheel.

'The trouble is, Qantas is still represented by fourteen different unions, covering fifty-four different [enterprise bargaining agreements],' Joyce continued. 'Some of the union names have changed, but it's exactly the same as it was back [in the 1970s].' He argued that 'some niche unions' had very blinkered views of the world, and on what job security meant.

'To the cabin crew, to the airport staff, job security means a successful business, and it's the only way you can guarantee job security. To others, it's building [more protections] into union agreements.' The only way of offering job security, he maintained, was to 'have a successful business'.[3]

Historically, legacy airlines like Qantas have been heavily vertically integrated, meaning they run everything inhouse – from strategy, marketing and sales at the top, through to customer service, operations management, asset ownership, maintenance and servicing. Newer airlines, over recent decades, have taken less risk than their forebears, farming services out to contracting companies to take on many of these tasks.

As a result, this century has witnessed an explosion in specialist services firms, which have become global players and very efficient in their domains, whether it's ground-handling services, aircraft leasing, catering or maintenance. Legacy carriers have felt obliged to adopt the practice too, outsourcing the 'non-core' parts of their operations to third-party service-providers, to reduce costs and lower their risks.

In mid-2020, with COVID pushing Qantas to the brink of bankruptcy, the airline announced a review of its ground-handling operations at ten airports across Australia. It invited bids for the services, arguing this could save the airline an estimated $80 million in annual operating costs and another

$80 million investment in ground-handling equipment over the ensuing five years. The move sparked a union outcry that would rumble all the way through the recovery phase.

'In August 2020, we didn't know when the pandemic was going to end,' explains Andrew David, who fronted the move. 'We didn't know how demand was going to come back. People might not have wanted to travel for years, [so] we had to make a series of tough calls.'

Two weeks after the muted 100-year anniversary, Joyce confirmed Qantas would indeed be pressing ahead with the outsourcing of its ground-handling operations at Australian airports. Qantas reviewed the external bids from specialist ground-handling suppliers and an in-house bid from employees and their TWU representatives. The TWU bid was rejected and Qantas outsourced the work, removing 1700 jobs from its employment roster, plus another 500 from Jetstar.

'It was a decision we had to make, but it is not a decision you make lightly,' says David. 'When you're in leadership roles, you have to make these calls for the majority. It was tough. There are people that get impacted – and they had been with us for a long time. We'd analysed everything, and the risks were greater of not making that decision than they were of making that decision.'

The Federal Court determined that Qantas's move to outsource the remainder of its ground-handling operation contravened the *Fair Work Act*. The timing of the move during the pandemic helped Qantas avoid industrial action from the TWU.

'This is the largest finding by a country mile of illegal sacking and outsourcing in Australian corporate history,' TWU national secretary Michael Kaine said.

Although the airline would not have to walk back the changes, it risked a big fine, and quickly announced plans to appeal the Federal Court's decision. (At the time of writing, the matter is before the High Court, after Qantas was granted leave to appeal in late 2022.)

All the while, Qantas was having a bruising encounter with the FAAA over a new four-year enterprise agreement for flight attendants. The airline, like many of its international counterparts, was attempting to switch to more dynamic schedules, where different aircraft types were deployed at short notice to deal with spikes in demand for passengers and freight – for example, replacing an A330 with a much larger A380.

Under its enterprise bargaining agreement, Qantas International crews were limited to working on one aircraft type only; now the airline wanted to train them to work across all three widebody aircraft types, to give it more flexibility in managing its international operations. Group international capacity was expected to be around 20 to 30 per cent of pre-COVID levels for January–March 2022, and then to double to 60 per cent in the April–June quarter. But this would be contingent on getting the right international crews in place at the right time.

Early into the new year in 2022, Qantas International applied to the Fair Work Commission to terminate its enterprise bargaining agreement with its long-haul cabin crew staff, citing 'outdated' rostering processes. Qantas argued that the complexity it was dealing with needed to be replaced by a more agile way of working.

These disputes were not about to go away, but a sounder financial platform could stabilise relations.

As the future began to look brighter and more predictable in the early stages of 2023, Joyce unveiled a vision for a bigger Qantas.

As it moves from recovery to growth, the Qantas Group expects to create new jobs over the next decade. 'Aviation is so important to a country like Australia and you need a big skills pipeline to power it.' Joyce says. Qantas expects to create 9500 new jobs, some 8500 of those in Australia, in the next ten years. That includes some 1600 pilots, 800 engineers, 4500 cabin crew and 1600 airport staff, driven by investments in new aircraft and increased flying. Almost a quarter of those new roles will be hired by the end of 2024.

The investment will see the establishment of the Qantas Group Engineering Academy in Australia, with capacity to train up to 300 engineers a year. A new flight training centre is also under construction in Sydney, which will train up to 4500 Qantas and Jetstar pilots and cabin crew each year from early 2024.

Union representatives were cautiously positive on receiving the news. ALAEA federal secretary Steve Purvinas said the engineering academy was 'great news', adding that the profession was 'in desperate need of replenishment'. The Australian Manufacturing Workers Union grudgingly told the *Australian Financial Review* that the move was a 'welcome step in the opposite direction' of recent history.[4]

If Joyce's vision comes to pass, the Group will have an estimated 32,000 people by 2033. The last time Qantas had a workforce that size was in the 2013 financial year, when full-time-equivalent roles numbered 33,265. Then came the swingeing cutbacks under Joyce's Accelerated Transformation Plan. That action took full-time-equivalent staffing levels to a low of 28,622 in 2015. Just prior to COVID, Qantas had 29,745 full-time-equivalent roles, which then fell to just 20,640 in 2021. Full-time equivalent numbers grew back to 25,426 at 30 June 2023. Qantas was much more efficient with fewer employees by the end of Joyce's time as CEO.

Now, as the airline begins to grow again, containing costs will always remain a fundamental, but the foundations are in place for a much more stable future.

In June 2023, Joyce sold 2.5 million Qantas shares, or 83 per cent of his stake in the carrier at the time, at $6.75 per share, netting him just under $17 million. It raised eyebrows in the investor community, as a CEO selling stock can signal that it has peaked and difficulties lie ahead. But there are many reasons for selling shares. It can simply mean, for instance, a clean slate ahead of the CEO's next career move.

For Joyce, the share sale followed a $9 million purchase days earlier of a 223-square-metre penthouse apartment in The Cove tower adjacent to the one he and Shane Lloyd had purchased earlier in The Rocks. The Mosman mansion – which the couple had never lived in – was put on the market for a reported $20 million, with the egg stains removed from the roof. It was just fifteen months after they had purchased it and set about extensively renovating and furnishing it.

These were the first occasions the working-class Dublin boy had a chance to tangibly enjoy the wealth he had earned. It was a step up from collecting airline schedules.

By many standards, Joyce has been richly rewarded during his time as Qantas CEO, earning over $130 million in salary and benefits in his fifteen years at the helm. Back in 2011, Joyce was asked about his salary and its role in motivating him to go above and beyond in doing the job. He responded: 'Well, I think for anybody that does these roles, the salary is always secondary on it.'[5]

Executive remuneration and bonuses were often in the headlines during his tenure. The 350 per cent surge in Qantas's share price over the three-year Accelerated Transformation Plan had put a rocket under the company's market capitalisation – and its executives' pay packets, given that bonuses were mostly paid in Qantas shares.

It was (and remains) a useful way of risk sharing and incentivisation, especially in the airline industry, where risk abounds. There's nothing to guarantee that shares will rise, given the constant shocks in the industry.

When the shares did make the target in the 2017 financial year, Joyce was the highest-paid executive of all the listed companies on the ASX200 for that year. That was when he reaped the rewards of a large long-term incentive allocation granted in 2014, when the share price was $1.26. It vested in full during the 2017 financial year, when the share price was $5.66. The rise in the share price more than doubled Joyce's total 'realised pay' to $23.9 million, according to the Australian Council of Superannuation Investors (ACSI).

Joyce had set a post-GFC high for CEO pay, and was one of just two CEOs in Australia to receive remuneration of more than $20 million that year, just beating out Macquarie Bank's Nicholas Moore. (For the Millionaires' Factory, though, that was standard fare – nothing exceptional.)

Qantas had been the best-performing stock of all ASX100 companies and the best-performing stock in the global listed airlines peer group over the period, but the size of its executives' pay packets was raising eyebrows. Hrdlicka and Evans each received $8.1 million that year.

Leigh Clifford felt it necessary to defend the largesse, saying that while there was no question the pay outcomes were high, 97 per cent of shareholders had voted for them, including the original performance targets. 'For a business that was facing an uncertain future three years ago, and was in no position to pay bonuses to any of its people, the fundamentals that underpin today's pay disclosures show how far we have come,' he argued.[6]

In September 2019, the TWU's Michael Kaine accused Qantas management of being 'more focused on executive bonuses and shareholder profits than on ensuring job security and safe conditions for the airline's workers'.[7]

Joyce's realised pay (salary plus short- and long-term bonuses) the previous year had come in at $12.2 million, according to ACSI. He ranked eighth on the ASX200 executive pay list that year. Joyce slipped to twelfth in 2020 to $10.7 million as the pandemic started to bite. In response to COVID-19, Joyce took a temporary salary cut, receiving no fixed pay for the last three months of the 2020 financial year. Joyce received no bonus in 2021 and was the only ASX100 CEO to receive zero bonus in 2022. He was, however, awarded a lucrative two-year retention equity allocation in 2022, which vested at the end of the 2023 financial year.

By comparison, Afterpay founders Anthony Eisen and Nick Molnar together pocketed $264 million in realised pay in the 2021 financial year, followed by CSL's then CEO, Paul Perrault, with almost $59 million. ResMed's Mick Farrell took top spot in 2022, netting over $47 million in realised pay, according to ACSI.

Words like 'obscene' are frequently used to describe executive pay in Australia. That's understandable, when staff are undergoing pay freezes or cuts, or being fired. Labor senator Tony Sheldon says 'big corporate gorillas' like Qantas are 'hoarding all the bananas'.[8] The discrepancy between senior executive pay and that of rank-and-file staff can be disproportionate in the extreme. But when seen through the lens of a business, where investors' money depends on successful results, things can look very different. Success often comes down to the CEO's performance.

In August 2023, the CEO of European LCC Wizz Air, József Váradi, was given an extension of the term in which to achieve his target bonus, against vociferous protests from some shareholders. The aim was to get Wizz Air's price above £100 by 2028; it was then at £23 (about the same multiple as Joyce's target in 2014–2017). Váradi's success bonus would be £10 million.

When Joyce was awarded his target bonus, as the Transformation Plan was underway, there was no guarantee whatever that the very high target share price would be achieved in the timeframe – nor, for that matter, that he would even still be employed. There were many calling for him to go.

As Váradi put it when arguing his corner, the return on investment was what counted. 'Common sense prevailed,' he said. '[Investors] voted for creating €10 billion of shareholder value at [a] 1 per cent commission rate. Wouldn't you do that?'[9]

29

The Sun Rises Again

Project Sunrise is more than Joyce's cherished innovative operation, it has been a masterclass in marketing. It has generated massively more global coverage than Qantas's advertising budget ever could.

One of Joyce's highlights as CEO was the delivery flight of the first Qantas Dreamliner to Australia in October 2017. 'It's an aircraft we've waited eighty years for,' he said, with a spring in his step. It wasn't because of the technology Boeing had put into this next-generation aircraft, nor how Qantas had designed the cabin, 'but because of what it will enable us to do'.[1] The aircraft represented a big part of the visible legacy Joyce would leave at Qantas.

The 787-9s, of which Qantas initially ordered eight, were a harbinger of what was to come. They were the entrée to Joyce's main course: linking Australia's east coast cities nonstop with London and New York. These are the main business routes, with higher-yielding travellers. The target year for those ultra-long-haul missions was 2022, but they needed an aircraft that didn't exist yet. In August 2017, Joyce threw down the challenge to Boeing and Airbus to deliver an aircraft capable of flying regular direct services like Sydney–London, Brisbane–Paris and Melbourne–New York nonstop with a full payload.

The name 'Project Sunrise' was a nod to the legendary double-sunrise flights operated by Qantas across the Indian Ocean during World War II. These remained airborne long enough for those on board to see two sunrises in what was an incredible feat of endurance.

It was a challenge the likes of which the manufacturers had not seen since the Boeing 747SP (for Special Performance). That aircraft smashed range barriers for airlines like PanAm, Iran Air, Qantas and South African Airways in the 1970s. It was a stubby, shortened version of the 747, designed for longer-distance flights. Boeing 777X and the Airbus A350ULR were in the manufacturers' plans, but further advances were needed.

The first step, though, was to link Perth with London – 14,498 kilometres of distance. The flights took off on 28 March 2018, linking Australia with Europe nonstop for the first time. The aircraft would have a spacious layout, with just 236 business, premium economy and economy seats, and had design features to improve passengers' comfort on such an extended mission. It wasn't the longest scheduled flight by any means: Singapore Airlines' New York flights, at 15,400 kilometres, takes nearly nineteen hours. But Project Sunrise connects the antipodes.

When Qantas created the Kangaroo Route to London in 1947, it took four days and nine stops. Now it would take just seventeen hours from Perth nonstop. In 1947, a return flight from Sydney to London cost £525, when the average weekly wage was £7. In March 2018, the average Australian weekly wage was $1600 and a return economy fare from Perth to London was priced from $1300.

The Perth–London link would eclipse the 13,730-kilometre Sydney–Dallas route as the longest sector in the Qantas network. Nonstop flights to Paris and Frankfurt were also in the frame, from Perth, but Joyce suggested that if it worked on Perth, 'it will work on Melbourne and Sydney to London, and Melbourne and Sydney to New York and Chicago, to Rio de Janeiro, to Cape Town'.[2]

Joyce was delighted with the initial financial performance of Perth–London, which was a stark contrast to the losses Qantas had racked up to Europe earlier that decade. Qantas hadn't made money on the London market for a decade since the global financial crisis, 'whereas Perth–London made money from day one,' he says. 'We're getting 94 per cent load factors and we're getting a premium. People are willing to play more to fly direct.'

This was a market in which there could be no competition. Under international rules, only the airlines based at each end of the route could fly nonstop, unless each of the two governments agreed to third-party entry. For now, at least, that isn't likely – neither British Airways nor Virgin Atlantic is in a position to reciprocate. For the other routes, Qantas is also likely to have the playground to itself.

The 787-9s offered a step-change in efficiency compared with the 747-400s that had been plying the long-haul routes. Their capability presented a way of further segmenting the market, providing a nonstop (more expensive) or one-stop (less expensive) option, just as the creation of Jetstar had done more than a decade earlier.

Qantas was providing a product with a unique value proposition, a premium offering that was more expensive to operate but that could be profitable. Joyce sees that as 'a win-win for everybody'.

Two months later, the airline upped its order for 787-9s, committing to six more, for a total of fourteen of the type by the end of 2020, to coincide with the retirement of the last six 364-seat 747-400s in its fleet.

Qantas has always loved aviation firsts. And in the modern world of social-media hype, they generate enthusiasm and free publicity. The Perth–London nonstop announcement in 2016 was massive. Joyce estimated it generated over $90 million worth of free publicity around the globe. It made the evening news in dozens of countries and was carried on blogs all over the world. Project Sunrise would be the publicity gift that just kept giving.

To keep feeding the publicity machine, in early 2019 Qantas opened the lid on research it had been conducting in conjunction with the University of Sydney's Charles Perkins Centre to capture passenger experiences and suggestions from their Perth–London flights. The stationary exercise bikes and virtual reality relaxation ideas expressed in interviews and focus groups were great fodder for morning news TV and the hundreds of articles and television clips that followed.

Delays to the 777X – the Boeing plane that could achieve the longer flight lengths – were rumoured, but both Boeing and Airbus put their aircraft offers on the table for Qantas to consider around the middle of 2019. The airline was also working with regulators to permit flights beyond twenty hours, while simultaneously negotiating with pilots to forge a deal that locked in some productivity gains, as it had with the Dreamliners.

Joyce made a veiled threat at the 2019 results announcement that, despite the enthusiasm for Sunrise, it was not a foregone conclusion; ultimately, it was a business decision. The economics have to stack up, he said, and a final decision would be made by the end of 2019.

In the meantime, Qantas had more free PR column inches, clicks and views in the form of three separate research trips, using 787-9s on glorified delivery flights from the Boeing factory in Seattle. The aircraft were positioned in New York and London and flown direct to Sydney, with plenty of camera operators, smartphones and influencers on board – plus some researchers from Monash and Sydney universities, running tests on social media engagement and passenger comfort (and crew wellbeing, to be sent to the regulator CASA, to help with approvals). Qantas didn't estimate the PR value of the flight 'experiments', but it would have been in the hundreds of millions of dollars.

The PR train kept rolling a week or so prior to Christmas 2019. The Airbus A350-1000 had been selected as the preferred aircraft and CASA saw no regulatory obstacles to the Sunrise flights. But the go/no-go decision would be deferred till

March 2020, as discussions with the AIPA were not resolved. Meanwhile, a mysterious respiratory illness was starting to circulate in Wuhan.

The early months of 2020 brought an early sunset to Sunrise. The project had been signed off by the board in early March 2020. 'We were two weeks from ordering the aircraft,' Joyce says. 'We had done the competition between the 777X and the A350, we had negotiated a deal for the airplanes, we had done a deal for our pilots. And then COVID hit.'

Two tumultuous years would pass before Joyce confirmed, in February 2022, that work had resumed on Project Sunrise. The latest customer research showed that, with health now an issue, demand for nonstop long-haul flights was even stronger than it had been pre-COVID. After the restart, the number-one route people were searching for on Qantas's international operation was Perth–London.

The Project Sunrise plan was dusted off and nonstop services were again on the cards between Sydney and Melbourne and New York and London. Joyce put the business case for Project Sunrise to the board: it showed an internal rate of return 'in the mid-teens' – a respectable margin for most businesses, but exceptional for an airline.

By May 2022, Qantas finalised a deal with Airbus for twelve A350s, which will start to arrive in late 2025. It was the second time the board had signed off on Project Sunrise – the only time the Qantas board has ever approved the same proposal twice.

'I think we have three of the top five longest routes in the world today,' Joyce enthuses. 'And they're a unique value proposition, they get the highest passenger scores, have the highest profitability and they're unique. And that's why Sunrise is just going to be a phenomenal opportunity.' Joyce later said Sunrise had been 'that close' in early 2020. 'We lost three years but it was the right call at the time.'

The deal was part of a massive order for Airbus aircraft, along with the renewal of Qantas's domestic narrow-body fleet. The Airbus planes will have the range for nonstop flights between Australia and any city in the world. Each aircraft will carry 238 passengers (compared to more than 300 seats on competitor airlines) across first, business, premium economy and economy classes. More than 40 per cent of the cabin is dedicated to premium seating, compared to 30 per cent for the 787-9.

Joyce stressed the green credentials of the new fleet, which would reduce emissions by at least 15 per cent if running on fossil fuels. The 'if' was small but significant. Project Sunrise also weaves together another pillar of Joyce's legacy: environmental sustainability. The flights will be carbon-neutral from day one – or so is the plan. To that extent, Sunrise is flying into the unknown. Environmental challenges will be greatly magnified in coming years.

30

Flygskam

Flight shaming – *flygskam* in Swedish – has blossomed across Europe since 2018, largely as a result of climate protests by Swede Greta Thunberg. The idea is to shame air travellers for contributing directly to global warming. The trend was impacting all air travel, but particularly long-haul flights to far-flung destinations like Australia, as people became more aware of, and concerned by, their personal carbon footprint.

Estimates vary on aviation's contribution to the world's carbon emissions, but they settle around 3 per cent. Long-haul flying, however, contributes as much as 40 per cent of that, and Australia's geography ensures a lot of long-haul flying.

Project Sunrise shone a much brighter light on emissions, particularly where the flights involved Europe, the leader in regulation and environmental activism. So ensuring that Project Sunrise did not run into environmental problems became a priority at Qantas, one that has coincided with a flurry of new actions by the airline.

First, Qantas announced plans immediately to offset 100 per cent of all Sunrise flight emissions from day one. A carbon price was built into the business case for the initial three Project Sunrise aircraft.

Qantas has been a long-term player in offset markets, launching its carbon offset program back in 2007. It doesn't reduce emissions, but accredited offset programs – and there are some that have been pretty dodgy in the past – are the only weapon available in the near term.

The industry's preferred system is to use sustainable aviation fuel (SAF). These can cut lifecycle emissions by up to 80 per cent compared with fossil fuels, but even the most optimistic projections for industry-wide use by 2030 only foresee it making up less than 10 per cent of total fuel use. Electric and hydrogen technologies are even more distant.

Newer aircraft burn up to 25 per cent less fuel, and Qantas now has them arriving in droves. Taken together, offsets, new planes and SAF would become Joyce's big bets in the sustainability stakes. They require massive investment.

Qantas's record on emissions reduction has been unimpressive, although the same can be said for most other major airlines. Joyce's bold moves towards making the airline financially sustainable have not been echoed when it comes to environmental sustainability. Inaction has been fostered by the tepid attitudes of successive Australian governments.

It wasn't always like this. Qantas had long believed Australia to be a prime candidate to develop its own sustainable fuel industry. Back in 2012, it joined a feasibility study into the potential for an Australian SAF industry, backed by funding from the Australian government. In April that year, Qantas operated Australia's first flight powered by SAF: a Sydney–Adelaide flight using a fuel type derived from recycled cooking oil.

In 2013, Qantas and Shell released a report that said an Australian SAF industry was technically viable, but significant obstacles remained. These included insufficient natural oil feedstock at a competitive price in Australia, a lack of refining locations requiring expensive new infrastructure, and a lack of policy and funding support – namely, biodiesel production grants to help make a commercial plant viable.

The report was released two months after the Coalition government of Tony Abbott was elected in September 2013, and with it momentum ceased on many environmental causes, this included.

At that time, Qantas was struggling financially, but as the Transformation Plan started to pay dividends, the airline began to make the right noises again. Qantas's head of environment, John Valastro, explained that 'Qantas's focus now is on making biofuel a viable alternative to conventional jet fuel. It won't be easy, but we are armed with a stronger and more detailed understanding than ever before of all aspects of the biofuel supply chain.'[1]

When profits started to flow again, Qantas proudly announced in early 2017 that its carbon offsetting program had offset more than 3 million tonnes of carbon, making it the world's largest such program. Qantas's emissions in that financial year alone were almost five times that figure, so it was clear the carrier still had a lot of work to do.

It's fair to say that, until very recently, the issue has not been top of mind at Qantas HQ. The word 'emissions' did not even appear in Qantas's annual report in 2017, but it did in the record-breaking profit year that was 2018: it was mentioned once in relation to fuel savings and transformation benefits. The word 'emissions' came up four times each in the 2019 and 2020 annual reports, and six times in 2021. When Qantas released its first Sustainability Report, in 2022, it appeared a bumper twenty-one times.

Towards the end of 2022, Joyce said that while the demand for SAF had never been higher, supply was lagging well behind, particularly as there was no local industry in Australia, and that was keeping SAF prices several times more expensive than traditional jet kerosene.

In other words, SAF was an unviable option, and would remain so for a long time. In the meantime, Qantas would rely on offsetting the enormous footprint of the Project Sunrise flights.

*

It is easy to say with the benefit of hindsight, but Joyce's and the Qantas board's actions on environmental sustainability have been incremental and cautious. Joyce's execution on sustainability decisions has lacked the boldness, tenacity and precision he has demonstrated in other strategic areas.

On emissions targets, Qantas was one of the first airlines globally, in 2019, to commit to net-zero emissions by 2050. Under the November 2019 banner 'QANTAS GROUP TO SLASH CARBON EMISSIONS', Joyce announced a $50 million investment over ten years to help develop a SAF industry in Australia.

After years of failure to get going on this crucial component of the emissions-reduction plan, committing to a $5-million-a-year investment over ten years scarcely cuts the mustard. It wasn't exactly greenwashing, but it wasn't far away.

Only in March 2022 was the interim 2030 target and meaningful detail on a pathway unveiled under the Qantas Group's Climate Action Plan. This integrated climate change considerations into the Group's financial framework for the first time, and linked performance against targets to executive remuneration (from the 2023 financial year), including considering the cost of carbon in all financial decisions.

Qantas also renewed its calls for all levels of government to lend their support to ensuring Australia manufactures SAF, something the United Kingdom, the United States and Europe are already doing.

Qantas upped its commitment in June 2022, when it unveiled its US$200 million Australian Sustainable Aviation Fuel Partnership with Airbus, following its enormous order for new narrow-body and widebody aircraft. (The financial contribution to the partnership included the $50 million commitment previously announced into the research and development of SAF in Australia.)

The five-year pact, with options to extend, was designed to accelerate the establishment of a SAF industry in Australia by investing in locally developed and produced SAF and feedstock initiatives. Meanwhile, Australia exports millions of tonnes of feedstock every year, such as canola and animal tallow, to be made into SAF in other countries.

For anything substantive to happen in Australia, it's going to require significant financial commitments by government. Given the current economic straits, that may be a forlorn hope. The Albanese government, elected in 2022, has offered a stronger focus on emissions reduction than its predecessors, and Joyce says encouraging discussions are underway. The aviation industry needs the right policy settings in place, he argues, to ensure the price of SAF comes down over time so that the cost of air travel doesn't rise.

So far, that has produced a commitment to a feasibility study towards the establishment of a Queensland biofuel production facility. So, more than a decade after launching its feasibility study with Shell into local biofuel production, with much fanfare, another feasibility study is – almost – underway.

Whatever the outcome, the news for travellers won't be good. It seems inevitable that SAF will cost considerably more than jet fuel, and, to aggravate the fare situation further, regulatory charges or levies will most likely add further to prices. A recent study by consulting group Bain anticipates that the 'airlines' cost of mitigating carbon emissions will cause material increases in ticket prices starting in 2026' – a result of both SAF costs and regulation.

With its aged fleet, Qantas is producing significantly more emissions and fuel burn per revenue tonne kilometre (RTK) than when Joyce took office in late 2008. Fuel usage was 40.1 litres per 100 RTKs in the 2009 financial year. By pre-pandemic 2019, that figure had eased to 36.2 litres, but it shot up to 55.4 litres in the 2021 financial year, when aircraft load factors plummeted. The figure remained elevated at 51 litres in 2022, although with higher load factors in 2023, and as the new aircraft arrive, the level will gradually reduce.

Climate activists and one UK government-commissioned study have called for the banning of frequent-flyer programs as they encourage flying. These views are outliers, but they do point to areas of concern for airlines in the future.

As a step in this direction, in late 2021 Qantas introduced a 'Green Tier' to reward its frequent flyers for making sustainable choices, such as offsetting their flights or selecting a hotel that has sustainable policies in place.

'We know that points can change a lot of behaviour, like people changing credit cards, changing home mortgages, changing supermarkets and energy companies,' says Olivia Wirth, the head of Qantas Loyalty. 'So the very essence of this idea is, "Well, can we use points to help change behaviour?" We're in conversations with our other partners about how we embed Green Tier into their own programs. How do we reward our Green Tier members through earning more points with our partners?'

At the other end of the spectrum, Qantas also richly rewards its most frequent and loyal flyers. In late 2019, Qantas introduced its most exclusive club yet: Lifetime Platinum, to retain its best customers and help maintain its stranglehold over the corporate market. Members must amass 75,000 status credits to qualify, or the equivalent of two decades of flying at platinum level, which is normally about two flights a week, fifty-two weeks a year. *Business Traveller* magazine estimated it would take 130 Sydney–London return business-class trips, or over 6000 hours of flying, to qualify.

One Sydney–London return trip in business class produces some 8.6 tonnes of CO_2 emissions, according to the IATA's emissions calculator, which is almost twice the global average annual carbon footprint of 4.7 tonnes of CO_2 per person. In effect, Qantas is lavishing rewards on its best travellers when they achieve carbon emissions equivalent to the combined annual output of 234 people.

It's a broader societal issue, Wirth says. At the moment, if you are doing business and you're choosing to travel and you have to travel, there's no other way of doing it. 'So, therefore, our approach is, "Well, how do you work with them to understand how you can offset the impact that you're having through flying?"' she asks. 'Because flying is going to be a necessity to connect communities, for essential services, and to grow business. That's a reality of the continent that we inhabit.'

The catastrophic events of 2023's northern summer have spread a more personalised understanding of the potential effects of global warming; UN Secretary-General António Guterres has described it as an existential problem that signals 'the era of global boiling has arrived'.[2]

Geographically remote Australia, more than any other developed nation, is most exposed to the inevitable pushback against the airline industry in the next few years. So it will be vital to Qantas's long-haul aspirations to be able to demonstrate 'clean' operations. It won't be easy. Nor will it be cheap, whether as a result of using more expensive SAFs, or regulatory impositions like carbon taxes, or both.

After years of complacency under an Australian government that didn't prioritise the issue, Qantas was not pressured to act. But change is afoot, as the airline addresses the climatic and commercial implications of long-haul flying, with orders for new, more fuel-efficient aircraft and plans to acquire SAF.

Although Airbus and Boeing are providing some support alongside the fleet orders, the fact that synthetic fuels will account for less than 10 per cent of Qantas's needs by 2030 means continued heavy reliance on offsetting emissions, an area which remains controversial. The next few years will provide complex new challenges.

31

Mind Games

Following the 2011–12, 2013–14 and 2020–22 dramas, Joyce was a hero to some but a villain to so many others.

Each episode had shown he was always determined to give as good as he got. He seemed impervious to the criticism and successive trials and never once considered resigning, despite the well-publicised calls for him to step down. There were plenty.

Andrew David says Joyce was the toughest person he worked with across his thirty-year career spanning five airlines. 'There's nobody tougher than Alan,' he reflects. 'That's just the way he's wired. People talk about the brave or courageous decisions he's made. I'm not sure Alan even thinks about them as brave or courageous – he just thinks of them as the *right* decisions.

'If you're an adrenaline junkie, aviation is the most wonderful industry. But you've really got to be on your A game every day to win in this business – you do have to work so hard. And that's what it's been like working for Alan. You're in the A team and you're making stuff happen.'

Despite the constant headlines and the media scrutiny that pursued him – or, some might say, that he sought – Joyce managed to maintain a healthy work–life balance. As he says, 'It's probably [grounded in my] problem-solving background – the physics, mathematics background that I came from, where you get so focused on one particular item that you block everything else out around it.'

Early in his career at Aer Lingus, when he was running network planning, the company put its managers through a mindfulness course. 'I found it unbelievably useful,' Joyce recalls. 'And I read a bit more about it and started practising it a lot more. It was a way of keeping all the distractions out – it's a form of meditation, and a bit more than that.'

The course honed Joyce's natural ability to 'compartmentalise' and dedicate his attention to one thing at a time. 'If you focus on it – if you train your mind – you can actually focus on the issue that's in front of you and not get distracted,' he explains. 'It helps you avoid the stresses of what could be very stressful times.'

Even during the stressful Fair Work Australia review in 2011, compartmentalising and delegating saw him through. 'We had different people doing different things at the time. And I think it did help. I was doing a lot of the media while Fair Work was hearing the case on arbitration, or the case to terminate. I felt really comfortable that we had people doing things, and that I could focus on this part of it and not worry about the rest. And I think that works really well once you have the ability to do that.'

Joyce believes his mindfulness skills also helped his decision-making processes during the pandemic, a time when at first it looked as if the world were caving in. 'It's actually being present in the moment when you're talking about issues,' he reflects. 'We were switching from managing cash, to restructuring, to safety issues, to issues that then related to future growth. Mindfulness does help you to spend your time on those things and not get distracted by a lot of the noise that's around you.'

John Gissing agrees. 'Alan is a great compartmentaliser, always has been,' he says. 'Blows me away how well he can just lock his focus on a problem until it's fixed and not let the noise get in the way. He took that leadership role through COVID. It's a tough gig for a group CEO in an environment like that.'

Joyce finds other ways to take his mind off the challenges of work. 'I do get to a stage where I can go home, I can completely switch off,' he says. 'I am an avid reader, which I do a lot . . . It annoys the hell out of my husband, because in the middle of these crises, I go home, and he says, "Do you want to talk about Qantas?" I say, "No, I just want to switch off." I don't bother with talking about work and you try to avoid [it] as much as you can, because the last thing you want to do is replay things over in your mind.'

Predictably, for someone with his interests, he finds books on maths a great way to switch off. 'I have Adam Spencer's books about the history of maths and any type of problem,' he told *The Australian*. 'I try to solve those problems and put my mind to them, which I find relaxing.'[1]

The physical side, too, is vital. Joyce credits regular exercise and early starts for his ability to sustain peak performance over such a long period. He usually hits the gym at 5 am each day. 'I've been doing that for a long time now, probably going back to just after the cancer in 2011,' he says.

Sleep is also important. 'You have to have that ability to sleep, to relax,' Joyce says. 'I go to bed pretty early. So I'm in bed around nine. So I again usually get seven hours. Getting poor sleep is really unhealthy, particularly in later life. My father had Alzheimer's just before he died. One of the worst things that you can do for your brain is not get a decent seven to eight hours of sleep. And so I try to do that as best as I can.'

As a CEO, Joyce was always a believer in making the big calls. His former bosses Eddington and Dixon modelled this and Joyce followed in their footsteps.

'Somebody said to me, "I get frustrated with leaders who, when they get the leadership role, they're like the dog that caught the car – they don't know what to do with it!"' Joyce says. 'You have to do something with the [CEO] role. I've always thought

I'm a custodian of this amazing company, an amazing brand. You could sit back, kick the can down the road, but shame on you for doing that. That's what a leader of an organisation like this shouldn't do! Along the way, there are difficult calls and you just have to bite them, but the big calls that we've made have always worked, and always helped the company on the other side of it.'

Joyce has always stressed the importance of having a strong team around him. 'I've done a lot of functions through the aviation industry . . . but you're hiring a lot of people to do those roles, and you've got great expertise across the organisation. It's your job as CEO to facilitate those people to do that activity, hire the right people, and get the right team around you.'

A key part of his thinking was operating at 35,000 feet, but getting down to 5 feet when necessary. But he maintains that 'if you're not operating at 35,000 feet most of the time, I don't think you're doing your job'.

Another key Joyce mantra was around accountability. At Group Management Committee meetings, Joyce was very clear about the areas each leader was responsible for.

Andrew David recalls that one of his first executive team meetings in the Domestic CEO role in early 2015 was particularly difficult, as he hadn't prepared his numbers. 'Alan made it very clear to me, in front of all my peers, that he fully expected me to come to the meeting with the numbers,' he says. 'So I learned early on that you've got to prep. You can't just front and say, "Oh, I'll trust my gut here." If you are going to win an argument with him, you've got to be prepped and have done your numbers. If you don't prep, you're in trouble.'

Olivia Wirth notes that, despite the close attention he paid, Joyce never interfered with his executives' responsibilities. 'He's not interested in getting in and running the businesses,' she explains. 'You're accountable for the business segment that you're running and you will bring key issues to the table at GMC or to the board if it's a strategic shift. But once the target is set and you discuss and debate major changes, responsibility is yours – he's not in the weeds. Alan is ambitious and has been ambitious for the business. But he also leaves each CEO to be running their business, which is why it's a great place to work.'

According to David, the matrix-style organisational structure works for Qantas because of the culture that has developed under Joyce. 'I know when I'm sitting at the GMC table, I'm held accountable for my area,' he says. 'But at the same time, you're also there representing the whole business and you're expected to have a view on the whole business.'

Joyce has the ability to stay totally focused and present, listening intently and learning, according to David. 'He's a fantastic listener . . . and he's always framing something in his head, working out how to get things done,' he says. 'He thinks about things as a mathematician would. "First of all, tell me what the problem or opportunity is. Then tell me what the solution is. Then let's understand what the risks associated with executing on that strategy are, and how we mitigate those risks."

'He would do that in an environment where we're all around the table, and he's triangulating with everybody. Then once he gets to that point of making a decision, he knows, "This is the only thing I can do. I understand the risks, and I understand how I can mitigate those risks, so I'm confident this is the right thing to do." That's why he goes home and sleeps at night, because for him there's nothing else he can do.'

'Alan relies on corridor conversations,' says Wirth. 'He likes talking through issues. An important part of the way he works is through those casual interactions. He processes, triangulates and gets different people's point of view.'

But when the COVID-19 pandemic struck, those corridor conversations ceased. Joyce and his team had the added complexity of not being in the room together.

'There were lots of challenging conversations, very sobering conversations, and some really lonely times because you don't get to debrief and share decisions that were being made that you knew were going to impact people's lives,' Wirth says. 'And you think about the decisions that had to be made in such an alien environment. They were some of the biggest decisions that we had to make, ever, frankly.'

Andrew David explains further. 'He's always been about creating that culture of high collaboration, but healthy conflict as well. You don't want a bunch of yes men. You want to create an environment where people stand up, but do it in a better way.'

According to Joyce, most organisations, and particularly a company like Qantas that's been around for many decades, try to modify things only slightly. 'They never try to break out of usual patterns,' he says. 'Or think big when it's needed.

'When World War II happened, we figured out how to link Australia with the UK when the Japanese invaded South-East Asia by flying amazing double-sunrise flights from Perth to Sri Lanka that spent thirty-two hours in the air. We did 270 of them successfully, and kept the links between the two countries, and not a single aircraft was lost during that period of time.

'But this was all about the organisation, the leadership team thinking big, thinking outside the box and thinking of new ways of doing things. This is one of the reasons we're keen to do Project Sunrise, to fly from Sydney and Melbourne nonstop to London, to Paris and New York, which is the final frontier in the industry, in terms of distance.'

Joyce likes to quote a famous line from pioneering car maker Henry Ford: '"If I asked my customers what they wanted, they would've said a faster horse." In business, CEOs and business leaders often think of that faster horse instead of the car. Sometimes you have to go for the car – it's something way out there that's different to make a change.'

Joyce tried to encourage people at Qantas to do this all the time. 'I think those big calls have always worked out for the airline,' he says.

The best people managers are humble people, Joyce says, because they don't believe they have all the answers. This is easily said: power in an organisation can quickly lead to autocracy. And in aviation, power can literally be dangerous. There are many examples in accident investigations where a main cause was found to be the captain – the 'officer in command' – ignoring inputs from their co-pilot, or the latter being afraid to contradict his or her commander. 'Crew resource management' is about working as a team and breaking down hierarchical barriers. It works.

For Joyce, the effective leader is 'open for debates and discussion – and open to changing their mind. So we try to surround ourselves with amazing people that are humble, not arrogant, that don't think they have all the answers to every problem. You know you're in trouble when people believe that that's the case.'

Yet there has to be a balance, and people in spotlighted leadership roles need a healthy ego. 'You have to believe in yourself,' says Wirth. 'And when you're under such scrutiny, when every single person, including people on the street, has an opinion of you, you have to be firm in who you are and what you stand for and the decisions that you're making. And, therefore, ego has to come into that.

'Power doesn't create, power exposes – and it brings out your true sense and self. Alan is incredibly humble,' she said. 'It's funny, when you're out with him talking to people at events, you constantly get people, having met him, saying, "Oh, he's actually really nice." He's just Alan – he's not one of those people where there's "boardroom Alan" or there's "Parliament House Alan" and "media Alan". He is who he is.'

Joyce's early Jetstar experiences taught him the importance of admitting when you're wrong. 'The one regret you'll have when you look back over your career,' he says, 'would be the time you didn't admit that something was wrong earlier and got on and fixed it.'

One of the things Jetstar did very early on was offer free seating on board – that is, no seat allocation. 'We were so insistent that the Ryanair way of doing things was the right way of doing things,' Joyce recalls. 'And I pushed hard for it.' The board and senior management preferred to go with assigned seating. Joyce didn't heed their advice and free seating was duly brought in.

'The free seating debate went round and round and round,' says John Gissing. 'The original strategic intention of Jetstar was to keep it simple. It would only be successful if we do a couple of things. So, one narrow-body fleet type, one simple production schedule. And so that decision on free seating was constantly being questioned.'

After the launch, and with free seating underway, Joyce attended a St Patrick's Day function, having a few drinks. 'A comedian came on stage and started his set saying he'd just flown in from Hobart on Jetstar – he didn't know the CEO of the airline was in the room,' Joyce recounts. 'The comedian said, "I was like everybody else, I was elbowing the little granny out of the way. I was elbowing the little kids out of the way. And I was running to the aircraft to get the best seat on board. I got on the aircraft and I sat in the best seat. But then this guy came up to me, tapped me on the shoulder and said, "Hey, you're sitting in my seat." And I said, "No, bugger off, it's free seating. I can sit anywhere I want." And he said, "Okay, if you want to fly the aircraft, you can!"

'I knew at that stage free seating had become such a big joke, there was no point in insisting on free seating after that. It just wasn't working. When you make a mistake like that, it's very hard to put your hand up and say, "It's wrong." But it was wrong. And I eventually admitted it was wrong and we got on and fixed it.'

Backing down can be difficult, particularly when you've worked all the angles and the answer is obvious. 'Alan is prepared to make decisions when he knows that he'll be the only one that thinks that it's the right thing to do,' says Andrew David. 'He's prepared to make calls that are ultimately right for the longer term of the Qantas Group. And there's obviously a few calls that he's made regardless of the unintended impact on others.'

Joyce says he frequently sought advice from his board members. 'Leigh has always been a good sounding board,' he says. 'James Strong always had great insights because he put Australian Airlines and Qantas together. I have been very lucky that I have had a number of people over the years who have been good sounding boards,' Joyce told *The Australian*'s *The Deal* magazine in 2018.[2]

Humour can play a vital role in breaking down stressful moments, and there have been plenty of those over Joyce's time. Having a good sense of humour is one of the things that keeps you sane in this industry, says Wirth. 'You have to, otherwise, the weight at certain times on the shoulders, it's heavy, and it's so public – look at the last fifteen years!'

During the early COVID days, the Group Management Committee Teams meetings had some lighter moments. With his guitar close at hand, Gissing composed a version of *The Brady Bunch* theme – 'Qantas GMC on the Telly'. After a particularly tense meeting, Gissing grabbed his guitar. 'I just threw that in at the end – they were singing along and it was really nice to have a bit of fun. A real strength of Alan's is that he can have a bit of fun and take the micky sometimes. I can point out that the tie he's wearing is awful and that he should get some better fashion advice, so be it. It's humour in the right place for the right reasons. It was a very stressful time.'

David and Gissing were often the recipients of Joyce's highjinks during company town halls. 'Andrew and John were always the grumpy, cantankerous old men,' he says, 'always challenging everything, so I started calling them Waldorf and Statler from *The Muppets*,' Joyce chuckles. 'The town hall audience looked confused. They were all under thirty and nobody knew who the Muppets were.'

Ultimately, Joyce created a very strong leadership culture at Qantas. 'I wouldn't have stayed ten years if he was a different type of boss,' David says. 'I've left companies and joined others in my career because of culture. I've enjoyed my job immensely, and I've enjoyed it because I'm with highly intelligent people and we're getting amazing stuff done.

'At the end of the day, you can fall out with Alan, don't talk to him for a couple of days, agree to disagree with him, but you know he's fair and he's strategic and he's tough and he's unrelenting. I think they're good qualities. Sure, he's got plenty of detractors and plenty of people have said things about him, but he never worries about that.

'Ultimately, he's about doing the right thing, which is why he pushes back so hard when he feels there's an injustice being done. I'm sure that goes right back to his school days. Can't have been easy being a small, gay Irishman growing up in a tough area and background. But he never takes a step back. And if he sees an injustice, he's in there. He's going to fix it and make it right.'

Joyce showed his true colours and made the big calls, and the team culture was comprehensively tested when COVID came to call.

There have been moments of intense personal turmoil for Joyce during the pandemic. His homeland, Ireland, experienced a massive surge in infections in late December 2021 and the country entered another lockdown – one of the strictest in the world – on Christmas Eve. His elderly mother was locked down and on the other side of the world.

'The one time – and there's not many – that I've seen him . . . not crack, but really struggling was during that time and being away from his family – away from his mum,' Wirth says. At the time, Joyce borrowed a line from Winston Churchill: 'I was sleeping like a baby. I was waking up screaming every three hours.'

Joyce's robust approach can become overly personal, even over the top, when he is roused or when his icon is attacked – as the deputy chairman of Rex Airlines, John Sharp, can attest.

In 2021, Rex had just commenced jet services on the major trunk routes between Sydney, Melbourne and Brisbane, raising the competitive heat. Joyce rubbished the move, saying Rex had presided over the worst launch of a new jet airline in Australia's aviation history, with empty aircraft and announced routes never flown. Joyce pointedly noted that Sharp had told media in March that passenger numbers on the jet services were 'better than expected', 'but he mustn't have seen the pictures that lonely customers were posting on social media of empty Rex cabins'.[3]

John Sharp wrote an opinion piece branding Qantas 'technically insolvent' and calling Joyce a hypocrite for going 'cap in hand' to the federal government for assistance. 'Qantas is now so desperate that it is willing to risk universal ridicule just to get its hands on more cash at any cost,' Sharp wrote.[4]

Joyce shot back venomously: 'Perhaps if you're used to running a small company, the accounts of a large company can be confusing. Otherwise, it begs the question whether Mr Sharp is trying to mislead the market about Qantas's financial position.' The Qantas CEO branded Sharp's claims as outlandish and said the frequency of the 'baseless' criticisms point to it being a key part of Rex's strategy. Joyce said Rex liked to say it is 'the most profitable airline in Australia, adjusted for size, but that's a dubious distinction when you have failed to invest in your fleet and propellers are literally falling off'.[5]

Joyce has also demonstrated he could move on from conflict or disappointment, and developed his own way of persisting. 'To me, that is a reflection of a strong culture, a healthy culture,' Andrew David says. 'We can have our differences and agree to disagree, or agree to agree – eventually.'

After Geoff Dixon's involvement in the destabilising bid for Qantas in 2012, Joyce didn't talk with him for many months. Dixon had made suggestions about Qantas's direction at the time, particularly criticising the Emirates partnership, which he'd seen as detrimental to the airline's future, a direct thrust at Joyce's judgement.

'Personal relationships and anything else around it are secondary,' Joyce said later that year. He thought Dixon was doing the wrong thing at the time, and he stuck to his guns. 'Part of the [bidding] consortium was going to be one of the Chinese airlines. I believe the [Chinese airline] was thinking, "This is government endorsed," because you've got the chairman of Tourism Australia wanting to do it. It was getting a bit confused. That's where we had a big problem. Either Geoff went for it, and that was fine, but not as chair of Tourism Australia at the same time. We agreed to disagree on that.'

Joyce reckons Dixon was 'persuaded by people that it was a good opportunity and business venture'. Joyce later says, 'I think it was the hangover from the [2007] Airline Partners Australia bid that didn't go through. It was an opportunity to go again – I think there was unfinished business on it.'

Despite that episode, Joyce still admired his former boss, and he contacted Dixon to wish him a speedy recovery from illness in early 2014. The pair then met at a business summit in Sydney in July that year, and in a Qantas lounge later that year both men displayed the characteristic warmth of their relationship.

'We had a bit of a chat – we talk when we meet. I always had the deepest respect for Geoff and what he did at Qantas. It is not aggressive in any way. It is very friendly. I love Geoff and he loves me and I'm sure one day when I retire and he retires we will have a good drink,' Joyce told the *Australian Financial Review* in late 2014.[6]

'There was never any personal animosity between the two of us,' Joyce says. 'But that was wrong and I just believe it was wrong. And I had to say and call it for what it was.'

Joyce eventually buried the hatchet with Tourism Australia, but not until almost a year after Geoff Dixon stepped down as chairman. Dixon was replaced by industry veteran Tony South, who oversaw the signing of a three-year $20 million promotional agreement with Qantas in August 2016.

Joyce thought Dixon was a great boss. 'Geoff gave us huge opportunities and I thought he was brave on a lot of things, which I took a lead from,' he reflects. 'Things like setting up Jetstar, when everybody else was probably telling him not to do it.'

Joyce also rates Rod Eddington highly. 'I thought he was phenomenal. I always really respected him. I've always talked to [him] because of his experience with Cathay and British Airways. I still talk to Rod regularly. Anytime we run into each other, he just is a fleet maniac. As a former head of fleet planning and (literally) a rocket scientist, he just wants to know all the performance issues on aircraft. He was phenomenal.'

That Joyce has survived fifteen gruelling years at the head of the Qantas Group, and done so with considerable success, speaks to a man who is capable of strong leadership, with solid strategic skills, and a long-term vision for Australia's number-one icon.

It is rare for any airline CEO to remain in the role for ten years. Fifteen years at the top is exceptional. As Joyce has said, they are like dog years, with the potential to exact an enormous personal toll.

32

The Joyce Legacy

In early 2015, after six and a half years in the role, Joyce conceded he'd had an up-and-down journey as Qantas CEO thus far. But he quickly added: 'I love this job. I love working for Qantas. I'm very passionate about its history – it gets me all the time. I think there's a great legacy in this company and a legacy that I want to make sure that when I'm passing it along to the next CEO, I leave Qantas in a better position than when I inherited it.'[1]

One immutable legacy of Joyce's fifteen years at Qantas is that he departs the airline on the back of the largest annual profit in its history. It helps greatly that the fingerprints of his successor, Vanessa Hudson, the chief financial officer during this period, are all over it too. That opens doors. And pays the bills. Qantas remains one of only a handful of airlines worldwide with an investment-grade credit rating.

His aspiration is that this result is not a one-off – that it will stand as a challenge to be bettered. For the final decade of his leadership, Joyce's overriding goal has been to make Qantas financially sustainable. That will be hard to achieve, but most fundamentals are now in place that might allow it to happen: solid strategies for the domestic and international airline operations, sturdy growth in non-flying revenue, particularly with Qantas Loyalty, and an efficient and highly skilled workforce.

Joyce hands over with a strong management team in place. The airline's board is balanced, with an impressive range of experience. Qantas is a leader in encouraging diversity and inclusiveness, and – despite loud voices to the contrary – the brand is highly resilient. Financially – the bottom line by which any CEO must be judged – the airline's share price has performed well in the Joyce era after a difficult beginning.

Yet airlines live in a permanently hostile environment – one that is predictably unpredictable. The two largest outgoings are salaries and fuel; one is partially manageable, the other at the whim of international oil prices.

In the short term, one foreseeable headwind is already gusting on the industrial front. The combination of an attractively large profit on the one hand and, on the other, economic hard times for labour as inflation and interest rates soar – along with new workplace bargaining terms under the Labor government – can only lead to a cost blowout or plenty of industrial strife. The least bad outcome is perhaps a compromise combination of the two.

Oil prices remain high. In 2019 the airline spent nearly $4 billion on fuel, a quarter of total costs. That was over $600 million more than the previous year, but with a broadly similar amount of flying. For a company with average annual profits below $1 billion, a doubling of prices, which happens from time to time, can destroy profitability. That's one reason Joyce has lavished so much attention on the loyalty program, which involves no flying.

Having guided Qantas through the extreme turbulence of COVID-19, Joyce was ready to step aside.

At the succession announcement, on 2 May 2023, Richard Goyder praised Qantas's twelfth CEO for his role in bringing about the transition at a time when the Group was extremely well positioned. 'Much of the credit for the bright future in front of

Qantas goes to Alan,' the chairman said. Joyce had 'faced more than his fair share of challenges as CEO, and he's managed them exceptionally well – from the GFC, to record oil prices, to intense competitive pressures and the COVID crisis. The company was restructured to deal with a number of external shocks and Alan led it to several record profits. He's overseen a lot of investment in aircraft, lounges, the creation of Jetstar, our cornerstone partnership with Emirates and innovations like the Perth–London route and Project Sunrise.'

As for Vanessa Hudson, the lucky thirteenth Qantas CEO – Goyder reckoned she would draw on her deep understanding of the business after almost three decades with the airline. 'She is extremely well rounded, serving in a range of roles both onshore and offshore, across commercial, customer and finance,' he said. 'She has a huge amount of airline experience and she's an outstanding leader.'

Joyce leaves Qantas amid a firestorm of controversy, but with record-breaking profitability and a repaired balance sheet. His final twelve months as CEO coincided with a time when travel was prioritised in the post-pandemic era, and households – many of them cashed up by government stimulus – began travelling again in big numbers.

But there are parallels with 2008, when Joyce became CEO, in the shadow of the record profits of his predecessor, Dixon, with the GFC poised to strike. Today, as interest rates take off in response to out-of-control inflation, the global and national economy faces headwinds that are hitting discretionary spending. Hudson will be hopeful that the wheels don't fall off the economy the way they did in 2009, and that she will have a smoother initial time as CEO than Joyce.

Her immediate task will be to repair the airline's image. One of her biggest challenges for the remainder of this decade will be getting to grips with the accelerating need to combat climate change. This brings with it practical – and expensive – consequences. Governments will begin to tax emissions in one way or another;

SAF will have to replace fossil fuel, with an expensive price leap. The new Airbus planes will deliver a step-change in fuel efficiency, but as global warming raises the stakes, expectations for action will intensify in tandem.

Setting the culture of an enlarged workforce will also be Hudson's task, as it regrows after years of slimming down to fighting shape. Addressing the 'people issues' quickly is crucial, according to Joyce, who admits that changing the culture and getting the right people around him took longer than he thought when he became CEO.

'It's not only getting your direct management team but throughout the organisation,' he recalls. 'We wanted a diverse and inclusive culture, one where you got things done. But *how* it was done was equally as important.'

A string of international airline partnerships Joyce established provides a strong foundation for the international operations, most notably with Emirates. As Sir Tim Clark also moves on after decades at the helm, Hudson will be looking to re-establish close ties at the top level with Clark's successor, a key factor in keeping that vital relationship healthy.

Funding the expensive commitments to new aircraft will be a task top of mind. Given her earlier involvement in the process as chief financial officer, it's hard to see any substantial change in direction. Most agree that Qantas will have to raise significant capital in the not-too-distant future to fund new orders; that will be Hudson's (and the Qantas board's) call.

There's also the issue of the brand. Many today question how intact it is, after a particularly torrid period in 2023. Are customers happy? And, more substantively, are the cancellations, delays, refunds (or not) and credits things of the past? As the world returns to 'normal', most airlines – including Qantas – are struggling to restore normal service. The good news is Net Promoter Scores are heading steeply back up again, but even so, Vanessa Hudson will have that issue near the top of her in-tray.

*

The arcane structure of the aviation industry – with its protectionism, its nationalism and its exposure to constant shocks – means it is unlikely ever to achieve true financial stability. At the same time, it is an industry with fundamentally important social and economic benefits, so it's in the interests of all of us that it continues.

The fifteen years of Alan Joyce's tenure at the helm of Qantas provide many examples of how the obstacles to industry efficiency make leading an airline such a complex challenge. As he exits his role as guardian of Australia's most iconic company, he's well aware that his legacy will be defined not by outspoken union officials, or by hostile members of the media, or even by contemporary popular opinion, but by his enduring achievements: the black and white of the numbers, the stability of the sophisticated airline model he has established, the standing he has among his peers, and the opinions of both his customers and his staff. Reaching beyond the airline, he's leveraged his influence to make a difference in diversity and inclusivity, both in his industry and in wider Australian society. He's Irish and Australian, married to a New Zealander, yet he genuinely feels a deep pride at having put the iconic Australian airline squarely on the map.

Joyce has been divisive, that's true. He's not broadly popular in the community. Mostly, quite the reverse. Yet it requires a special sort of courage to look beyond the present when those with present needs resist, often vocally and actively. He has made mistakes and, when he has, they've always been public ones, with plenty of critics on hand to magnify his failings. Meanwhile, the long-term successes he has engineered rarely make headlines.

Whatever he says, no man is an island. At a personal level, he must at times have felt pained by the more virulent attacks over fifteen years that frequently propelled him to being Australia's most wanted/hunted/vilified CEO. Although, one of the best.

If you can't be universally loved, well, transforming a national icon for the better is some consolation. Priceless, even.

*

Aviation is a cyclical business. Joyce likes to talk of seven-year cycles, which means he effectively completed a double stint as CEO.

John Gissing reckons there is something incredibly powerful about having such longevity. 'You get time to develop a deep understanding of things, as well as deep relationships,' he observes. 'Until you've seen a few cycles in aviation, you might fall into the trap of thinking, "This is new."'

Sooner or later in the 2020s, a new crisis will appear on the horizon, and Qantas will confront it with a well-managed cost base and a strong balance sheet. The good times never continue forever in aviation, and the next challenge will be for Hudson and her team to manage.

Joyce, meanwhile, is taking a six-month break after leaving Qantas. He can expect many new offers to come in. 'Leigh called me and said, "Alan, you've got one dance card, don't fill her up too soon – make sure you pick the right ones,"' he says. He knows that is good advice, and he plans to take some time to 'decompress'. He will stay well away from aircraft and cruise around the Antarctic.

As for what lies beyond – Joyce is not sure. 'Is it another executive role? Is it board roles? Is it something completely different, like going into education and supporting the community?' he says. 'Maybe some of each of those, or maybe one focus, but we'll see at the end of six months.'

His lieutenants think Joyce will pop up again soon.

'Let's see how long Alan's six-month sabbatical goes for – six weeks? Six hours?' says Gissing. 'Would I be surprised if he resurfaces in aviation? No. It would be great for the industry to see some of Alan's learnings put back in at some stage. That's a personal wish. But he's just got to get through that transition and work out what he wants to do next. He is still young, so he's still got time on his side.'

Rob Gurney believes Joyce is a brilliant chief executive. 'I think you could put Alan in a number of different environments and businesses and he'd thrive,' he says. 'It's just his passion is aviation and has been for a long time, but I think he could assimilate into pretty much any industry. He's got a tremendous breadth of skills and possesses this great ability to turn the complex into simple and explain things very simply.'

Aviation is in Joyce's blood, agrees Olivia Wirth. 'It is absolutely who he is,' she says. 'He loves it and he cares deeply about it at every level. It's not just about the aircraft, it's about the policy settings. It's about the contribution of aviation as an industry. The love and deep affection that he has for the industry will not stop the day he walks out of Qantas or Jetstar – that will continue.'

Andrew David believes Joyce will be back, if not in aviation then in some other executive role. 'I think he's got more to give and more fire in the belly,' he says, 'and I can think of plenty of colourful characters in this industry that he could work with and will be approached by, I'm sure. He'll be in very high demand.'

Back in 2008, the Qantas Group had four businesses. Imagine a table with four legs, three of them sturdy, the other one shorter. Qantas Domestic, Jetstar and the frequent-flyer program were robust, but the international operation was performing ever more poorly, losing hundreds of millions of dollars annually. It was no particular failing of the operation, just that it was operating in a competitive inferno.

Says Joyce, 'What I wanted was the senior management people coming up with business transformation ideas, business growth opportunities. Look at it now, with Project Sunrise, with the Domestic business going for the A220s and the A321s, and with Loyalty and Jetstar.' The four legs are now equally dynamic. 'And that's where we wanted to get to. It took a bit longer probably to get there, but here we are.'

There have been other wins. Joyce believes the business community has been getting better in recent years at discussing policy issues that affect their employees, customers or shareholders – not just on economic issues, but on social and environmental issues too, all of which are intertwined. 'I am a firm believer that business leaders have a duty to speak up,' he says. He's certainly walked the talk.

Social activism by CEOs definitely received a shot in the arm in Australia during the Joyce era. But there is still work to do. Joyce observed in early 2023 that 50 per cent of LGBTIQ+ people are 'uncomfortable coming out in work still, even to this day. Since I've been CEO of Qantas, I've heard from many young Australians who still face discrimination and don't feel like they can come out at home or work. It's the same way I felt as a young man growing up in Ireland, and I absolutely know how isolating and scary that can be. My message to you is that you're not alone. Change is happening and things will get better.'[2]

Diversity and inclusion have been constant themes of Joyce's leadership. 'I hope that we've made a big difference on diversity and inclusion, both in the company and worldwide,' he says. 'It's great that we've got three women – Jayne, Vanessa and Steph – running airlines in Australia. That's phenomenal.

'And an openly gay man running this company, the diversity that we've led the way on, what we did on marriage equality – hopefully it's that diversity and inclusion which makes the business better, makes society better, and will be another legacy out of it.

'Then I hope also at the end of the day that we've got an amazing, iconic company, the most iconic company in Australia that's set up for success for at least another 100 years. At the end of the day, that's what the job was.'

Epilogue

In today's rapid news cycle, history rarely plays a part in our perception of events and people. As this book prepares for printing, a flurry of anti-Qantas and anti-Joyce news has filled the media. It's nothing new. Media storms have accompanied Joyce for most of his time at the helm of Qantas. This was to be the last. He left two months earlier than planned – on 5 September 2023 – just short of his fifteenth anniversary as CEO.

In this final media storm, it's only too easy to take for granted his achievements over those often enormously difficult years.

Airlines have no pre-ordained right to survival; today they exist in a hostile and unpredictable competitive environment. To emphasise that fact, all of the other major Australasian airlines have collapsed this century: Ansett Australia, Air New Zealand and Virgin Australia. Ansett could not adapt and folded, leaving 16,000 staff out of work; Air New Zealand imploded and had to be re-nationalised; Virgin failed during COVID, destroying equity and impacting 6000 staff.

The fact is that over the course of his leadership, Joyce, supported by his board, has been responsible for transforming Qantas from an unwieldy operation, wholly unsuited to the new competitive environment, into one of the most successful airline groups in the world. In many of those fifteen years, Qantas lost money, yet remarkably it has been among the most profitable airlines in this brutal industry.

Most recently, in the relatively calm light of day, it's easy to overlook the intensity, complexity and uncertainty of the desperate years of COVID. And, for Qantas, the extraordinarily difficult recovery period that followed. After nearly $7.5 billion in statutory losses before tax between FY2020 and FY2022, everything was suddenly expected to simply return to normal.

The operational shortcomings of 2021 and 2022 are fully understandable, especially when considered alongside the entire global aviation industry's struggles with the same circumstances, in this instance short-notice border closures compounded by supply chain and staff health issues. The same could be said of Joyce guiding Qantas through the post-GFC environment of 2009–2011, or the crisis of record-high fuel prices in an extremely competitive domestic environment in 2013–2014.

But by any standards, the post-COVID response by Qantas has been sadly lacking. It suggests a disproportionate focus on rebuilding financial stability. Even so, it would be inappropriate and unfair to judge Alan Joyce, the board or the airline by the failings of this extraordinary post-pandemic period.

In recent months, Qantas has been in the firing line of consumer complaints, lawsuits, allegations of political interference, questions over exorbitant executive remuneration, and much more. But today Qantas is well positioned to continue to be profitable, and without that there is no airline. It is placed to grow its operations, create employment and provide social connections. In seeking to make the airline bulletproof, Joyce surely couldn't have done much better.

And, despite short-term appearances, history strongly suggests that the brand will recover. Virtually every airline in the world saw its brand trashed in the aftermath of COVID; Qantas's reputation will recover faster than most would expect.

Yet there will be more enduring reverberations from these recent ructions. There is the matter of a long overdue need to install better consumer protections for flight delays and cancellations, and refunds. Reform is needed to provide better consumer protection and transparency, and at last there is an ACCC that seems determined to act – although it will be up to Canberra to lift its game when it comes to implementing regulation.

Equally, the competition body has begun to address the inequities created by the current airport slot system (or the abuse of that system), a matter that will only grow in importance as Sydney's second airport nears completion.

And there are rightly questions about the political influence of the Chairman's Lounge. Even its name is outdated. It has no place in a fair, competitive marketplace.

All of this has coincided with high international fares, partly because seats are still limited as airlines recover, leading to pressure to increase foreign airlines' capacity to service Australia. Whether or not it's purely about protectionism, as it appears to be, it raises more profound questions about the future role of government in stabilising competition in the domestic market. Virgin becoming a viable competitor to Qantas is very much in the national interest.

Did Joyce stay too long? Probably. But it should be remembered that he was preparing to leave when COVID struck in all its fury, and the board specifically requested he remain for a further three years to see the airline through this uniquely challenging period.

Perhaps his greatest failing has been an inability to connect with the popular mood – Joyce the mathematician, with his often tin ear. But there's no doubting his peers in the global airline industry hold him and his achievements at Qantas in the highest regard. They've all been through the mill, making the big calls and copping the criticism as they fight to survive. Throughout, Alan Joyce has been single-mindedly passionate about securing the future of Qantas.

By reviewing the many challenges Joyce has faced over the last fifteen years, and his responses to them, this book has hopefully delivered a broader perspective on the history of what will continue to be an iconic Australian brand. It is in this context – his role in transforming Qantas – that Joyce's legacy should be judged.

Peter Harbison
6 September 2023

APPENDIX A

Data

When Geoff Dixon handed down his final annual report, for the 2007/08 financial year, the Qantas Group had some 33,670 full-time-equivalent (FTE) staff, a shade below the all-time-record headcount of 35,224 in 2005.

In staff productivity and efficiency terms, back in FY2008, Qantas was producing 3.04 million revenue passenger kilometres (RPKs, the average distance a paying passenger was flying) per full-time employee.

Eleven years later, in FY2019 – the last year of 'normal' activity just prior to the COVID pandemic – Qantas was producing approximately 4.29 million RPKs per full-time employee, a 41% increase. By comparison, Air New Zealand produced a 24% increase in RPKs per FTE over the same eleven-year period.

Qantas's revenue per FTE went from just over $464,000 in FY2008 to $604,000 in pre-COVID FY2019, a 30% improvement. Air New Zealand achieved just a 16% improvement over the same period. Qantas's revenue per FTE soared to $779,320 in FY2023.

Employees' productivity was rewarded over the Joyce era. Qantas's staff and manpower cost per FTE was just under $105,000 in FY2008. That figure rose to $143,486 by FY2019,

outstripping average annual revenue growth – and inflation –
during the period. Measured against the Reserve Bank of
Australia's inflation calculator, Qantas's staff costs at the base-
line FY2008 would have reached $131,660 in FY2019 if they
were running in line with the national inflation rate. In other
words, Qantas staff were rewarded above inflation during the
pre-COVID era under Joyce. The figure reached $167,584 in
FY2023.

APPENDIX B

Share and Fuel Prices

A shareholder in Qantas through the Joyce era since 2008 has fared much better than one in its peers in the region, Air New Zealand under Rob Fyfe, Christopher Luxon and Greg Foran, or Singapore Airlines under Chew Choon Seng and Goh Choon Phong.

Unlike the open share register of Qantas, both Air New Zealand and Singapore Airlines are majority government-owned. Air New Zealand had the early lead for much of the 2010s, but its shares – and Singapore Airlines' – have lost ground over the Joyce era.

The legacy in numbers: Qantas, Air New Zealand and Singapore Airlines share price indexes (100=28 November 2008)

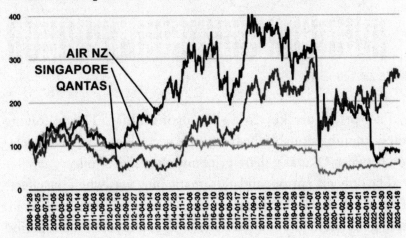

Source: Yahoo! Finance

Meanwhile, for another comparison, the US major airlines powered on, thanks in large part to their bankruptcy reorganisations and mergers in the 2000s and 2010s. While Qantas was struggling to generate a more cost-effective operation, the US airlines just walked away from their obligations and restarted with a clean slate.

Qantas shares outperformed American Airlines over the Joyce era, but shareholders in all four carriers in the US oligopoly have enjoyed big gains in the world's biggest protected market, after losing everything when the airlines went into bankruptcy protection.

Qantas, Delta, American and United share price indexes (100=28 November 2008)

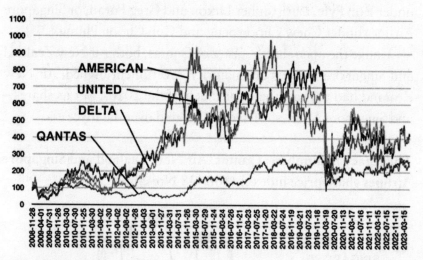

Source: Yahoo! Finance

Fuel prices are key to airline profitability. The following graph unambiguously illustrates the very close inverse correlation between Qantas's share price and the price of oil.

The only exception, and a dramatic one, was when the effects of Qantas's 2014 Accelerated Transformation Plan kicked in, driving the share price higher even as oil prices rose for the period between 2015 and 2017. There could scarcely be a more graphic vindication of the controversial policy's effectiveness! From being an airline near collapse, the turnaround was remarkable.

Until COVID spoiled the party, the share price then rose to three times the stock price Joyce had inherited in 2008. Then COVID took the share price all the way back to November 2008 levels, before staging a rapid comeback and, at the time of writing, ending roughly two and a half times higher than on Joyce's first day.

The legacy in numbers: Qantas share price index and Jet Fuel Price index (100=28 November 2008)

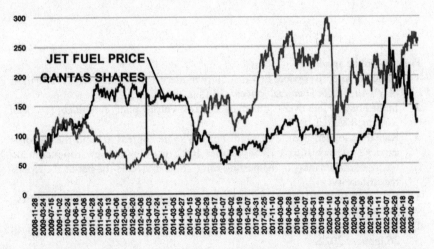

Source: Yahoo! Finance & US Energy Information Administration (US Gulf Coast Kerosene-Type Jet Fuel Spot Price)

Notes

Preface – In the Spotlight

1   Anne Hyland, 'Revealed: Private equity bidders had doubts over $11b Qantas play', *Australian Financial Review*, 24 June 2017.
2   Jamie Freed, 'High flyer Clifford defends cost-cutting plan', *Australian Financial Review*, 8 March 2014.
3   Richard Goyder, 'Qantas Op-ed: Putting some context around the national carrier's recent history', 13 September 2022. www.qantasnewsroom.com.au/media-releases/qantas-op-ed-putting-some-context-around-the-national-carriers-recent-history/
4   Rachel Browne, 'If I'd waited for my test, I may have been dead in 10 years', *Sydney Morning Herald*, 4 September 2011.
5   'Leading from the Skies', in conversation with Linda Doyle for Trinity Alumnus, 26 January 2022.
6   'Meet the CEO' event for the Australian School of Business, University of New South Wales, 22 November 2011.
7   Tony Sheldon, 'Transport union puts its case on Qantas', *Sydney Morning Herald*, 27 October 2011.
8   Alan Joyce, 'CEO's Report', Qantas Annual Report 2009.

Chapter 1 – Shaping the Future Leader

1   Stephanie Quine and Alan Greenfield, 'On clouds of data – Alan Joyce on steering Qantas, Mathematics and Business Leadership', interview for the Actuaries Institute, 16 April 2015.
2   Michael Smith, 'Qantas Airways chief executive Alan Joyce says no plans to go out on a high', *Australian Financial Review*, 21 August 2015.
3   Jared Lynch, 'How maths helps the Joyce brothers fly', *The Australian*, 28 May 2023.
4   'Meet the CEO' event for the Australian School of Business.
5   Ibid.
6   Jared Lynch, 'How maths helps the Joyce brothers fly'.

7   'Leading from the Skies', in conversation with Linda Doyle for Trinity Alumnus.
8   'Meet the CEO' event for the Australian School of Business.
9   CAPA World Aviation Summit, interview with Siew Hoon Yeoh, 7 October 2015.
10 Michael Hogan, 'Michael O'Leary's 33 daftest quotes', *The Guardian*, 9 November 2013.
11 'Looking at the stars', Alan Joyce speech at Wings Club, Dublin, 10 March 2009. www.qantas.com/au/en/about-us/news-room/news-room-archives. html?archive=mar-2009/Speech

Chapter 2 – Time to Move
1   'Being young and LGBTIQ can be tough. But take it from us, it gets better', *Sydney Morning Herald*, 12 May 2023.
2   Geoff Dixon, 'The Modern Qantas', speech at Australian Institute of Company Directors, Brisbane, 24 November 2008. www.qantas.com/au/en/about-us/ news-room/news-room-archives.html?archive=nov-2008/Speech
3   David Knibb, 'Executive appointments – Qantas Airways', *FlightGlobal*, 28 February 2005.

Chapter 3 – An Australian, an Italian and an Irishman . . .
1   Joanne Gray, 'Tenure undone by perceived arrogance', *Australian Financial Review*, 18 May 2007.
2   'Meet the CEO' event for the Australian School of Business.
3   Geoff Dixon, 'The Modern Qantas'.
4   Ibid.
5   'Looking at the stars', Alan Joyce speech at Wings Club, Dublin.

Chapter 4 – The Tipping Point
1   Geoff Dixon, 'The Modern Qantas'.

Chapter 5 – Plotting the Future
1   'Flying above the turbulence', Alan Joyce speech at Australia–Israel Chamber of Commerce, 8 December 2008. www.qantas.com/au/en/about-us/news-room/ news-room-archives.html?archive=dec-2008/Speech
2   'Looking at the stars', Alan Joyce speech at Wings Club, Dublin.
3   Matt O'Sullivan, 'Last of the Dixon-era lieutenants leaves Qantas', *Sydney Morning Herald*, 8 April 2009.

Chapter 6 – Reshuffle and Reset
1   Alan Joyce, 'Qantas: Agenda 2011', speech at Melbourne Press Club, 03 February 2011. www.qantas.com/au/en/about-us/news-room/news-room-archives.html?archive=feb-2011/S12011
2   Michael Smith, 'Joyce says Qantas prepared to take on challengers', *Australian Financial Review*, 21 August 2009.

Chapter 7 – QF32
1   Gerard Frawley, 'TBT: Worth the wait – the Qantas A380 era begins', *Australian Aviation*, 20 September 2018.
2   Richard Champion de Crespigny, *QF32*, Pan Macmillan, 2012, p158.
3   'Joyce discusses A380 engine failure', *The 7.30 Report*, 4 November 2010.
4   Ibid.
5   'Qantas CEO Alan Joyce addresses media after halving its full-year loss', *ABC News*, 25 August 2022.

Chapter 8 – The Slow Bake

1 Andrew Cleary, 'Qantas chief is fed up with unions', *Australian Financial Review*, 20 April 2011.
2 'Engineers' union cancels planned strike action', 12 May 2011. www.qantas.com/au/en/about-us/news-room/news-room-archives.html?archive=may-2011/5106
3 'Future of Qantas in jeopardy: Joyce', *AAP*, 27 May 2011.
4 'Qantas troubles come to a head at AGM', *Sydney Morning Herald*, 28 October 2011.
5 CAPA Australia Pacific Aviation Summit 2016, Brisbane, interview with CNN's Richard Quest, 5 August 2016.
6 'Extended Alan Joyce interview', *ABC 7.30*, 23 August 2012.

Chapter 9 – At the End of the Line

1 Andrew Cleary, 'Asian carrier promises new levels of luxury', *Australian Financial Review*, 17 August 2011.
2 Mark Skulley, 'Union backlash over Qantas job cuts', *Australian Financial Review*, 16 August 2011.
3 'Unions vow to fight Qantas plans', *Sydney Morning Herald*, 16 August 2011.
4 'Qantas CEO Alan Joyce on today's announcements', *ABC News*, 17 August 2011.
5 'Qantas reports strong full-year profit in challenging conditions', 24 August 2011. www.qantas.com/au/en/about-us/news-room/news-room-archives.html?archive=aug-2011/5168a
6 'Union targets busiest weekend to delay and disrupt customers', 26 September 2011. www.qantas.com/au/en/about-us/news-room/news-room-archives.html?archive=sep-2011/5183
7 Ibid.
8 Simon Benson, 'Guards for Qantas boss Alan Joyce after death threats', *The Daily Telegraph*, 5 October 2011.
9 'Engineers' union plays cynical games with Qantas passengers', 10 October 2011. www.qantas.com/au/en/about-us/news-room/news-room-archives.html?archive=oct-2011/5202
10 'Industrial relations update', 13 October 2011. www.qantas.com/au/en/about-us/news-room/news-room-archives.html?archive=oct-2011/0000
11 'Meet the CEO' event for the Australian School of Business.

Chapter 10 – Grounding the Fleet

1 'Anatomy of a grounding: Qantas seeks immediate and lasting concessions to secure future', *CAPA – Centre for Aviation*, 29 October 2011.
2 David Flynn, 'Qantas shutdown: CEO Alan Joyce's statement in full', *Executive Traveller*, 29 October 2011.
3 AAP with Alexandra Back, 'Qantas grounds all flights', *Sydney Morning Herald*, 29 October 2011.
4 'Alan Joyce stands by grounding', *ABC News*, 5 November 2011.
5 'Qantas CEO has "gone mad" say pilots', *Sydney Morning Herald*, 30 October 2011.
6 'How Alan Joyce Screwed His Workers & Ruined Qantas', *Supportah TV*, 14 August 2022.
7 CAPA Australia Pacific Aviation Summit, interview with Peter Harbison, 3 August 2015.
8 'Meet the CEO' event for the Australian School of Business.

9   Steve Creedy and Mitch Nadin, 'Suspension of Qantas death threat probe predictable end to stunt: TWU', *The Australian*, 23 November 2011.
10   'Qantas CEO Alan Joyce and his tough call', *ABC News*, 1 December 2013.
11   Steve Creedy, 'Damage to Qantas only temporary, says Alan Joyce', *The Australian*, 13 December 2011.

Chapter 11 – Escaping the Niche
1   Ingrid Pyne, 'Can Qantas resist the urge to merge?', *Australian Financial Review*, 23 November 2009.
2   Doug Nancarrow, *Game Changer*, HarperCollins Publishers, 2015, p142.
3   Praveen Menon, 'UAE's Etihad buys stake in Virgin Australia', *Reuters*, 5 June 2012.
4   'Weathering the storm', *Australian Financial Review*, 6 June 2012.
5   Matt O'Sullivan, 'Qantas prepares for hostile takeover bids', *Sydney Morning Herald*, 12 June 2012.
6   Andrew Cleary, 'Qantas looking at Emirates tie', *Australian Financial Review*, 26 July 2012.

Chapter 12 – Seismic Events
1   Alan Joyce speech at Qantas AGM, 2 November 2012. www.qantasnewsroom.com.au/speeches/annual-general-meeting-alan-joyce/
2   'The World's Leading Airline Partnership', 6 September 2012. www.qantasnewsroom.com.au/speeches/the-worlds-leading-airline-partnership-alan-joyce-qantas-group-ceo/
3   'Kicked in the seats', *Australian Financial Review*, 7 September 2012.

Chapter 13 – Line in the Sand
1   Michael Smith, 'If at first you don't succeed', *Australian Financial Review*, 23 May 2009.
2   Tansy Harcourt, 'Virgin means business in war on Qantas', *Australian Financial Review*, 29 June 2010.
3   Jenny Wiggins, 'Qantas chief Joyce takes potshots at airline rivals', *Australian Financial Review*, 29 July 2010.
4   Michael Smith, 'If at first you don't succeed'.
5   Michael Smith, 'Airline rivalry will hurt Qantas more: Virgin's Borghetti', *Australian Financial Review*, 31 January 2014.

Chapter 14 – Juggling with Chainsaws
1   'New Qantas Airlines structure, executive team', 22 May 2012. www.qantas.com/au/en/about-us/news-room/news-room-archives.html?archive=may-2012/5399
2   Ewin Hannan, 'Union bosses end law suit to fight common enemy', *The Australian*, 19 October 2012.
3   'Geoff Dixon accuses Alan Joyce of lack of strategy', *The Australian*, 14 May 2012.
4   Damon Kitney, 'We eyed Qantas stake: ex-CEO Geoff Dixon', *The Australian*, 26 November 2011.
5   Andrew Cleary, Sarah Thompson and James Chessell, 'Dixon group sells Qantas holding', *Australian Financial Review*, 30 January 2013.
6   Speech at Australian Institute of Company Directors, Brisbane, 18 October 2012. www.qantas.com/au/en/about-us/news-room/news-room-archives.html?archive=oct-2012/00000

7   'Qantas Group financial result – First Half 2012/13', 21 February 2013. www.
    qantas.com/au/en/about-us/news-room/news-room-archives.html?archive=
    feb-2013/5502

8   'Annual General Meeting, CEO's Address', 18 October 2013. www.qantasnews
    room.com.au/speeches/annual-general-meeting-18-october-2013-ceos-address/

Chapter 15 – The Capacity Wars Turn Nasty

1   Jamie Freed, 'Doubts whether Qantas cuts will be effective', *Australian Financial
    Review*, 28 February 2014.

2   'Armchair experts in the cockpit', 24 January 2014. www.qantasnewsroom.
    com.au/media-releases/commentary-from-qantas-cfo-gareth-evans/

3   Michael Smith, 'Airline rivalry will hurt Qantas more'.

4   'Qantas Group market update', 5 December 2013. www.qantasnewsroom.com.
    au/media-releases/qantas-group-market-update/

5   'Alan Joyce speech to Tourism and Transport Forum Friends of Tourism Event,'
    13 February 2014. www.qantasnewsroom.com.au/media-releases/alan-joyce-
    speech-to-tourism-and-transport-forum-friends-of-tourism-event/?print=1

6   Jemima Whyte, 'Street Talk', *Australian Financial Review*, 25 November 2008.

7   'Qantas Group Strategy update', 27 February 2014. www.qantasnewsroom.
    com.au/media-releases/qantas-group-strategy-update-2/

8   Quoted in Matt O'Sullivan and Courtney Trenwith, 'Branson slams Qantas boss
    over domestic air travel', *Australian Financial Review*, 12 February 2014.

9   'Qantas Group Strategy update', 27 February 2014.

10 Mathew Dunckley, 'ACTU presents Qantas wish list', *Australian Financial
    Review*, 5 March 2014.

11 'A Dark Day for the Qantas Group', Australian Services Union, 27 February 2014.
    www.asu.asn.au/news/categories/qantas/140227-dark-day-for-qantas-group

12 Jamie Freed, 'Qantas chief slams "alarmist" unions', *Australian Financial
    Review*, 19 March 2014.

13 Jamie Freed, 'Carrier under fire but CEO plans to stay', *Australian Financial
    Review*, 5 March 2014.

14 Ibid.

15 Anne Hyland, 'Qantas mayday: Where to now?', *Australian Financial Review*,
    1 March 2014.

16 Leigh Clifford, 'Opinion Piece', 3 March 2014. www.qantasnewsroom.com.au/
    speeches/leigh-clifford-opinion-piece/

17 David Tweed, 'Bloomberg Turnaround: Qantas Airways', *Bloomberg*, 5 June
    2019.

18 Tansy Harcourt, 'The life of Alan: loved, loathed, late and lost', *The Weekend
    Australian*, 26 August 2022.

Chapter 16 – The Capacity Wars End

1   Michael Smith, 'Alan Joyce pilots Qantas from turbulence to clear skies',
    Australian Financial Review, 15 December 2014.

2   Robyn Ironside, 'Qantas v Virgin Australia: The war that cost $8.75m a day',
    News Corp Australia Network, 29 August 2014.

3   Michael Smith, 'Alan Joyce pilots Qantas from turbulence to clear skies'.

4   Jamie Freed, 'Qantas eyes new investor for international arm', *Australian
    Financial Review*, 28 August 2014.

5   Anne Hyland, 'Alan Joyce, Qantas's boxing kangaroo', *Australian Financial
    Review*, 29 August 2014.

6 Michael Smith, 'Qantas chairman says CEO Joyce not going anywhere', *Australian Financial Review*, 15 December 2014.
7 'Two-hats Todd a breath of environmentally fresh air for Qantas board', *Australian Financial Review*, 19 January 2015.
8 'Joyce's pinch of salt at lunch', *Australian Financial Review*, 6 March 2014.
9 CAPA Australia Pacific Aviation Summit, Brisbane, interview with Richard Quest, 5 August 2016.

Chapter 17 – The Best of Times?
1 CAPA Australia Pacific Aviation Summit, Sydney, interview with Peter Harbison, 3 August 2015.
2 Michael Smith, 'Alan Joyce pilots Qantas from turbulence to clear skies'.
3 'Alan Joyce on Market Freedom', Centre for Independent Studies, 21 September 2016.
4 CAPA Australia Pacific Aviation Summit, Brisbane, interview with Richard Quest, 5 August 2016.

Chapter 18 – Bulletproofing the Icon
1 CAPA Australia Pacific Aviation Summit, interview with Peter Harbison, 7 August 2019.
2 Will Horton, 'Jetstar Loses Its Shine For Qantas In Vietnam, But Singapore's Jetstar Asia Still Strong', *Forbes*, 15 June 2020.
3 Damon Kitney, 'The art of the deal: Alan Joyce, CEO, Qantas', *The Deal, The Australian*, 19 October 2018.
4 Will Horton, 'Jetstar Loses Its Shine For Qantas In Vietnam, But Singapore's Jetstar Asia Still Strong'.

Chapter 19 – Walking the World Stage
1 Angus Whitley, Benjamin Katz and Kyunghee Park, 'Boys' club on parade as women struggle for top airline positions', *Australian Financial Review*, 4 June 2018.
2 Deena Kamel, 'Fuel and fury dominate IATA boys' club gathering in rainy Sydney', *The National*, 6 June 2018.
3 Colin Kruger, '"Very challenging position": Qatar Airways chief says a woman can't do his job', *Sydney Morning Herald*, 6 June 2018.
4 Julia Kollewe, 'Qatar Airways CEO apologises for suggesting a woman could not do his job', *The Guardian*, 6 June 2018.
5 'Adam Goodes announced as new Qantas ambassador', 28 October 2013. www.qantasnewsroom.com.au/media-releases/adam-goodes-announced-as-new-qantas-ambassador/
6 'Qantas unveils new I Still Call Australia Home campaign', 25 March 2022. www.qantasnewsroom.com.au/media-releases/qantas-unveils-new-i-still-call-australia-home-campaign/

Chapter 20 – Redefining the Airline Leader
1 'Meet the CEO' event for the Australian School of Business.

Chapter 21 – The Long Road to Marriage Equality
1 Michael Smith, 'More work to do on gay equality: Joyce', *Australian Financial Review*, 14 December 2014.
2 Geoff Winestock, 'Wesfarmers chief Richard Goyder backs marriage equality', *Australian Financial Review*, 5 August 2015.

3 'Qantas CEO Alan Joyce on Work Life Balance and Social Influence of CEOs', Actuaries Institute, 10 April 2015.

4 CAPA Australia Pacific Aviation Summit, Brisbane, interview with Richard Quest, 5 August 2016.

5 'Do it without anti-gay vitriol', 8 October 2016. www.qantasnewsroom.com. au/speeches/alan-joyce-opinion-piece-do-it-without-anti-gay-vitriol/

6 Miranda Devine, 'Qantas Chairman's Lounge is where the elites hang out', *The Daily Telegraph*, 7 December 2016.

7 Joe Aston, 'Miranda Devine and Alan Joyce to face off at Lachlan Murdoch's Christmas party', *Australian Financial Review*, 12 December 2016.

8 'Peter Dutton Doorstop Interview, Cairns', 18 March 2017. www.minister.home affairs.gov.au/peterdutton/Pages/Doorstop-Interview-Cairns.aspx

9 'From economics to equality, why companies speak up on the big issues', 21 March 2017. www.qantasnewsroom.com.au/speeches/alan-joyce-opinion-piece-from-economics-to-equality-why-companies-speak-up-on-the-big-issues/

10 'Pie Protest', *9 News Perth*, 9 May 2017.

11 Fiona Carruthers, 'Qantas boss tells Cricket Australia to deal with scandal', *Australian Financial Review*, 17 March 2018.

12 Jemima Whyte, 'Israel Folau: Qantas boss backs breach verdict', *Australian Financial Review*, 9 May 2019.

13 Ibid.

14 Robert Gottslieben, 'Risks to company directors who support voice without checking', *The Australian*, 11 August 2023.

Chapter 22 – Before the Storm

1 'Qantas Group CEO's address – 2017 full year results', 25 August 2017. www. qantasnewsroom.com.au/speeches/qantas-group-ceos-address-2017-full-year-results/

2 Michael Smith, 'Qantas reshuffles senior executive ranks', *Australian Financial Review*, 29 August 2017.

3 'Qantas announces new Loyalty CEO and new chief customer officer', 24 January 2018. www.qantasnewsroom.com.au/media-releases/qantas-announces-new-loyalty-ceo-and-new-chief-customer-officer/

4 Tony Boyd, 'Leigh Clifford leaves Qantas in good shape', *Australian Financial Review*, 9 October 2018.

5 Jemima Whyte, 'How far will Virgin's cost cutting go?', *Australian Financial Review*, 29 August 2019.

Chapter 23 – Descent into Chaos

1 'Qantas' new "survival of the fittest" moment', *Australian Financial Review*, 10 March 2020.

Chapter 24 – Eleven Weeks Left

1 'Qantas Group update on additional liquidity', 25 March 2020. www.qantas newsroom.com.au/media-releases/qantas-group-update-on-additional-liquidity/

Chapter 25 – Turnaround – Again

1 'Alan Joyce on why 6000 Qantas jobs have been cut', *ABC 7.30*, 26 June 2020.

2 'A better future for all', Griffith University thought leadership series, in conversation with Kerry O'Brien, 30 July 2020.

3   Geoffrey Thomas, 'Qantas slashes 6000 staff, to raise billions, to stay in the air', *Airline Ratings*, 25 June 2020.
4   'Joyce to remake Qantas again', *Australian Financial Review*, 25 June 2020.

Chapter 26 – Twists and Turns
1   Stuart Layt, 'Virgin CEO calls for open borders, even if "some people may die"', *Sydney Morning Herald*, 17 May 2021.
2   CAPA Live, interview with Peter Harbison, 14 April 2021.
3   Mark Ludlow and Jemima Whyte, 'Ramp up vaccine rollout or get left behind: airlines', *Australian Financial Review*, 20 May 2021.
4   Lucas Baird, 'Alan Joyce warns WA on travel plans', *Australian Financial Review*, 26 August 2021.
5   'Qantas marks 100 years of serving Australia', 16 November 2020. www.qantas newsroom.com.au/media-releases/qantas-marks-100-years-of-serving-australia/

Chapter 27 – Another Whopping Loss
1   'HY22 results speech', 24 February 2022. www.qantasnewsroom.com.au/speeches/hy22-results-speech-qantas-group-ceo-alan-joyce/
2   'Qantas boss says travellers just "not match fit" amid Sydney Airport queue chaos', *7NEWS*, 7 April 2022.
3   'How Alan Joyce Screwed His Workers & Ruined Qantas'.
4   Tansy Harcourt, 'The life of Alan: loved, loathed, late and lost'.
5   'Explaining what's happening with air travel right now', 17 July 2022. www.qantasnewsroom.com.au/media-releases/qantas-op-ed-explaining-whats-happening-with-air-travel-right-now/
6   Angus Whitley, 'Late-night egg attack shows traveller fury at Qantas CEO', *Bloomberg*, 11 August 2022.
7   Ibid.
8   *Airline competition in Australia Report 11*, Australian Competition and Consumer Commission, March 2023, p2.
9   Tansy Harcourt, 'The life of Alan: loved, loathed, late and lost'.
10   'FY22 results speech', 25 August 2022. www.qantasnewsroom.com.au/speeches/fy22-results-speech-qantas-group-ceo-alan-joyce/
11   'How Alan Joyce Screwed His Workers & Ruined Qantas'.
12   'Full Interview: Qantas CEO Alan Joyce', *CNBC International*, 20 June 2022.
13   'The inside story of the chaos at Qantas', *Four Corners*, 5 September 2022.
14   'Qantas statement on claims in Four Corners story', 5 September 2022. www.qantasnewsroom.com.au/media-releases/qantas-statement-on-claims-in-four-corners-story/
15   Aaron Patrick, 'The ugly truth about Alan Joyce', *Australian Financial Review*, 12 September 2022.
16   Terry McCrann, 'Attacks on Alan Joyce are silly and totally unfair', *Herald Sun*, 12 September 2022.
17   'Putting some context around the national carrier's recent history', 13 September 2022. www.qantasnewsroom.com.au/media-releases/qantas-op-ed-putting-some-context-around-the-national-carriers-recent-history/
18   Lucas Baird, 'Could Qatar Airways swoop on Virgin?', *Australian Financial Review*, 20 April 2023.
19   Robyn Ironside, '"Fierce competition" at the heart of airline CEOs' friendship', *The Australian*, 5 March 2022.

Chapter 28 – The Gorilla Hoarding the Bananas

1   'HY23 results speech', 23 February 2023. www.qantasnewsroom.com.au/speeches/hy23-results-speech-qantas-group-ceo-alan-joyce/
2   Vesna Poljak and James Chessell, 'Qantas chief flags final union showdown', *Australian Financial Review*, 5 May 2008.
3   'Meet the CEO' event for the Australian School of Business.
4   Lucas Baird and Gus McCubbing, 'Qantas to hire thousands as it reverses pandemic cuts', *Australian Financial Review*, 3 March 2023.
5   'Meet the CEO' event for the Australian School of Business.
6   'Statement on executive remuneration', 15 September 2017. www.qantasnewsroom.com.au/media-releases/statement-on-executive-remuneration/
7   'Qantas profits soar as jobs and safety standards hit the wall', TWU Australia press release, 25 September 2019.
8   'Alan Joyce is a "big corporate gorilla": Labor Senator', *Sky News Australia*, 24 November 2022.
9   Leke Oso Alabi, 'Wizz Air chief hails "capitalist spirit" behind £100mn bonus package extension', *Financial Times*, 4 August 2023.

Chapter 29 – The Sun Rises Again

1   'CEO's address at Annual General Meeting', 27 October 2017. www.qantasnewsroom.com.au/speeches/ceos-address-at-annual-general-meeting-27-october-2017/
2   *Bloomberg Turnaround*, 5 June 2019.

Chapter 30 – *Flygskam*

1   'Qantas and Shell Release Biofuel Report', 3 December 2013. www.qantasnewsroom.com.au/media-releases/qantas-and-shell-release-biofuel-report/
2   Catherine Clifford, '"The era of global boiling has arrived," says UN boss', *CNBC*, 27 July 2023.

Chapter 31 – Mind Games

1   Jared Lynch, 'How maths helps the Joyce brothers fly'.
2   Damon Kitney, 'The art of the deal: Alan Joyce, CEO, Qantas'.
3   'Claims, counterclaims, but most importantly, credibility', 22 April 2021. www.qantasnewsroom.com.au/media-releases/op-ed-claims-counterclaims-but-most-importantly-credibility-qantas-group-ceo-alan-joyce/
4   John Sharp, 'No Mr Joyce, Qantas' "best game" doesn't beat Rex', *Australian Financial Review*, 20 April 2021.
5   'Claims, counterclaims, but most importantly, credibility'.
6   'Alan Joyce pilots Qantas from turbulence to clear skies'.

Chapter 32 – The Joyce Legacy

1   CAPA Australia Pacific Aviation Summit, Sydney, interview with Peter Harbison, 3 August 2015.
2   'Being young and LGBTIQ can be tough. But take it from us, it gets better'.

QUARTERLY ESSAY
BACK ISSUES

BACK ISSUES: (Prices include GST, postage and handling within Australia.) *Grey indicates out of stock.*

Please include this form with delivery and payment details overleaf.
Back issues also available as eBooks at **quarterlyessay.com**

SUBSCRIBE TO RECEIVE
10% OFF THE COVER PRICE

☐ **ONE-YEAR PRINT AND DIGITAL SUBSCRIPTION: $89.99**

- Print edition × 4
- Home delivery
- Full digital access to all past issues, including downloadable eBook files
- Access iPad & iPhone app
- Access Android app

DELIVERY AND PAYMENT DETAILS

DELIVERY DETAILS:

NAME:

ADDRESS:

EMAIL: PHONE:

PAYMENT DETAILS: Enclose a cheque/money order made out to Schwartz Books Pty Ltd.
Or debit my credit card (MasterCard, Visa and Amex accepted).
Freepost: Quarterly Essay, Reply Paid 90094, Collingwood VIC 3066
All prices include GST, postage and handling.

CARD NO. ☐☐☐☐ ☐☐☐☐ ☐☐☐☐ ☐☐☐☐

EXPIRY DATE: /   CCV: AMOUNT: $

PURCHASER'S NAME: SIGNATURE:

Subscribe online at **quarterlyessay.com/subscribe** • Freecall: 1800 077 514 • Phone: 03 9486 0288
Email: subscribe@quarterlyessay.com (please do not send electronic scans of this form)